Post-war Architecture between Italy and the UK

Post-war Architecture between Italy and the UK

Exchanges and transcultural influences

Edited by

Lorenzo Ciccarelli and Clare Melhuish

UCLPRESS

First published in 2021 by
UCL Press
University College London
Gower Street
London WC1E 6BT

Available to download free: www.uclpress.co.uk

A CIP catalogue record for this book is available from The British Library.

ISBN: 978-1-80008-085-0 (Hbk)
ISBN: 978-1-80008-084-3 (Pbk)
ISBN: 978-1-80008-083-6 (PDF)
ISBN: 978-1-80008-086-7 (epub)
ISBN: 978-1-80008-087-4 (mobi)
DOI: https://doi.org/10.14324/111.9781800080836

Contents

List of figures vii
List of contributors xi

1 Editors' note 1
Lorenzo Ciccarelli and Clare Melhuish

2 The complexity of cultural exchange: Anglo-Italian relations in architecture between transnational interactions and national narratives 4
Paolo Scrivano

3 On the wave of the welfare state: Anglo-Italian town-planning strategies in the post-war years 20
Lorenzo Ciccarelli

Part I: Personae and Debates

4 Banham's Italy 45
Davide Spina

5 From neoliberty to postmodernism 57
Benjamin Chavardès

6 Franco Albini and Leslie Martin: 'a parallel working life' 70
Antonello Alici

7 Superstudio, the sign and the problem of architectural education 86
Da Hyung Jeong

Part II: Designing the Post-war City

8 Reweaving the city: the CIAM summer schools from London to Venice (1949–57) 107
Lorenzo Mingardi

9 The influence of Patrick Geddes in post-war Italy through Jaqueline Tyrwhitt and Giancarlo De Carlo 127
Maria Clara Ghia

10 Domenico Andriello and the 'città dell'uomo' 145
Gemma Belli

11 From futurism to 'town-room': Hodgkinson, the Brunswick and the low-rise/high-density principle 156
Clare Melhuish

Part III: Building the Welfare State

12 A Janus-faced approach to the new universities of the 1960s: monumentality and pedagogy at Sussex and Essex 179
Jack O'Connor

13 Italy assessing the UK assessing Italy: a battle of perspectives on cities and learning 199
Francesco Zuddas

14 The jewel of the Triennale: dialogues between Italy and the UK around a school 213
Gabriele Neri

15 Post-war British church architecture and the Italian model 236
Lorenzo Grieco

Index 255

List of figures

2.1 Frontispiece of Pugin, Augustus Charles, Augustus Welby Northmore Pugin and Edward James Willson, *Examples of Gothic Architecture: Selected from Various Antient Edifices in England: Consisting of Plans, Elevations, Sections, and Parts at Large; Calculated to Exemplify the Various Styles, and the Practical Construction of this Admired Class of Architecture: Accompanied by Historical and Descriptive Accounts* vol. 2 (London: Henry George Bohn, 1836). Private collection. 7

2.2 Postcard depicting the Swiss Village at the Exposition Nationale de Genève, 1896. Private collection. 8

2.3 Abraham Darby III and Thomas Pritchard, Iron Bridge over the River Severn, Coalbrookdale, Shropshire, 1779. RIBA Architecture Image Library. 13

2.4 Charles Henry Holden and William Graham Holford, Model of St Paul's Precinct development, City of London, 1952. RIBA Architecture Image Library. 15

2.5 Cover of *Metron* no. 1, 1945. Private collection. 16

3.1 The London 'living and organic communities' as shown in Forshaw, John Henry and Patrick Abercrombie. *County of London Plan*. London: Macmillan and Co., 1943. 25

3.2 The neighbourhood unit of Eltham as shown in Forshaw, John Henry and Patrick Abercrombie. *County of London Plan*. London: Macmillan and Co., 1943. 26

3.3 A suburban organic district as designed in the Turin master plan by Giovanni Astengo, Nello Renacco and Aldo Rizzotti. Published in 'Concorso per il piano regolatore di Torino', *Urbanistica*, 1 (1949). 27

4.1 Reyner Banham, portrait, 1980. © RIBA Collections, image number 5808. 54

5.1 Roberto Gabetti and Aimaro Isola, Bottega d'Erasmo, Turin, 1953–7. © Benjamin Chavardès. 58

5.2 BBPR, Torre Velasca, Milan, 1956–8. © Benjamin Chavardès. 63
6.1 Franco Albini with Luigi Colombini, Albergo-rifugio per ragazzi, Pirovano, Cervinia, 1948–52. Fondazione Franco Albini, Milan. 75
6.2 Franco Albini and Franca Helg, Grandi magazzini 'La Rinascente', piazza Fiume, Rome, 1957–61. Fondazione Franco Albini, Milan. 76
6.3 Leslie Martin, Patrick Hodgkinson and Colin St John Wilson, Harvey Court, New student accommodation for Gonville and Caius College, Cambridge, 1960–2. *Casabella-Continuità*, 268, October 1962. 79
7.1 Superstudio, *Manhattan, photomontage final (Monumento Continuo)*, 1969. Centre Pompidou, AM 2000-2-141. 88
7.2 Cover of *Op. cit.* 18 (May 1970). Image courtesy of Renato De Fusco. 93
7.3 Superstudio, *Terza città: New York of Brains*, 1971. Centre Pompidou, AM 2000-2-157. 96
7.4 Advertisement for the International Institute of Design's 1971 Summer Session. The 'conflicting attitudes … toward education' had already been underscored at this previous iteration of the event. Image courtesy of AA Print Studio, London. 97
7.5 Cover of the first issue of the *Global Tools* bulletin, 1974. Image courtesy of Archivio Ugo La Pietra, Milan. 100
8.1 Ernesto Nathan Rogers at CIAM 7 in Bergamo (1949). From Tentori, Francesco. 'I CIAM per il Cinquecentenario del Congresso di Bergamo: L'architettura, l'arte e l'importanza decisiva della libertà', *La Rivista di Bergamo* 18 (1999), 18. Courtesy of *La Rivista di Bergamo*. 108
8.2 Designs by students of the CIAM summer school (1949). From the *Architects' Journal*, 15 September (1949), 276–7. Courtesy of the *Architects' Journal*. 110
8.3 Le Corbusier at CIAM summer school in Venice (1952). Source: Università Iuav di Venezia, Archivio Progetti, fondo Egle Renata Trincanato. 116
8.4 Designs by students of the CIAM summer school (1956). From Scimemi, Gabriele. 'La quarta scuola estiva dei CIAM a Venezia', *Casabella-Continuità* 213 (1956), 73. Courtesy of *Casabella*. 121

9.1 The urban-geographical structures of Athens and Edinburgh, as represented by Patrick Geddes in 1911. Published in Welter, Volker. *Biopolis: Patrick Geddes and the city of life*. Cambridge, MA: MIT Press, 2002, 67. 130
9.2 Balrampur, an example of conservative surgery applied by Patrick Geddes to a city quarter, 1917 (at lower left). Published in Welter, Volker. *Biopolis: Patrick Geddes and the city of life*. Cambridge, MA: MIT Press, 2002, 117. 135
9.3 Giancarlo De Carlo, the urban regeneration of Colletta di Castelbianco, elevations and sections, Indian ink on tracing paper, 1994. The drawings underline De Carlo's attention towards certain Geddesian key principles, such as the conservative surgery and the unfruitfulness of city–country opposition. Courtesy of Università Iuav di Venezia, Archivio Progetti, Fondo Giancarlo De Carlo. 140
11.1 The Brunswick precinct, view to north, newly refurbished in 2006 by Levitt Bernstein, with the retail frontage extended by canopies: 'a high street for Bloomsbury'. © C. Melhuish 2006. 157
11.2 View looking due south of winter gardens to Foundling Court, prior to refurbishment. © C. Melhuish 2001. 161
11.3 View through apex of concrete A-frame structure supporting housing block, with access level to atrium below. © C. Melhuish 2001. 162
11.4 Outline Planning Scheme 1963, showing a more formalized axial emphasis to the public space, with circular recital hall at centre between two linear blocks. © RIBA Collections. 171
12.1 Falmer House, North Entrance. The classical arched entrance to the Falmer House courtyard and great court beyond, echoing the arches of the Colosseum. © University of Sussex. 189
12.2 Drawing of square at University of Essex by Conrad Schevenels, Architects Co-Partnership c. 1963. The architect's conceived vision for the Essex squares as a social space. University of Essex Collection. Used courtesy of the Albert Sloman Library, University of Essex. 192
12.3 The monumental residential towers at Essex, on the skyline and contrasting with the trees in the parkland. University of Essex Collection. Used courtesy of the Albert Sloman Library, University of Essex. 193

13.1 'A Florentine Fiasco'. *Architectural Review* 900 (1972): 79–82. Endorsing the critique by juror James Gowan, the editors of the *Architectural Review* polemicize with the premises and results of the international competition for the expansion of the University of Florence. The illustrations in the article are from the winning project by Vittorio Gregotti, Edoardo Detti *et al*. Courtesy of the *Architectural Review*. 200
14.1 CLASP British School at the XII Triennale, Milan, 1960. Courtesy of Triennale Milano – Archivio Fotografico. 214
14.2 Patience Gray. 'A Lesson in English', *The Observer*, 14 August 1960. Courtesy of CASVA – Archivio Francesco Gnecchi Ruscone. 218
14.3 The Italian Minister of Public Education representatives, visiting a CLASP building in the UK in September 1960, puzzled by British bureaucratic recklessness. Courtesy of CASVA – Archivio Francesco Gnecchi Ruscone. 225
14.4a Francesco Gnecchi Ruscone, CLASP School in Biella, Italy. Aerial view, 1960. Courtesy of CASVA – Archivio Francesco Gnecchi Ruscone. 227
14.4b Francesco Gnecchi Ruscone, CLASP School in Buccinasco, Italy, 1962. Courtesy of CASVA – Archivio Francesco Gnecchi Ruscone. 228
14.5 Francesco Gnecchi Ruscone, IRCOM School in Rome, early 1960s. Courtesy of CASVA – Archivio Francesco Gnecchi Ruscone. 229
15.1 Luigi Figini and Gino Pollini, Church of Our Lady of the Poor, Milan, 1952–4. Photo by Lorenzo Grieco. 241
15.2 Augusto Baccin, Church of St Basil, Rome, 1952–63. Photo by Lorenzo Grieco. 242
15.3 Angelo Mangiarotti and Bruno Morassutti, Church of Our Lady of Mercy, Baranzate, 1956–8. Photo by Lorenzo Grieco. 248
15.4 Guido Maffezzoli, Church of the Holy Heart, Milan, 1962–6. Photo by Lorenzo Grieco. 249
15.5 Giovanni Michelucci, Church of St John the Baptist, Campi Bisenzio, 1960–4. Photo by Lorenzo Grieco. 249

List of contributors

Lorenzo Ciccarelli is Research Fellow in History of Architecture at the University of Florence and member of the Scientific Committee of the Renzo Piano Foundation. In 2019 he was Visiting Fellow at the University of Queensland, Australia. He studies Italian architecture of the twentieth and twenty-first centuries in a global context with particular attention to cross-cultural exchanges and labour organization strategies. He is the author of *Renzo Piano before Renzo Piano: Masters and beginnings* (2017) and *Il mito dell'equilibrio* (2019). He is member of the editorial team of *Opus Incertum, Histories of Postwar Architecture* and *Studi e Ricerche di Storia dell'Architettura.*

Clare Melhuish is Principal Research Fellow and Director of the UCL Urban Laboratory, where she has been working since 2013 on the role of university spatial development projects in urban regeneration and the production of cosmopolitan urbanism and imaginaries in the UK and abroad. She is a co-ordinator of the Curating the City research cluster in the Centre for Critical Heritage Studies. Her background lies in architectural history and criticism, anthropology, and cultural geography, drawing on ethnographic and visual research methods to interpret and understand architecture and the built environment as social and cultural setting.

Antonello Alici is Architect, PhD, Associate Professor in History of Architecture at Università Politecnica delle Marche, Ancona and Visiting Professor at the International Doctoral Programme in Architectural Heritage Management and Tourism, Silpakorn University, Bangkok. He has been Visiting Scholar at St John's College and at the Martin Centre for Architectural and Urban Studies, University of Cambridge. His research and teaching interests are mainly in nineteenth- and twentieth-century architecture in the Nordic countries, Great Britain and Italy, and on the theory of Heritage and Architectural Conservation. In 2019–20 he promoted the international research project GDC 100 on the legacy of Giancarlo De Carlo based at the National Academy of San Luca in Rome.

Gemma Belli is Architect, PhD, Associate Professor in History of Architecture at the Department of Architecture of the University of Naples Federico II, where she teaches History of the City and Landscape and History of Settlement Forms. Since 1998 she has carried out research activities in Italy and abroad, participating in the organization of exhibitions and national and international conferences. Her studies have been widely published and recognized in Italy and abroad: her book *Narrare l'urbanistica alle élite: 'Il Mondo' (1949–1966) di fronte alla modernizzazione del Bel Paese* received more than 10 reviews from national and international specialized journals. Since 2018 she has been a member of the scientific committee of the journal *Storia dell'Urbanistica*.

Benjamin Chavardès is Lecturer at the École Nationale Supérieure d'Architecture de Lyon. His work focuses on the history and theory of postmodern architecture, built heritage and religious architecture. He is the author of *Quand le post-modernisme expose* (Éditions de l'Espérou, 2015) and *L'Italie postmoderne: Paolo Portoghesi, architecte, historien, théoricien* (Presses universitaires de Rennes, 2022). He has taught and lectured in Bath, London, Paris, Lyon, Avignon, Como, Rome and Naples.

Maria Clara Ghia holds a PhD in Architectural Theory and Design (Sapienza University) and in Philosophy (Université Jean Moulin Lyon 3). She currently teaches History of Architecture at Sapienza University. She has been Senior Lecturer at Umeå University in Sweden. Dealing in general with the history of architecture of the twentieth and twenty-first centuries, her research focuses chiefly on Italian post-war architecture and the relationship between ethics and design. She has curated exhibitions and participated in conferences in Italy, Sweden and France. She is author of numerous essays and monographs, mainly concerning the work of Bruno Zevi, Luigi Moretti and Leonardo Ricci. In 2011 she won the Bruno Zevi International Prize and in 2019 the Enrico Guidoni Prize.

Lorenzo Grieco is PhD candidate in History of Architecture at the University of Rome Tor Vergata, and the University of Kent, Canterbury, UK. His studies deal with renaissance and contemporary architecture, especially the technological conception of historical buildings. His current research focus is on post-war church architecture in Britain and its relationship with interdenominational and cross-geographical factors, whose impact can be traced in the layout, form, and conception of sacred buildings.

Da Hyung Jeong is a doctoral candidate and Adjunct Professor at New York University. His dissertation, entitled *Soviet Architectural*

Postmodernism: 1977–1991 and supervised by Professor Jean-Louis Cohen, is the first book-length study devoted to the subject. He has given conference talks on the international legacy of Superstudio's radical design, the convergence between postmodernism and a politicized regionalism in the architecture of the Soviet 'peripheries', references to Japanese Metabolism in late Soviet architecture, and other topics. His essay 'The First World War and Nationalist Primitivism in Russian Architecture', analysing the use of architecture as war propaganda, will appear in *States of Emergency: Architecture, urbanism, and the First World War*, which is forthcoming with Leuven University Press.

Lorenzo Mingardi completed a PhD in History of Architecture and Urban Planning from the IUAV Università di Venezia in 2016. He was then awarded a fellowship at the Ragghianti Foundation in Lucca (2018–19). He is currently Adjunct Professor at the University of Florence. His main research field is history of modern and contemporary European architecture. He is the author of *Sono geloso di questa città: Giancarlo De Carlo e Urbino* (2018) and *Contro l'analfabetismo architettonico: Carlo Ludovico Ragghianti nel dibattito culturale degli anni Cinquanta* (2020).

Gabriele Neri is an architectural historian, curator and architect. He is Mâitre d'enseignement et de recherche at the Accademia di architettura, Mendrisio, Switzerland. Since 2011 he has been Adjunct Professor of History of Design and Architecture at the Polytechnic of Milan. He holds a PhD in History of Architecture and Urban Planning. He is currently a member of the Board of Directors of the Fondazione Museo del Design (Triennale Milano). In 2020 he was awarded the Weinberg Fellowship in Architectural History and Preservation of the Italian Academy for Advanced Studies in America, Columbia University, New York.

Jack O'Connor is a History PhD candidate at the University of Sussex. His project – *The University and the Public Sphere: Pedagogy, architecture and lived experience of the new universities at Sussex and Essex, 1960–1979* – is a critical historical investigation that engages with the University as a whole; from how it was *conceived* and *perceived* by founders and architects, to how it was *lived* in by staff and students. The project's conceptual framework is based on a conception of the public sphere, to develop an understanding of the university as part of a plural public sphere of action, debate and contestation.

Paolo Scrivano is Associate Professor of History of Architecture at the Polytechnic of Milan. He received a PhD degree in architectural history from the Polytechnic of Turin and held teaching positions at the University of Toronto, Boston University, and Xi'an Jiaotong–Liverpool University. A specialist in twentieth-century architecture, he has authored numerous publications on history, historiography and criticism, including the volumes *Storia di un'idea di architettura moderna: Henry-Russell Hitchcock e l'International Style* (2001), *Olivetti Builds: Modern architecture in Ivrea* (2001, as a co-author), and *Building Transatlantic Italy: Architectural dialogues with postwar America* (2013).

Davide Spina is a Postdoctoral Researcher at the Institute for the History and Theory of Architecture, ETH Zurich, where he also completed his doctorate. Prior to this, he completed the architectural history MA at The Bartlett, UCL. Davide was a Collection Research Grant recipient at the Canadian Centre for Architecture, Montreal (2016), a Visiting PhD Scholar at the Columbia University Graduate School of Architecture, Planning and Preservation (2017), and a Fellow at the Swiss Institute in Rome (2018–19). At ETH, he co-organizes *The Architecture of Research*, a yearly symposium on research methods, and *DocTalks*, an international online platform for early-stage researchers in architectural history and theory. His research has appeared in *AA Files* and *gta Papers*.

Francesco Zuddas is Senior Lecturer in Architecture at Anglia Ruskin University. He has taught architectural design and history and theory at Università degli Studi di Cagliari, the Architectural Association, Central Saint Martins and the Leeds School of Architecture. In 2014, he was visiting research scholar at GSAPP, Columbia University. His writings on post-war Italian urbanism and architecture, space and higher education, architectural pedagogy, and the spatial implications of changing production paradigms towards the knowledge economy, have appeared in *AA Files*, *Domus*, *Oase*, *Architecture and Culture*, *San Rocco*, *Territorio*, and *Trans*, among others. His book *The University as a Settlement Principle: Territorialising knowledge in late 1960s Italy* (Routledge) was published in 2020.

1
Editors' note

Lorenzo Ciccarelli (University of Florence)
and Clare Melhuish (UCL)

In the catalogue of the exhibition *Italian Contemporary Architecture* organized at the Royal Institute of British Architects (RIBA) in March 1952, Robert Furneaux Jordan wrote that 'to an architect, contemporary Italy is perhaps the most interesting of all countries', while Ernesto Nathan Rogers defined British architecture as 'a happy complement to the Italian'. Rogers and Furneaux Jordan were among the most interesting and refined architectural critics in Italy and the UK during the 1940s and 1950s, and these words are just some of the crumbs that invite the reader to continue the explorations of the cultural exchanges between the two countries during and after the Second World War. Indeed, while scholars have studied the transnational connections and sharing of models and ideas with America and Scandinavia, there has been no comprehensive publication focused on the exchanges and transcultural influences between British and Italian architects, town-planners and historians. This volume is a first and partial contribution in this field, with the aim of fostering further research.

Two introductory essays by Paolo Scrivano and Lorenzo Ciccarelli outline the parameters of the debate, and the main topics through which Italian and British architects, historians and town-planners engaged with each other and contested their positions, while the main part of the volume is divided into three parts. The first part – *Personae and Debates* – focuses on some of the characters who fostered and animated the (sometimes harsh) debates between Italy and the UK, such as Reyner Banham, Ernesto N. Rogers, Franco Albini, Leslie Martin and Adolfo Natalini. The second part – *Designing the Post-war City* – deals with the sharing of town and country planning strategies for reconstructing and designing post-war cities with special attention to housing schemes; while the third part – *Building the Welfare State* – addresses the design and construction of schools, universities and churches framed by the social and political expectations of the Welfare State.

This book arrives at the end of a long path through a research project co-ordinated by Lorenzo Ciccarelli at the Department of Architecture of the University of Florence between 2017 and 2019. Among the outcomes there were the book *Il mito dell'equilibrio: Il dibattito anglo-italiano per il governo del territorio negli anni del dopoguerra* (Franco Angeli, 2019) and the international conference *Italy and the United Kingdom: Exchanges and transcultural influences in postwar architecture,* organized by Lorenzo Ciccarelli and Martina Caruso and held at the University of Florence and the British School at Rome on 27 and 28 November 2019.

The collaboration with Clare Melhuish came about following an introduction by Dr Florian Mussgnug, Academic Director of UCL Cities Programme (Rome). Clare's track record of research and publication in the field of UK post-war architecture and planning intersected with more recent work at UCL Urban Laboratory on contemporary developments in the planning and design of universities, which had led to a fruitful exchange with UK-based Italian academics working on the history of university architecture in Italy in the post-war period (Zuddas, see chapter 13 in this volume). She joined and helped to expand the conference Scientific Committee, and contributed as a member to the circulation of the call for papers and selection of abstracts, with a view to collaboration on an edited volume arising from the proceedings. She subsequently chaired one of the conference sessions at the British School at Rome in November 2019 – which as it turned out would be a final academic research trip abroad before the outbreak of the global COVID-19 pandemic.

After the conference, we invited the presenters – from Italy, the UK, France and the US – as well as a number of additional distinguished scholars, to re-work their papers within the framework of an edited book for an international audience. It has proved to be a productive and enriching transcultural and cross-linguistic collaboration that has generated a significant contribution to the body of knowledge in this field, and to the understanding of the shared cultural and political histories and processes embodied in the field of architecture and design. From a UK perspective, particularly, it highlights the depth of the intellectual and artistic entanglement that historically binds the UK to its European neighbours, and shapes our common urban futures, notwithstanding the repetitive historic rifts caused by political and religious dissent and warfare. Architecture and urban design across the UK and Italy present everyday material evidence of those historical collaborations and exchanges that frame contemporary lives and interactions.

As the process of compiling this volume reaches its conclusion, it is pleasing to reflect on one such positive outcome of a year of enforced home-working and isolation, and the possibilities that it has nevertheless offered to pursue such fruitful collaborative initiatives. It only remains to express our thanks to all the colleagues, friends and reviewers who accepted and joined us in the invitation to participate in this venture, and in the publication that has emerged from it, thanks to Chris Penfold who handled the editorial process as representative of UCL Press.

2

The complexity of cultural exchange: Anglo-Italian relations in architecture between transnational interactions and national narratives

Paolo Scrivano

British and Italian cultures have interacted for several centuries, and often with fruitful results, as plenty of studies have well documented. They have moulded a history of exchanges that includes examples of both 'high' and 'low' culture and that extends to recent times, embracing literature, art, music and even cinema and sports.[1] It is also a history that at times encompasses misunderstanding, ambiguity and stereotyping, if not plain prejudice. In architecture, the relations between Italy and the UK have followed very similar patterns, as is attested by some of the best known cases of interplay between the two countries, Palladianism and landscape gardening: popularized by British amateurs and collectors about a century later, the work of Andrea Palladio generated a word-wide process of imitation that spread out in the English-speaking world, likewise affecting everyday building practices;[2] the English Garden, for its part, not only significantly influenced Italy's nineteenth-century architectural design, but also played an important role in launching the long season of European eclecticism.[3]

Rich and captivating in results and outcomes, the Anglo-Italian exchange is of equally critical importance in terms of the questions it raises. In the first place, its study forces an interrogation of the intensity over time of the relations between the UK and Italy and the extent of their reciprocity; then it compels a probe into the forms of an exchange that materialized between two ambits referring to very different ideas of self-identity and diverse understandings of 'nationality'. Addressing these questions might prove even more challenging when dealing with the post-war years: the passage from a context of prevalently bi-national relations – or multi-national relations, but with a limited number of key players – to an increasingly transnational one renders a reconsideration of the mechanisms of cultural exchange almost inevitable.

Indeed, addressing problems concerning processes of cultural exchange entails questioning the very essence of what one could call the 'original elements' of the latter – in a way, the 'poles' or 'extremes' between which cultural relations normally develop. Talking of cultural exchange – as in this case, between Italian and British architectural cultures – implies to discuss the different ways of viewing itself and the other, to evaluate the 'self-reflections' and the narratives put in place by each participant in the exchange, and to consider how these self-reflections and narratives have interacted and still interact.[4] In a few words, it requires tackling the question of how transnational exchanges unfold and, in a way that might appear at first somewhat paradoxical, also of how these exchanges consolidate national narratives.

Some questions can serve as a guideline for a discussion on these themes. What role do national narratives play in the transnational processes of cultural exchange? Do they limit or support, if not favour, the transmission of knowledge? And do national identities – the self-reflections mentioned above – facilitate or hamper the circulation of information and the establishing of mutual influences between different cultures? Considering the role that buildings and the built environment can play in creating and affirming cultural values, the contacts between British and Italian architectural cultures in the post-war years are an invitation to explore these questions from the perspective of a specific disciplinary field, architecture.

Cultural exchanges and national narratives: A dynamic relationship

A first important consideration is that, typically, cultural exchanges and national narratives co-exist in a dynamic relationship. In this respect, it might be useful to start from well-established (and largely accepted) definitions of national narrative and of nationalism, such as those advanced by British historian Eric Hobsbawm, perhaps the foremost authority on these points. In his 1990 book *Nations and Nationalism since 1780*, Hobsbawm identified the nineteenth century as the key moment for the formation of a new idea of nation, one that replaced those that had previously existed and that were grounded in a strict identification between the nation and the limits and extents of royal or princely powers.[5] Hobsbawm emphasized the element of artificiality and social engineering in the making of nations, together with an equally important component of invention: it was the latter aspect that was debated in another seminal work, the volume *The Invention of Tradition*, edited with Terence Ranger and first published in 1983.[6]

Central to *Nations and Nationalism since 1780* was the assertion that the definition of nation as it developed during the nineteenth century derived from a process of acquisition of mass support, from mechanisms – that is – that can be assimilated to those at the basis of the construction of national narratives. For Hobsbawm, nation building was essentially the outcome of a process of expansion and, in his view, the national movements that emerged during the nineteenth century in Western Europe and North America converged toward a form of unification, following a transnational trend. Contained in Hobsbawm's discourse were implications of spatial nature: the nation, he wrote, '... is a social entity only insofar as it relates to a certain kind of modern territorial state ... in the context of a particular stage of technological and economic development.'[7]

Another author who investigated the notions of nationalism and nationality, in particular in connection to the creation of a sentiment of national consciousness, was political scientist and historian Benedict Anderson in his *Imagined Communities: Reflections on the origin and spread of nationalism* of 1983.[8] Addressing the issue within a larger discussion around the formation of national languages, Anderson claimed that the diffusion of 'print-languages' created the conditions for the development of, in his words, 'unified fields of exchange and communication', based on the sharing of common idioms that derived from the birth of non-local audiences for books, journals, periodicals and printed documents and, later, from the institution of large bureaucratic apparati, schooling systems and national bodies of laws.[9] Despite selecting different 'inception' times (late eighteenth and nineteenth century for Hobsbawm and the so-called printing revolution during the sixteenth century for Anderson), both authors pointed at the nineteenth century as the key moment for the creation of national identities – in the case of Anderson's position because of the acceleration in the circulation of paper-based information that took place during the nineteenth century.

What counts, at least for the sake of this discourse, is that the nineteenth century set the stage for a deliberate and elaborated process of invention of traditions that had a nationalist agenda but that was also transnationalist in scope. By underlining possible continuities with the past, invented traditions contributed to the building of national narratives: but, while inward looking, these attitudes were often propelled by some form of transnational exchange. In architecture plenty of examples illustrate this point, most obviously the neo-historicist movements that flourished during the nineteenth century. The interest in the national past that characterized the nineteenth century, in fact, manifested itself through local forms, even though there was an international inspiration at its origin. Mitchell Schwarzer, for example, argues that the construction of nationalist architectural languages in France and Germany progressed in very different directions: in France it followed an already-defined course of nation building through the impositions of a centralized state; in Germany, on the contrary, it had

Figure 2.1 Frontispiece of Pugin, Augustus Charles, Augustus Welby Northmore Pugin and Edward James Willson, *Examples of Gothic Architecture: Selected from Various Antient Edifices in England: Consisting of Plans, Elevations, Sections, and Parts at Large; Calculated to Exemplify the Various Styles, and the Practical Construction of this Admired Class of Architecture: Accompanied by Historical and Descriptive Accounts* vol. 2 (London: Henry George Bohn, 1836)

Private collection

the difficult task of supporting, culturally more than politically, a project of national unification in a context where most of the potential symbols of nationhood had a less than certain German origin (and this explanation might apply to Italy as well).[10] This struggle is exemplified by the reconstruction of Cologne Cathedral during the nineteenth century, an endeavour that was driven by an effort to create a complex yet fictional historical narrative. After all, the one staged in Cologne was the same kind of imaginary framework that propelled the attempt in the 1830s by Augustus Charles Pugin and his son Augustus Welby Northmore to classify the largest possible spectrum of 'specimens' and 'examples' of English gothic architecture.[11]

Other cases, perhaps less frequently mentioned, provide further evidence of how political actions involving architecture often developed in a transnational perspective – and how the construction of national narratives conformed to transnational trends. One case, for example, is the Swiss chalet as described by Jacques Gubler in his *Nationalisme et internationalisme dans l'architecture moderne de la Suisse* – a book of 1975 sometimes overlooked when it comes to questions of nationalism in architecture.[12] In this text Gubler compellingly explained that the Swiss chalet, a typology that has risen to the level of worldwide iconological proxy for mountain architecture, was a nineteenth-century invention

Figure 2.2 Postcard depicting the Swiss Village at the Exposition Nationale de Genève, 1896

Private collection

loosely connected to local traditions but patently instigated by transnational trends. The public debut of the *chalet suisse* took place in 1896, when it was introduced as part of the *village suisse* at the Swiss National Exhibition at Geneva, an imaginary and ephemeral installation aimed at reflecting the cultural diversity of the Swiss Confederation, condensed in a summarized architectural formula.

While embedded in a project meant to produce an all-comprehensive national message, the Geneva initiative was by no means original. One of the first experiences of this kind, in fact, had occurred in Turin in 1884, when, in concomitance with the Italian General Exhibition, a fictional 'medieval borough' had been erected by assembling replicas of fifteenth-century architectures found in the region of Piedmont and in the Aosta Valley. In its attempt to promote a 'national language', Geneva's national exhibition imitated an Italian initiative that, in turn, just followed a transnational trend. In an amusing spiralling of international connections, Turin's medieval re-enactment had been organized by Alfredo de Andrade, an architect, painter and archaeologist who, while trained in Italy, was born in Lisbon.[13]

To use Benedict Anderson's interpretative framework, cases such as the one of the Swiss chalet attempted to 'compact' in a limited number of features very diverse forms of local and regional distinction into a national formula, contributing to create national identities and narratives. As an endeavour of deep social relevance, architecture in fact represents a persuasive symbolic receptacle for collective identity. Carmen Popescu argues that, from the end of the eighteenth century onward, increased individual and cultural mobility altered the perception of space and time and that the consequent 'loss of references' fostered a new demand for distinction that architecture had the potential to fulfil.[14] Since then, what Popescu calls 'identitarian architecture' has offered the prospect of resolving the divide between past and present through the establishment of a link between different time perspectives: to simplify, the narratives that architecture contributed to build participated in a process of 'domestication of the new', during times of unprecedented societal transformations.

So, if in the post-war years some sort of exchange did take place between Italy and the UK – as the essays included in this volume illustrate – it is essential to analyse it by reflecting on the forms it assumed, by identifying what each architectural culture had to offer to the other, and by looking at the way each national distinctiveness contributed to the cultural exchange in relation to a peculiar quest for self-representation. As already remarked, Britain and Italy arrived to shape their ideas of nationality in very different fashions – and the Italian path to national identity had been much more tortuous that the one of its counterpart.[15] Differences between the two countries had by no means been reduced in 1945, and this condition of disparity appeared evident in architecture too. Indeed, the key questions that in this respect should be addressed concern how Italian and British architectural cultures had evolved by the end of the war, in which way they presented themselves to the other (and to the rest of the world) in those crucial years, and how their respective national narratives resounded internationally.

Directions, aims, attitudes, ideals, as well as practices that distinguished the Italian and British cases would deserve an analysis beyond the scope of this essay. What needs to be underlined, however, is that after the war specific issues emerged in each of the two camps, affecting the role architecture could play in consolidating national identification. For instance, one question that was indisputably dominant in post-war Italy centred on the dilemma about how to promote societal change while preserving existing, and supposedly inviolable, traditions.[16] After the Second World War, Italian designers were forced to confront the weighty legacy of Fascism's support of modernism, while at the same time rejecting the regime's rhetorical use of ideologized notions of national identity. The fact was that, in 1945 (but also during the following decade), Italian national identity escaped any precise definition in the same way as it had done before and during the war. A good case in point is an article that architect, theorist, and educator Pasquale Carbonara published in *Architettura: Rivista del sindacato nazionale fascista architetti* in 1942. Titled 'La cucina nella tradizione della famiglia italiana' (The kitchen in the tradition of the Italian family), it provided extremely generic definitions of what could be deemed as 'traditionally Italian' in design.[17] To indicate the 'typical' Italian kitchen, Carbonara listed a long and rather generic series of examples: a house in Roman times, a renaissance farm in Tuscany, and a 'stufa' or 'Stube' from the Alpine region.

As a matter of fact, in the case of Italy the construction of a renewed national identity in the post-war years intersected intricate processes of exchange, of 'give and take', with other cultures. One direction was, of course, the one that defined Italy through the perception of others and that found its roots in well-established traditions, such as the *Grand Tour*. The other one was to some degree 'self reflective', involving the way Italy (or parts of it) looked at itself and produced a patronized gaze that could be called 'orientalism in one country'.[18] In many ways, these two attitudes co-existed, combining views from outside and from inside in the construction of a national and somewhat unified narrative.

National identities' transnational projections

It is important to remember that these processes of narration building were in no way limited to Italy or the UK. Arata Isozaki, for example, in *Japan-ness in Architecture*, a book published in 2006, elaborated on how Japanese identity (in general, and in the particular case of architecture) was the result of – in Isozaki's words – a 'contact with an external gaze' and the ensuing reaction to it.[19] This reaction consisted in 'restraining, draining off, and removing the energy conceived in each earlier transformative period', a process of 'sophistication and purification' that Isozaki called 'Japanization'.[20] The case of the architecture and the garden of the Imperial Villa of Katsura, near Kyoto, well exemplifies this course of action. In the eyes of German architect Bruno Taut, Katsura materialized the aesthetic values of many modern architects in the West – minimalism, pure geometry, simplicity of forms; his external gaze, in turn, prompted a reaction, the rediscovery of the villa as well as of Japanese traditional architecture on the part of Japanese architects and then of the Japanese public.[21]

This Japanese digression serves to further highlight the dynamic relation with the 'other' that lies behind the construction of national narratives. The case of Japan, by the way, draws an interesting parallel with that of Italy and of other countries in what concerns the conditions (or constrictions) that led to the partial remodelling of national architectural identities after the end of the Second World War. In fact, the post-war development of an export-oriented economy, whose ultimate goal was to contribute to a rapid payment of the war reparations and of the debts contracted to sustain the military effort, went hand in hand with the expansion of the handicraft sector, posing the conditions for the success of the so-called 'made in Italy' in the years to come. It is around this time that an almost rhetorical image of Italian industrial design and architecture took shape, coincident with the 'invention' of a fashionable idea of Italian style and the commodification and commercialization of the concept of 'Italianness'. Events such as the exhibition 'Italy at Work', presented in 1950 and 1951 at the Brooklyn Museum and at the Art Institute of Chicago, and co-ordinated by the Italian Ministry of Foreign Commerce, should indeed be considered in this light.[22] This post-war concoction of 'Italianness' was in many ways equivalent to the contemporary inventions of 'Germanness' and 'Japaneseness' – and perhaps 'Britishness' – in design, insofar as they were induced by very similar social and economic conditions.

To discuss the 'projections' of British national identity in architecture in the post-war years would be as difficult as for Italy's case. However, a text containing important reflections on these issues can come to our help, owing specifically to the time when it was conceived and written: it is *The Englishness of English Art* by Nikolaus Pevsner, the volume collecting the notes that the German-born but British-naturalized historian prepared for the Reith Lectures, broadcast by the British Broadcasting Corporation in October and November 1955.[23] Leaving aside, of course, the misleading identification between 'English' and 'British' identities, this volume is of particular significance since it addresses the question of national identity in both visual arts and architecture: 'Is there such a thing at all as a fixed or almost fixed national character?' was indeed the question that Pevsner posed in the opening pages of the volume.[24]

Developing a discourse beginning in the sixteenth century but extending to cover contemporary times (that is, when the notes were written, the mid-1950s), Pevsner underlined the mobile, dynamic character of national identities. His assertion – probably prompted by the reading of *The Illusion of National Character* by journalist and writer Hamilton Fyfe[25] – that nothing like a national character can be considered 'consistent over centuries' is one of the key statements of the entire publication. In debating whether unchangeable and permanent elements could be identified as intrinsic components of any national narrative, Pevsner confuted the role of climate, for long considered '… among the premises of national character.'[26] To prove that climatic conditions are not permanent, Pevsner reminded the reader of the changing perception of places like London, not only a foggy urban area as it could have appeared to visitors in the mid-1950s, but a polluted city in the eyes of foreign travellers during the eighteenth and nineteenth centuries.

In his book, Pevsner sought to define the elements that supposedly characterize British (or, in the case of his discourse, English) art and architecture by connecting contemporary times to the past, in this way contributing to delineate the traits of a hypothetical national artistic and architectural identity through the establishment of a persuasive historical narrative. For him, in fact, it was the passage 'from craftsmanship to quantity production' in the eighteenth century that defined British architectural identity, but that also substantiated the value of British architecture in comparison to other Western architectural cultures. Pevsner identified specific architectural and technological features to support his claim: '… the architecture of the spinning-mill, that most matter-of-fact, most utilitarian, most workaday architecture of the eighteenth and early nineteenth centuries, is originally English, and so is

Figure 2.3 Abraham Darby III and Thomas Pritchard, Iron Bridge over the River Severn, Coalbrookdale, Shropshire, 1779
RIBA Architecture Image Library

the architecture of the dock warehouse, the iron bridge, and the Crystal Palace.'[27] According to him, these examples testified to a 'distinction between utilitarian and ornamental, that is useful art', something that in his view was quintessential of the British Isles. To illustrate this statement, Pevsner used the example of the iron bridge in Coalbrookdale, an infrastructure indicated in most books of architectural history as one of the first examples of application of metal technology to the building industry.

While it might raise questions to refer to Coalbrookdale as an example of distinction between 'utilitarian' and 'ornamental' since the structure functioned almost as a wood scaffold, Coalbrookdale points to the fact that infrastructures of this kind successfully contributed to build a national British architectural narrative as early as the beginning of the nineteenth century.[28] Karl Friedrich Schinkel, for example, travelled to Britain in the 1820s with the precise purpose of learning about the most recent achievements in the infrastructural field – the evidence of the already established consolidation of the image that British architecture projected internationally. While officially abroad to visit the British

Museum and acquire knowledge to be applied in the realization of the Museum am Lustgarten in Berlin, Schinkel extended his architectural investigations to factories, docks, urban estates and structures characterized by the application of innovative building systems, visiting the Royal Pavilion in Brighton built by John Nash and the Conway and Menai bridges built by Thomas Telford among others.[29]

But it is in the parts dedicated to architecture and planning – in particular in the chapter entitled 'Picturesque England' – where Pevsner more convincingly digressed on the elements marking British national identity in architecture.[30] In these pages, Pevsner argued for the existence of a relation between the tradition of Picturesque gardening, developed since the late eighteenth century, and the political concept of liberty, in a conceptual short circuit between architecture and ethical values whose persistence in architectural discourse was first analysed in 1977 by David Watkin in his book *Morality and Architecture*.[31] Pevsner extended to the mid-twentieth century his theoretical construct linking political culture to architectural discourses. For him, in fact, the major problems that the UK faced after the end of the Second World War could be identified in '… those of improvements in towns, including the metropolis, and the laying out or, as it is now called, the planning of new towns or new parts of towns.' Still, in Pevsner's view, the challenges that British society had to confront in the mid-1950s remained situated within a solid political and philosophical tradition: '… even with regard to these urgent problems, so much more serious and portentous than those of the country-house and its grounds, the English Picturesque theory – if not the practice – has an extremely important message. We are in need of a policy of healthy, attractive, acceptable urban planning. There is an English national planning theory in existence which need only be recognized and developed,' he concluded.[32]

Retracing the roots of the tradition to which he made reference in the writings of eighteenth-century authors such as Alexander Pope, Uvedale Price and Richard Payne Knight, Pevsner remarked on a British peculiarity of giving importance to the geographical but also to 'the historical, social, and especially … aesthetic character' of a site. Nothing could be more indicative of a British approach to design and planning, in Pevsner's opinion, than 'treating each place "on its own merit"'. This, he explained, 'may indeed be called the principle of tolerance in action, and there is no more desirable element of Englishness than tolerance.'[33] While it perhaps contradicted previous statements about the mutability of national characters (a contradiction that probably reflected his own anxieties as an individual straddling different cultures, languages and cultural identities), this commendation of British tolerance, which seemed to pair an assumed public virtue with civic attitudes, was indicated by Pevsner as being at the very origin of architectural and planning practices and policies in the UK of the post-war years.[34]

In any event, Pevsner's most significant conclusion was that the lesson of the past could be of use for the present too if past principles were to be applied, instead of just replicating past solutions. For Pevsner this precept was of universal applicability, in particular at urban scale. 'The situation in planning in all countries today calls for two things in particular, both totally neglected by the nineteenth century: the replanning of city centres to make them efficient as well as agreeable places to work in, and the planning of new balanced towns, satellite towns, New Towns,' he proclaimed.[35] Adding a few lines below: 'These are urgent problems for all countries, but what has been said about English character shows that no country is aesthetically better provided to solve them and thereby leave its imprint on other countries than England.'[36] Among the best examples of the successful British approach to urban design, Pevsner indicated Charles Holden and William Holford's plans for St Paul's, the South Barbican scheme (as the Barbican was then known), and the projects for

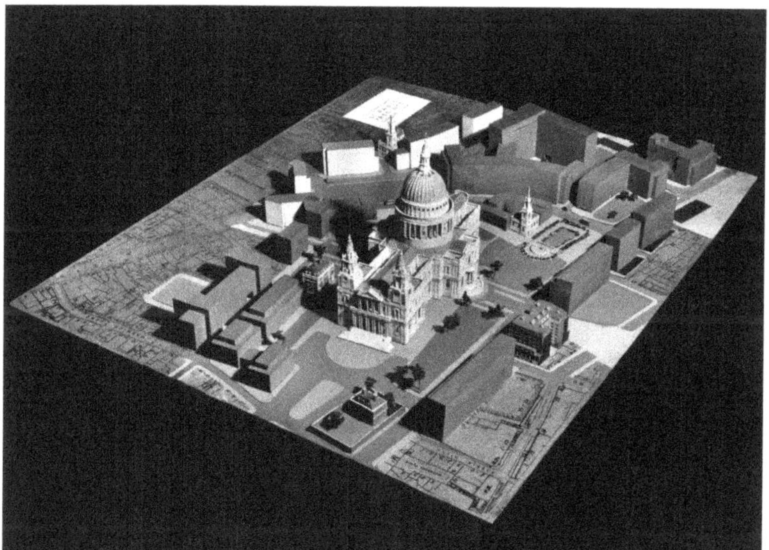

Figure 2.4 Charles Henry Holden and William Graham Holford, Model of St Paul's Precinct development, City of London, 1952

RIBA Architecture Image Library

Roehampton, Harlow New Town and Leonard Vincent's market place for Stevenage New Town – curiously, an array of interventions that, in the UK itself, would be subjected to criticism in the following decades.

Anglo-Italian relations in architecture as cross-cultural interaction

It would be beyond this text's aims to dwell on how, by the time Pevsner formulated them, these views about the potential universal value of British planning – based on ethical and political stances – had already been accepted and consolidated internationally. In Italy, for example, they had been appropriated and applied since the end of the war.[37] As early as 1945, in an article published in the first issue of the journal *Metron*, Bruno Zevi had equated the British and Italian situations at the end of the war pointing to common 'reconstruction problems', only to remark that if Britain had won the war it was because it possessed 'the organs and the habit to plan in time of peace'. Italy, on its part, having lived 'in Fascist inefficiency, in both peace and war', needed now to

Figure 2.5 Cover of *Metron* no. 1, 1945
Private collection

retrieve, in Zevi's words, '... the energies and the work culture necessary to plan for the reconstruction.'[38] Zevi's praise of the cultural climate characterizing the UK after 1945 – artfully juxtaposed to the Italian situation – exposed the short circuit between architecture and ethical and political values that defined how foreign information was processed in post-war Italy, regardless of its actual applicability.[39]

The crucial point, however, is that since the nineteenth century, transnational cultural exchanges both stimulated the construction of national narratives and nourished them from a variety of points of reference or, at times, of confrontation. This articulated phenomenon increased in significance after the end of the Second World War, when relations such as those between Britain and Italy could no longer be simply confined to the limited sphere of bilateralism, but had to be considered within a more complex network of worldwide actors. We do know that the construction of national narratives serves internal purposes, to no small extent related to questions of domestic social control and of cultural cohesion building. No national identity, however, has a reason to exist if it is not placed in dialogue with external interlocutors, with counterparts located outside national borders. Studying the exchanges that occurred in the post-war years between the architectural cultures of the UK and Italy implies therefore addressing issues that pertain to this more problematic – because more nuanced – sphere of cross-cultural interactions. Before and after the Second World War, Anglo-Italian relations might have unfolded in non-linear trajectories, not always based on effective mutual understanding, and not always sharing identical cultural agendas. But the way in which British and Italian architectures intersected proposes a possible paradigm for the study of processes of cultural exchange to a degree that extends well beyond the perspective offered by the essays included in this volume.

Notes

1 Some of these aspects are analysed in the essays included in: Pfister and Hertel 2008.

2 On this subject see the still essential work by Rudolf Wittkower: Wittkower 1974.

3 Roberto Gabetti has written on the significance of imported notions of garden design in the shaping of Continental European and Italian eclectic architectural cultures; see: Gabetti and Griseri 1973, 36–50; Gabetti and Olmo 1989, 216–51.

4 There obviously exists a vast literature on the question of how individuals and social groups relate to the 'other', from the works of Jacques Lacan on the notion of alterity to those by Edward Said on the internalization of romanticized Western views of the East (Lacan 2006 and Said 1978).

5 Hobsbawm 1990, 1–45.

6 Hobsbawm and Ranger 1983.

7 Hobsbawm 1990, 9–10.

8 Anderson 1983, 41–9.

9 Anderson 1983, 47.
10 Schwarzer 2012.
11 'Specimens' and 'examples' were the words included in two of the Pugins' most famous publications: Pugin and Willson 1821–3; Pugin, Pugin and Willson 1831–6. On Augustus Welby Northmore Pugin's activity as a writer see: Belcher 1994.
12 Gubler 1975.
13 Gubler 1975, 30.
14 Popescu 2006. A good example of how increased individual mobility changed the perception of space is provided by the nineteenth-century diffusion of railway as a means of public transportation: see Schivelbusch 1986.
15 On the problems accompanying the construction of Italy's national identity see: Graziano 2010.
16 Scrivano 2013.
17 Carbonara 1942.
18 'Orientalism in one country' is the title of the book edited by Jane Schneider in 1998: Schneider 1998.
19 Isozaki 2006.
20 Isozaki 2006, xv.
21 Scrivano and Capitanio 2018.
22 Rogers 1950.
23 Pevsner 1993.
24 Pevsner 1993, 15.
25 Fyfe 1940; Fyfe's book is quoted in one of the notes of Pevsner's text: Pevsner 1993, 208.
26 Pevsner 1993, 18.
27 Pevsner 1993, 48.
28 With all elements performing as rafters and no part being subject to stress, the bridge alluded to a form – that of the stone arch – rather than to its potential utility, if this is one of the possible meanings of the adjective 'utilitarian' used by Pevsner.
29 Riemann 1993.
30 Macarthur and Aitchison 2010.
31 Watkin 1977.
32 Pevsner 1993, 181.
33 Pevsner 1993, 181.
34 On Pevsner's overlapping (and sometimes conflicting) German, British, and Jewish identities see: Muthesius 2004.
35 Pevsner 1993, 186.
36 Pevsner 1993, 188.
37 Examples of appropriation and adaptation of British models in post-war Italian planning are in: Ciccarelli 2019.
38 Zevi 1945. See also: Scrivano 2018.
39 An illustration of the distance existing between imported planning models and references and their potential use in the receiving context is provided by the American experience of the Tennessee Valley Authority, which took the form of authentic myth in post-war Italy: Scrivano 2013, 139–44.

References

Anderson, Benedict. *Imagined Communities: Reflections on the origin and spread of nationalism.* London: Verso, 1983.

Belcher, Margaret. 'Pugin writing'. In *Pugin: A gothic passion,* edited by Paul Atterbury and Clive Wainwright, 104–16. New Haven–London: Yale University Press–Victoria and Albert Museum, 1994.

Carbonara, Pasquale. 'Analisi degli elementi dell'abitazione 1. La cucina nella tradizione della famiglia italiana', *Architettura: Rivista del sindacato nazionale fascista architetti* 7–9 (July–September 1942): 16–21.

Ciccarelli, Lorenzo. *Il mito dell'equilibrio: Il dibattito anglo-italiano per il governo del territorio negli anni del dopoguerra.* Milan: Franco Angeli, 2019.

Fyfe, Hamilton. *The Illusion of National Character*. London: Watts, 1940.
Gabetti, Roberto and Andreina Griseri. *Architettura dell'eclettismo: Un saggio su G. B. Schellino*. Turin: Einaudi, 1973.
Gabetti, Roberto and Carlo Olmo. *Alle radici dell'architettura contemporanea: Il cantiere e la parola*. Turin: Einaudi, 1989.
Graziano, Manlio. *The Failure of Italian Nationhood: The geopolitics of a troubled identity*. New York: Palgrave Macmillan, 2010.
Gubler, Jacques. *Nationalisme et internationalisme dans l'architecture moderne de la Suisse*. Lausanne: L'Age d'Homme, 1975.
Hobsbawm, Eric J. *Nations and Nationalism since 1780: Programme, myth, reality*. Cambridge: Cambridge University Press, 1990.
Hobsbawm, Eric J. and Terence Ranger (eds). *The Invention of Tradition*. Cambridge: Cambridge University Press, 1983.
Isozaki, Arata. *Japan-ness in Architecture*. Cambridge, MA: MIT Press, 2006.
Lacan, Jacques. *Le séminaire de Jacques Lacan: Livre XVI: D'un Autre à l'autre*. Paris: Seuil, 2006.
Macarthur, John and Mathew Aitchison. 'Pevsner's townscape'. In *Visual Planning and the Picturesque*, by Nikolaus Pevsner, 1–43. Los Angeles: Getty Research Institute, 2010.
Muthesius, Stefan. 'Germanness, Englishness, Jewishness, scientificness, popularization?'. In *Reassessing Nikolaus Pevsner*, edited by Peter Draper, 57–69. Aldershot: Ashgate, 2004.
Pevsner, Nikolaus. *The Englishness of English Art: An expanded and annotated version of the Reith Lectures broadcast in October and November 1955*. London: Penguin, 1993 [orig. ed.: London: Architectural Press, 1956].
Pfister, Manfred and Ralf Hertel (eds). *Performing National Identity: Anglo-Italian cultural transactions*. Amsterdam: Rodopi, 2008.
Popescu, Carmen. 'Space, time: Identity', *National Identities* 8, no.3 (September 2006): 189–206.
Pugin, Augustus Charles, Augustus Welby Northmore Pugin and Edward James Willson. *Examples of Gothic Architecture: Selected from Various Antient Edifices in England: Consisting of Plans, Elevations, Sections, and Parts at Large: Calculated to Exemplify the Various Styles, and the Practical Construction of this Admired Class of Architecture: Accompanied by Historical and Descriptive Accounts*. London: Bohn, 1831–6.
Pugin, Augustus Charles and Edward James Willson. *Specimens of Gothic Architecture: Selected from Various Antient Edifices in England: Consisting of Plans, Elevations, Sections, and Parts at Large: Calculated to Exemplify the Various Styles, and the Practical Construction of this Admired Class of Architecture: Accompanied by Historical and Descriptive Accounts*. London: Taylor–Pugin–Britton, 1821–3.
Riemann, Gottfried. 'The 1826 journey and its place in Schinkel's career'. In *Karl Friedrich Schinkel: 'The English Journey': Journal of a visit to France and Britain in 1826*, 1–11. New Haven, CT–London: The Paul Mellon Centre for Studies in British Art–Yale University Press, 1993.
Rogers, Meyric R. *Italy at Work: Her renaissance in design today*. Rome: Istituto Poligrafico dello Stato, 1950.
Said, Edward. *Orientalism*. New York: Vintage Books, 1978.
Schivelbusch, Wolfgang. *The Railway Journey: The industrialization and perception of time and space in the 19th century*. Berkeley: University of California Press, 1986.
Schneider, Jane (ed.). *Italy's 'Southern Question': Orientalism in one country*. Oxford: Berg, 1998.
Schwarzer, Mitchell. 'The sources of architectural nationalism'. In *Nationalism and Architecture*, edited by Raymond Quek, Darren Deane and Sarah Butler, 19–38. Farnham: Ashgate, 2012.
Scrivano, Paolo. *Building Transatlantic Italy: Architectural dialogues with postwar America*. Farnham: Ashgate, 2013.
Scrivano, Paolo. 'Against the contingencies of Italian society: Issues of historical continuity and discontinuity in Italy's postwar architectural periodicals'. In *Modernism and the Professional Architecture Journal: Reporting, editing and reconstructing in postwar Europe*, edited by Torsten Schmiedeknecht and Andrew Peckham, 184–96. London: Routledge, 2018.
Scrivano, Paolo and Marco Capitanio. 'West of Japan/East of Europe: Translating architectural legacies and the case of Bruno Taut's Hyuga Villa', *Built Heritage* 2, no. 2 (June 2018): 50–61.
Watkin, David. *Morality and Architecture: The development of a theme in architectural history and theory from the Gothic Revival to the Modern Movement*. Oxford: Clarendon Press, 1977.
Wittkower, Rudolf. *Palladio and English Palladianism*. London: Thames and Hudson, 1974.
Zevi, Bruno. 'La ricostruzione edilizia in Inghilterra', *Metron* 1 (1945): 33–40.

3

On the wave of the welfare state: Anglo-Italian town-planning strategies in the post-war years

Lorenzo Ciccarelli

At the end of the Second World War few people in either Britain or Italy could have imagined the long period of economic expansion and social upheaval that their two countries would experience in the following decades. The need for reconstruction and massive public building projects catalysed the growth and success of many architects both in Italy and Britain who gained international recognition. In the post-war years, despite differences in geography, climate, social structure and the degree of economic and industrial development, the dialogue and exchange between Italian and British architects, urban planners and critics was intense and fruitful, as this book illustrates.[1]

By examining publications, journals, and discussions, it appears that the exchanges between the urban planning culture of Britain and Italy moved in both directions. However, Britain exerted an attraction and influence that was much more pervasive and long-lasting than that which Italy transmitted. And while, year after year until the late 1960s, the Italian urban planners were interested in what was proposed and experimented with across the Channel, their British colleagues looked mostly to the past of the Italian peninsula, to the immense historical and artistic heritage of the towns and cities of previous centuries.

To understand the reasons for this imbalance, it is necessary to look beyond the boundaries of the field. For the Italian intellectuals who were preparing to launch new republican institutions, Britain embodied the perfect model of civil life, of democratic secular institutions and firm judicial steadiness. It was the only European country that had emerged victorious from the war, pushing back the Nazi invasion, and in the election of 1945, even elected a Labour Government. Clement Attlee, as Prime Minister, led the executive branch which, over just a few years, launched an extensive programme of social reforms, instituting the most ambitious welfare state system of the time in which urban planning and the construction of public housing had a major role. The enormous disparity between this political agenda and what the architects and urban planners of Italy struggled to achieve was a constant in the Anglo-Italian discourse of the 1950s and 1960s. And the lasting influence of British city planning was carried, therefore, on the shoulders of a more general admiration for the democratic institutions of the country and the reforms of the welfare state, which, despite the alternating Labour and Conservative governments, remained almost intact until the end of the 1970s. While British observers looked at architecture, at engineering structures, and at Italian cities untethered by the more general political situation of the country, the Italian architects, urban planners, and historians sought out British design culture because they were attracted above all by British political and social customs. In the following pages, I will examine some characters, events, and publishing initiatives that in the final stages of the war, and in the years immediately following, contributed to orienting the exchanges between British and Italian urban planning culture along quite precise trajectories, introducing the specific events that are the subjects of the next chapters.

The primacy of British urban planning

Bruno Zevi was the undisputed driving force for the penetration of Anglo-Saxon design in Italy in the 1940s and 1950s.[2] He tenaciously propagated British models through the publication of books of immediate and lasting fortune – from *Verso un'architettura organica* (1945) to *Saper vedere l'architettura* (1948) and *Storia dell'architettura moderna* (1950) – as well as writing articles for journals that he founded or encouraged like *Metron*, *Urbanistica* and *L'Architettura: Cronache e storia*, and participated in debates held by the Associazione per l'Architettura Organica (APAO), l'Istituto Nazionale di Urbanistica (INU) and l'Istituto Nazionale di Architettura (In/Arch).

Of less impact, though not negligible, was Zevi's presence in Britain. *Verso un'architettura organica* was translated in 1950 by the publishing house Faber and Faber and the diffusion of its texts and the relationships that he was able to establish in London earned him the prestigious appointment of Honorary Corresponding Member of the RIBA for Italy.[3]

Looking through the blunt judgements Zevi issued on the British context, he seems unimpressed in comparison with what was happening in other countries. Unlike in the United States and in Scandinavian countries – which could boast architects of the calibre of Frank Lloyd Wright, Richard Neutra or Alvar Aalto – Britain did not have equally prominent figures. The buildings designed by Frederick Gibberd, Richard Sheppard, Gordon Taylor, Eric Lyons, Basil Spence and the firm Lyons Israel Ellis showed design composure and an excellent quality of execution (and were constantly published in Zevi's journals) but did not have that spark of biting genius that the Italian critic sought.[4] For Zevi, British excellence resided in the well-organized professional associations and in the solid tradition of urban planning, summed up in the 'triumphal example' of the County of London Plan (1943) of Patrick Abercrombie and John Henry Forshaw.[5]

Unlike the other Italian architects and urban planners of the post-war period, Zevi had lived in Britain during the conflict. Fleeing Rome, he reached London on 22 March 1939 and remained until early in 1940, working in the office of the Finnish architect Cyril Sjöstrom and attending courses at the Architectural Association School.[6] After a period in the United States, Zevi again stopped in London in 1943 where, while waiting to return to Italy on 31 July 1944, he diligently worked in the library of the RIBA to complete drafting *Verso un'architettura organica*.[7] The months spent in the British capital allowed him to master the English language in a period in which the language of culture in Italy was French. He also established relationships with British architects and politicians and participated in the animated debate on reconstruction.[8]

Following the German bombardment in the summer of 1940, an intense discussion was triggered in Britain over reconstruction. Accustomed to the rigid strictures of Fascist propaganda, Zevi was particularly struck by how the topics of architecture and urban planning were subjects of public interest with wide participation. Citizens were encouraged to weigh in on how the country should be rebuilt after the war, through opinion pieces in the pages of the *Herald* and the *Mirror*, educational exhibitions like 'Living in Cities' (1940) and 'Rebuilding Britain' (1943), and the series of broadcasts, *Making Plans* (1941), by BBC Radio.[9]

The strategic guidance that British architects and urban planners exercised both in public discussions and in parliamentary actions was favoured by proven institutions like the Town and Country Planning

Association and the RIBA, which fuelled discussion through the promotion of meetings, conferences, debates and exhibitions. In particular the RIBA institute at Portland Place offered a model to Zevi of a free and independent association of architects that supported a rich library, the publication of a journal (the *RIBA Journal*), the promotion of competitions and legislative proposals, the organization of prizes (the RIBA Gold Medal) and mediation with political powers, the organization of exhibitions and the promotion of public debates, the expansion of academic-level courses and examination for professional qualification.[10] And there were countless conferences on foreign experiences, debates, meetings with members of the government, exhibitions of prefabricated components, and competitions for housing like those organized between 1941 and 1945.[11] These were occasions that Zevi, as seen from his diaries, was able to take advantage of in the months that he spent in London, often visiting the RIBA and its valuable library.[12]

Back in Italy, Zevi worked to set up similar institutions that could concentrate the efforts of anti-Fascist architects and urban planners and make their voices heard in the debate on reconstruction. On 28 March 1945, as evidence of Zevi's co-ordinated efforts, the Scuola di Architettura Organica opened, which merged in the following July with the Associazione per l'Architettura Organica. Contemporaneously, the journal *Metron* was launched promoting the association's activities.[13] If the Architectural Association of London was the model for the Scuola di Architettura Organica – an association independent of ministerial direction and financed solely by student fees – the RIBA remained the lodestar for Zevi in his subsequent role as Secretary General of the INU from 1951 to 1958 and founder of In/Arch in 1959. Not infrequently *Metron* published texts from conferences held at the London institute. Editorials that opened the issues of *L'Architettura: Cronache e storia* documented the debates, the exhibitions, and the meetings that took place there.[14] During the months in which Zevi was planning the organizational structure and the aims of In/Arch, he claimed peremptorily that 'the RIBA was the best organization of architects that exists today in the world'.[15] And like the British institution, the mission of In/Arch, which was soon mostly disregarded, was to 'establish a bridge between producers and consumers of architecture' and spread knowledge of architecture among institutions and the general public through the promotion of national and regional prizes, exhibitions, conferences, and professional development meetings.[16]

Even British superiority in the field of 'democratic' urban planning was regularly reaffirmed by Zevi. On the cover of *Verso un'architettura organica* above Frank Lloyd Wright's Fallingwater, Zevi inserted Abercrombie and Forshaw's map of the County of London Plan, tellingly clarifying the models that he proposed for Italian architects and urban planners. Again in *Storia dell'architettura moderna* he reiterated how 'the sector in which the English have originally made their mark is that of urban planning', and that the London plan had 'triumphally inaugurated beyond the existing tentative attempts, a new phase of modern urban planning'.[17]

Zevi was in London when the County of London Plan was published in a luxurious volume by Macmillan and he probably saw the exhibition of the plan organized at County Hall in London, visited by over 75,000 in a few months, including King George VI and Queen Elizabeth.[18] With the material he collected, as soon as he returned to Italy Zevi wrote a detailed article for the journal *Urbanistica* in which he promoted Abercrombie and Forshaw's plan as the model for a new 'organic urban planning'.[19]

What were the radical, new elements identified by Zevi? And how could the methodological proposal of the County of London Plan be better suited to the problems of the Italian reconstruction with respect to other contemporary prefigurations like Le Corbusier's plan for Saint-Dié?

If for Zevi, the hygienic or functionalist plans considered the fabric of the city subordinate to the hand of the architect, ready to be sliced and gutted to open monumental avenues and build large-scale buildings, the plan of Abercrombie and Forshaw proposed a radically different approach. Weighing the financial difficulties that the country would have to face post-war, the two urban planners set out to scrupulously respect the existing road network and private property rights, and use their resources, not for expensive expropriations, but for a series of limited changes that would allow them to 'retain the old structure, where discernible, and make it workable under modern conditions'.[20] The emphasis on the plan was thus shifted from the design vision to the enormous undertaking of preliminary analysis to determine which parts of the urban fabric were to be saved, which parts partially changed and which replaced. This series of preliminary analyses allowed Abercrombie and Forshaw to discover that the urban fabric of London still retained a series of 'living and organic communities' that had survived through the rapid industrial development of the previous two centuries. A series of communities, of cohesive territorial and social units, inherited from the old villages that the city absorbed over the course of its expansion, which had resisted homogenization, each maintaining its specific social character, grouped around symbolic buildings like factories, neighbourhood markets, or civic buildings.[21] Once the cellular structure of the city was unveiled, the

Figure 3.1 The London 'living and organic communities' as shown in Forshaw, John Henry and Patrick Abercrombie. *County of London Plan*. London: Macmillan and Co., 1943

purpose of the plan was to preserve the qualities of each community – Camden Town, Islington, Hackney, Battersea, Peckham, Greenwich, and so on – encouraging their independent and separate natures, inserting barriers like railways, green spaces and waterways, and preventing new roads from breaking them up.[22]

Even the expansion of the city toward the outer London region had to be accomplished through the design of analogous 'separate and definitive entities' or *unità organiche compatte* as Zevi translated it. These were self-sufficient zones, further structured to provide the basic requirements of a neighbourhood unit – that is a population sufficient to furnish the right number of children for a primary school without them having to cross roads with fast traffic. Experiments with organized neighbourhoods and *neighbourhood units* appeared, as is known, in Scandinavian countries and in the United States in the 1920s and 1930s. However, the County of London Plan collected these instances and applied them in the design of a large European capital, furnishing a reconstruction model on a large scale for those, like Zevi, who were in search of an urban design model for the new democratic Italy that was an alternative to functionalist proposals.

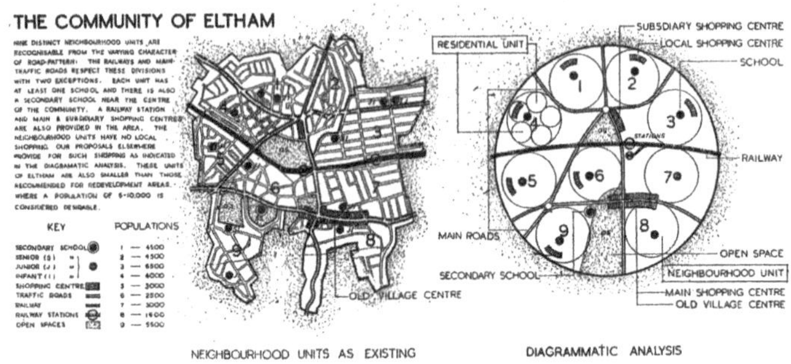

FIG. 2.

27

Figure 3.2 The neighbourhood unit of Eltham as shown in Forshaw, John Henry and Patrick Abercrombie. *County of London Plan*. London: Macmillan and Co., 1943

The myth of the self-sufficient neighbourhood – fed by the spread of the British New Towns and Scandinavian neighbourhoods – fed urban planning culture in Italy until the mid-1950s, leaving its mark on the first generation of INA-Casa neighbourhoods. However, to appreciate the considerable influence of Abercrombie and Forshaw's plan it is enough to look at the early projects of Italian urban planners in the immediate post-war period: especially the regulatory plan of Turin (1948) by Giovanni Astengo, Nello Renacco and Aldo Rizzotti.[23] It was a particularly meaningful proposal because it was based on the broader Piedmontese regional plan (1944–6) drawn up a few years earlier by the same planners with the help of Mario Bianco; because it was widely published in the first issue of the new series of *Urbanistica* and because two of its drafters – Astengo and Renacco – played a major role in the development of Italian urban planning in the 1950s and 1960s.[24]

The Piedmontese regional plan foresaw the formation from scratch of 'new organic civic units perfectly equipped and economically active' which, on the one hand, could instil an order in the countryside and small towns, on the other, could 'enliven the large existing centres', in particular Turin.[25] The influence of the model of the County of London Plan is evident even in the first lines of the text of the regulatory plan, where Astengo, Renacco and Rizzotti declare to have 'abandoned the purely geometric and spatial conception of the old regulatory plans', to embrace an 'organic, elastic and positive approach'.[26] The urban fabric was taken on as the subject of analysis and interpreted as 'sum and association of elements proportionate to the community life of the inhabitants'.[27] The

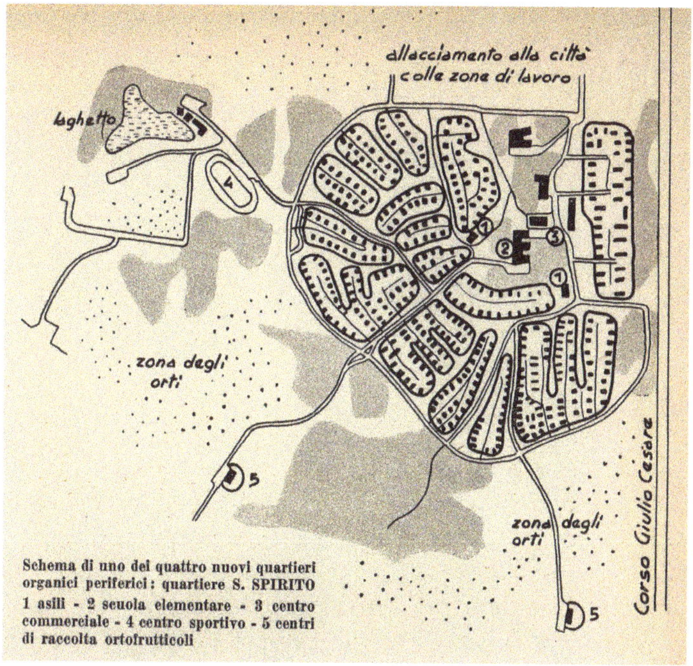

Figure 3.3 A suburban organic district as designed in the Turin master plan by Giovanni Astengo, Nello Renacco and Aldo Rizzotti. Published in 'Concorso per il piano regolatore di Torino', *Urbanistica*, 1 (1949)

INU Edizioni, Rome

large changes included in the plan – setting out a 'belt of green areas' and laying out an outer ring road and artery of high speed, north–south transit – were clearly inspired by the *Greenbelt* and the traffic axes that Abercrombie and Forshaw had imagined for London. And the problems to be addressed – evacuating residences, redesigning urban neighbourhoods, co-ordinating urban expansion, rationalizing connecting and communicating roads for new industrial areas – were no longer separately addressed with zoning as in the plans of functionalist inspiration, but integrated and resolved with the tools of the 'organic unit' clearly modelled on the communities of the County of London Plan. These units were sized to accommodate between five and ten thousand people – and not by chance the same population that Abercrombie and Forshaw had determined for the London communities – and served both to organize the growth of the first peripheral ring, and to fertilize the surrounding region by integrating industrial sites, residential areas and services for primary needs through the tool of the neighbourhood unit.

The competition for the Turin regulatory plan of 1948 came to nothing, and the formulations so clearly inspired by the London example were not fully included into the plan for Turin that Astengo and Giorgio Rigotti drafted in 1953 and 1956, mainly because of indiscriminate development of key areas around the periphery that happened in the meantime.[28] However, the principle of organizing the growth of the city through the establishment of compact and self-sufficient communities – that Zevi knew from the County of London Plan – heavily influenced many urban experiments in Italy in the 1950s.

Monuments Men

When Zevi was in exile in London from 1943 to 1945, a generation of young British specialists crossed Italy, from Sicily to the Alps, following the Eighth Army led by General Montgomery.[29] Together with the soldiers, there was also a group of architects, archaeologists, art historians and archivists engaged in the Italian campaign, earning experience and knowledge that later they did not hesitate to share at home. In this sense, the war became an important opportunity through which British architects and art historians could see in person the most important cities and monuments of the Italian peninsula.

Since 1941, some archaeologists had been called by the Civil Department of the War Office in London to consult on safeguarding archaeological sites that the British military encountered during their advance in North Africa.[30] In 1943, following the landing in Sicily, the requests became more and more pressing, and involved not just archaeologists but also art historians and archivists. In October of 1943, these informal opinions were given an official framework with the establishment of the Monuments and Fine Art Sub-Commission, under the Department of Civil Affairs of the War Office.[31]

What was the work of the members of the Sub-Commission? For library collections and artworks, in large part already moved to safety by Italian cultural ministry superintendents early in the conflict, their security and preservation had to be ensured. Furthermore, it was necessary to draw up lists of artworks destroyed or stolen by the Germans so that when the conflict was over, it would be possible to ask for their return.[32] As for the monuments, the main work was to make lists, working with the local superintendents, of the most important structures in the region, annotating the damage and the condition, and initiating urgent remedial actions, such as repairing roofs or shoring up unstable sections.[33]

Thomas Brooke, Edward Croft-Murray, and Roger Ellis were some of the officers of the Monuments and Fine Art Sub-Commission engaged in Italy.[34] In the context of this work, though, Colonel Leonard Woolley and Captain Roderick Enthoven were particularly important. Unlike some of their colleagues mentioned, once they returned to Britain they wrote articles, published books, held conferences on the months spent in Italy, spreading a particular *image* of Italy in which the monumental heritage was of pre-eminent interest compared to that of the contemporary, and where the walled towns of the central regions – Lazio, Umbria, the Marches, Tuscany – embodied the archetype of Italian landscape and art.

Between September 1944 and February 1945 the *RIBA Journal* published three detailed reports 'from the Civil Affairs Department of the War Office' detailing with minute description the damage and the condition of the most important buildings and monuments of the cities of central and north Italy.[35] These articles were published unsigned but from research in the files of the War Office at the National Archives of London, it emerges that they were written by Leonard Woolley.[36]

Woolley was, in the 1930s, probably the most famous British archaeologist thanks to his extensive excavation campaigns in Turkey, Syria, Egypt and Iraq where, beginning in 1922, he brought to light the remains of the ancient Mesopotamian city of Ur.[37] In June of 1943, Woolley was called to head the Archaeological Advisory Branch of the Department of Civil Affairs.[38] He was sent to Algeria and in December of the same year, Sicily, to supervise the archaeological division of the Monuments and Fine Art Sub-Commission, and spend the first months of 1944 at the Allied Command, first in Naples and then Rome, during the Italian campaign.

Although the work of the commission concerned practically the whole peninsula, the three articles only covered the central Italian regions: Lazio, Abruzzo, Umbria, the Marches and Tuscany. Though the reason for the choice is not known, it was fraught with consequences for British design culture, which even in the 1950s and 1960s devoted particular interest to the cities of central Italy, to the detriment of those in the north and south of the peninsula. The telegraphic notes on the damage to the monuments was supported by a series of photographs, taken directly by members of the Sub-Commission during their inspections. Besides the main cities, a myriad of little towns and tiny villages were documented, and sometimes photographed, with their churches, palaces, as well as views of the historic centres. The material included churches of Bolsena, Chiusi, Terni, Cortona, Gubbio, Volterra, Loreto and Pistoia besides a 'great number of smaller towns and isolated buildings visited by the officers' like Avezzano, Ferentino, Sutri, Veroli, Foligno, Acquapendente, Alatri, San Quirico d'Orcia, Pienza, Gradara, Fano, Fossombrone and many others.[39]

After the war, between 1945 and 1947, Woolley wrote detailed articles and also published a book on his experiences in Italy.[40] Besides describing the formation of the Sub-Commission and its aims, he records the activities in North Africa, Austria and Germany, the monuments visited and the urgent preservation repairs carried out. Much of the text and photography focused on Italy, and in particular, again emphasizing the central regions, contributing to reinforce the interest of British architects toward these perhaps less well-known centres.[41]

The information that Woolley conveyed in his publications came from the reports that the different teams of experts of the Sub-Commission compiled each month, on a regional basis.[42] In fact, teams were formed made up of art historians, architects, archaeologists and archivists, assigned to the areas of 'Sardinia and Sicily; Apulia, Campania, Calabria, Lucania; Abruzzi and Lazio; Le Marche, Toscana, Umbria; Liguria and Piedmont; Emilia and Lombardia; Le tre Venezie'.[43]

From the reports with his signature, it is also possible to reconstruct the places Captain Roderick Enthoven visited in Italy.[44] He studied at the Architectural Association School of London from 1919 to 1924 where he then taught, alternating with work in the Pakington Enthoven and Gray studio, which, in the 1930s, designed several commercial and residential buildings.[45] In 1940 Enthoven became a Civil Camouflage Officer in the Air Ministry, then enlisted in the Monuments and Fine Art Sub-Commission and was sent to Italy in August 1944, to Florence, where he worked as the Monuments Officer for Tuscany and Umbria. Afterwards, from 5 May to 15 October of 1945, he was assigned to the Piedmont and Liguria regions and finally, from 30 October to 1 December, to the Veneto and Friuli-Venezia Giulia. Shortly thereafter – 8 December 1945 – he was released from service and was able to return to London.[46]

From the mid-1950s, Enthoven dedicated himself mainly to his independent professional work, but in the early post-war years he held top positions, first at the Architectural Association School, which he directed in 1948–9, then at RIBA as vice president from 1951–3 and director of the Education Board from 1956–8.[47] Here he became, in fact, the sought-after expert for dealing with issues related to Italian artistic and historic heritage. It was Enthoven who, during the 1950s, reviewed the books of Italian authors or wrote on Italian subjects for the *RIBA Journal*, and it was again Enthoven who curated the extensive and detailed *Exhibition on Italian Architecture*, the first after the war.[48]

The exhibition was open from 7–29 October of 1949 in rooms of the Portland Place headquarters where a selection of more than 500 photographs taken in the 1930s by Ralph Deakin, foreign correspondent of *The Times* in Italy was displayed.[49] It was Enthoven who made the selection and organized the exhibition layout, with the aim of showing, not just masterpieces of Italian heritage, but also the many 'little known gems of Italian architecture' that he had discovered during the war.[50] It was not possible to find images of the exhibition itself, nor does there seem to have been a catalogue. However, in the article published in the *RIBA Journal* that described the opening of the exhibition, some of the photographs chosen by Enthoven were published. Almost exclusively, they show the regions he visited during the conflict: Tuscany, Umbria, and the Veneto. Enthoven chose photographs in which the cathedrals of Prato, Lucca, Perugia, the Basilica of San Francesco in Assisi, and San Marco in Venice were seen in the widest possible urban context. The piazzas, the winding streets – the stairways of Perugia – the historic centres descending harmoniously into the landscape like at San Gimignano and Assisi, were for Enthoven the essence of the Italian lesson. This was a lesson that he still considered relevant for British architects and urban planners, so much so that the exhibition was simply called *Exhibition on Italian Architecture*. It implicitly suggested that the Italian architecture to see was not the contemporary, though this was admired, but that of the historic patrimony, that of the town centres of the art cities that grew over time, in which it was difficult to separate monument from the urban context.

Italian lessons in townscape

In a famous 1950 editorial, the editor-in-chief of the *Architectural Review* James Maude Richards asked what the next steps were for British design.[51] Though the long road to establish modern architecture seemed to have ended, 'the way forward is not clear'.[52] And since the 'pioneers of modern design' had opened 'a brave new world', it was the moment to contaminate the functionalist lexicon with the national traditions of each different country.

As the magazine's directing editor since 1935, Richards had spent time disseminating functionalist architecture in Britain, publishing extensively the white-rendered buildings of European masters and of the MARS group, and at the same time watching with growing interest the peculiar character of the British territories and traditional constructions.[53] The search for 'cultural continuity' – and the difficult balance between the requirements of modernity and the legacy of spatial and construction solutions inherited from the past – became the load-bearing beam of the critical production of Richards during the 1950s and 1960s, to which the editorial lines of the *Architectural Review* also conformed.[54] The fine-tuning of the Townscape discipline was instrumental to this critical operation: a long-lasting editorial campaign that deeply engaged the magazine and its leading experts: Richards, the publisher Hubert de Cronin Hastings, and the editors Nikolaus Pevsner, Gordon Cullen and Kenneth Browne.[55]

Despite the emphasis placed on the purely British origin of the new discipline, the medieval city and the Italian renaissance acted as a constant point of reference for the development of Townscape. And that, not by chance, the growing interest in the *Architectural Review* and of the publisher, The Architectural Press, (both of which were headed by Hubert de Cronin Hastings) toward the historical, artistic and urban patrimony of Italy coincided with the ever sharper criticism that James Maude Richards and Ian Nairn directed toward the first generation of new towns.

Complementing the article of Hastings – 'Townscape' – published in 1949, Gordon Cullen contributed the first of a long series of 'Casebook' essays, expanding on all the perceptual effects that were seen in the design of 'urban scenes'.[56] The photographs and quick sketches Cullen made showing foreshortened views of British roads and squares, enlargements of the Houses of Parliament and Westminster, aerial views of Bath's crescents, and details of Kent cottages reinforced the idea that it was just these specific features of British cities and landscapes that shaped the new discipline.[57]

However, two months later, the *Architectural Review* published a detailed report on the city of Rome by the American critic Henry Hope Reed; this was especially important in that for the first time the Townscape principles were applied to a non-British city.[58]

The choice was not by chance. In the opening note, by the editorial staff, Rome was presented as 'the most perfect example in Europe of a capital that carries out its capital functions without loss of historic continuity'.[59] Despite the 'series of disasters after 1870 culminating in Mussolini's grandiose devastation' the Eternal City still embodied, for the editors of the *Architectural Review*, the model of a 'reconciliation of the ancient and modern'.[60] In particular, it was the historic centre of the city that we wanted to look at as 'the place in which to show how the historic centre of a capital city can serve modern needs without loss of character'.[61]

These judgements were framed in the ongoing bitter debate on the reconstruction of London and other British cities. The bombings of 1940–1 had destroyed large portions of the eastern neighbourhoods of London and areas of many of the main cities in the south of the country, sparking extensive debate on what to preserve in the ruins, how to do it, and what to demolish and rebuild; in particular regarding the churches of the City of London and Coventry Cathedral.[62] Richards, Hastings and Cullen also weighed in on how to reconstruct parts of London that were particularly delicate from a historical and monumental point of view – like the area behind Saint Paul's Cathedral and that of Covent Garden market – proposing on several occasions to fashion an urban fabric different from that proposed by functionalist inspiration, seeking instead the visual strategies *enclosure-exposure, truncation, change of level, building as sculpture* characteristic of the nascent Townscape.[63]

Rome could offer, in this sense, a series of valuable lessons. The American critic took into account the neighbourhoods of Spina of Borgo, Santa Maria Maggiore, Piazza di Spagna, Piazza del Popolo, Via del Corso, Via del Tritone, Piazza Venezia and Via dei Fori Imperiali – eight junctions in the urban fabric of Rome that showed how it was possible to shape a vibrant public place, or instead, through the wrong choices, destroy it completely. The latter category includes the demolition of the Spina of Borgo, which broke 'the whole effect of St Peter's that depends upon a sudden entrance into the sunlit piazza from the gloomy street', and the reorganization of the Piazza Venezia and Via dei Fori Imperiali, which, due to the heavy demolition and the construction of new buildings completely out of scale like the Altare della Patria, betrayed the character of 'secretive and intricate planning' that characterized the urban fabric of baroque Rome.[64]

If 'in French Baroque planning there are no surprises', said Henry Hope Reed, 'the unexpected transition from obscurity to magnificence is Roman' and the urban planning and architecture choices were attributed to respect for character.[65] Virtuous examples were the Piazza di Spagna and Piazza del Popolo which, changed into elliptical and trapezoidal forms allowed quick glimpses and changing views, and could also be admired from above from stairs and the belvederes that overlooked them. Despite being positioned at crucial junctions in the city, inside them, 'little boys can play games, the little girls can walk and the tourist can study his guide book without fear of the roadsters'.[66] The close connection between the street and the care for the buildings that faced onto it, with shops on the ground floor, opening out, were evident walking along Via del Tritone. Meanwhile, as an example of the unexpected change of scale between a street and the piazza where it opens up, Reed identified the junction between Via del Corso and Piazza Colonna; but there were many others so that 'practically every yard of the old city of Rome has a lesson relevant to the practice of townscape today'.[67]

Reed's text inaugurated a long series of historical essays, articles, travel reports and reviews that the *Architectural Review* dedicated in the 1950s to Italian heritage.[68] This interest in Italian monumental and urban heritage coincided with the publication, again in the pages of the *Architectural Review*, of the ruthless critical analysis of the first New Towns and residential neighbourhoods of the London County Council, which also ironically inspired Zevi and Italian post-war planners as an 'organic' model for the post-war reorganization of Italian towns during the same period.

As is well known, the initial enthusiasm for the urban design of the Labour Government of Attlee gave way to disenchantment. The failure that Richards encountered in 1953 in the New Towns of Harlow and Stevenage was attributable to low residential density and the dispersal of houses in the country; this worked against the formation of a compact city, and instead became 'groups of housing estates separated by empty spaces'.[69] The lack of a recognizable shape, of clearly defined full and empty spaces, of buildings and places in which citizens could recognize each other and identify themselves, prevented these aggregates of buildings from becoming real cities, regressing to places of transit and dormitory neighbourhoods. Two years later, again in the pages of the *Architectural Review*, Ian Nairn applied the same criticism to the whole British territory, where building speculation, low-density new housing, and uncontrolled growth of the suburbs had created a new type of characterless landscape, identified with the neologism of 'Subtopia'.[70] Both Richards and Nairn prioritized inverting the tendency for de-urbanization typical of the first generation of New Towns, instead designing neighbourhoods and pieces of city that were 'high-density and small area'.[71] And more than the American suburbs and the co-ordinated Scandinavian and Dutch neighbourhoods, the Italian historic centres were those that provided British design culture with unsurpassed models of recognizable urban forms, contained within a circle of walls that identified a discrete separation between city and country, and examples of a suitable urban density punctuated by quality public spaces. Not by chance, one such working interpretation of the historic patrimony of the Italian cities in the light of the studies on British Townscape would be pursued a few years later by Hubert de Cronin Hastings in *The Italian Townscape* (1963).[72]

Epilogue

The examination of publications and articles in Italian and British journals allows for the appreciation of the points that Zevi on the one hand, and Woolley, Enthoven and the circle of the *Architectural Review* on the other, impressed on the Anglo-Italian debate that lasted until at least the end of the 1960s. Although there was no lack of appreciation for individual architects – James Stirling and Denys Lasdun in particular – Italian design continued to dedicate attention to urban planning across the Channel and the New Towns. British design, meanwhile, was interested in the contemporary resonance with the vast historical, artistic, and urban patrimony of the Italian peninsula rather more than in what was actually happening there.

This emerges with clarity both in the fundamental book of 1959 of Giuseppe Samonà, *L'urbanistica e l'avvenire della città negli Stati europei*, and in the monographic 1968 issue of *Zodiac* dedicated to Great Britain. In both publications, it is British planning that plays a leading role in the development of Italian design, which especially admired the experiment of the New Towns defined as the 'most spectacular operation of planning from above that took place after the war'.[73]

In particular, the new town centre of Cumbernauld was extensively published in Italian journals, from the first announcements to its inauguration in 1967.[74] It abandoned the restricted dimension, the small-scale buildings, the rural temptation and de-urbanization of the first generation of the New Towns, to embrace large-scale territorial problems and the urban phenomenon of road traffic. The principle of neighbourhood unity was completely abandoned and the city was planned as 'a compact town set upon a hilltop', suggestive of central Italy, characterized by a high population density and residential areas collected and connected to an impressive public centre.[75]

Although this public centre was never entirely completed, it had a wide influence in Italy – where for the first time the major questions of the expanding city and automobile circulation were being faced – and it became a common undertaking for Italian architects and urban planners travelling by car as far as Scotland to see with their own eyes the mighty civic centre raised in the countryside.[76]

However, despite its fame, the Cumbernauld town centre was the last remnant of the British myth in Italy: the myth of an architectonic urban design capable of absorbing and rebalancing economic, social and residential dynamics over a vast area. The failure of the town centre, the altered economic and social panorama that 1968 brought to Italy as well as to Great Britain, sparked a decisive change of course to the British–Italian exchange.

The disasters of the Agrigento landslide, the Arno flood, and the high water in Venice in 1966 and the large general strike for housing in November 1969 showed how the aspirations of the Italian urban planners after the war toward the creation of a more equal city, better planned, and in which there was housing for everyone, remained unfinished.[77] In the same months, in Britain, the tough editorial campaign 'Manplan' launched by the *Architectural Review* harshly criticized the living conditions of residents in post-war residential estates and neighbourhoods, suggesting implicitly the failure of those state bodies and those architects that had shaped the old and new post-war cities.[78]

The energy crisis of 1973 and the following years of economic stagnation put a rapid end to that era of growth, social reform and optimism about the future that will be embedded in the definition of the 'trente glorieuses'.[79] Increasingly in crisis, even the machinery of the British Welfare State began to be under attack by the 1970s and would be progressively dismantled by the end of the decade.

Radically changed by this economic and social context, the contours of Italian–British exchanges were also affected in terms of architecture and urban planning. While the myth of British urban design persists in Italy at least up to the second half of the 1970s, British observers, occupied with the problem of towns and historic centres devastated by the massive residential neighbourhoods of the post-war era – as symbolized by the uproar of the publication of *The Rape of Britain* in 1975 – began to determine in the Italian architectonic debate that particular quality of insertion in the urban context that they were seeking.[80] This perhaps explains the growing interest of British journals and architects in the work of Giancarlo De Carlo in Urbino and Carlo Scarpa in the countryside and cities of the Veneto – interest in two architects, that is, who had made the search for a refined insertion of contemporary architecture in consolidated urban and natural contexts the hallmark of their work.[81] And in the other direction, the disruptive new language proposed by James Stirling made him the standard bearer of British architecture in Italy.[82] This renewed pathway of exchange seems intertwined though only at the level of architectural research, going beyond the political, economic context and the social aspirations that mix urban British culture with that of Italy in the early post-war period, and is therefore not covered here. However, the research pathways left open by these pages should lead to other fertile ground, suggesting how, despite the many differences, architects, urban planners and historians in Italy and Britain have continued to see themselves as interlocutors with mutual interests in the last decades of the twentieth century.

Notes

1 Ciccarelli 2019.
2 Dulio 2008; Ciorra and Cohen 2018; Bello 2019.
3 Bruno Zevi Foundation (Rome), Sottoserie 02 Onorificenze, busta 2, 02/08.
4 James 1957; Anichini and Grima 1960; A. Gentili 1960; G. Gentili 1960; Pedio 1962.
5 Forshaw and Abercrombie 1943.
6 Bruno Zevi Foundation (Rome), Serie 01, busta 1, 01/03 The Architectural Association School di Londra, and Serie 04, sottoserie 01, busta 5, 04.01/01 Studio Cyril Sjöstrom di Londra.
7 Dulio 2008, 30.
8 Zevi 1993, 34–5; Dulio 2008, 9–13.
9 Bullock 2002, 3–22. See also Mack and Humphries 1985.
10 Mace 1986; Richardson 2004.
11 The RIBA Journal issues report the monthly appointments and the full transcript of the conferences and debates.
12 Bruno Zevi Foundation (Rome), busta 75, 11/02 Agendine e rubriche di Zevi, agendine 1943–4.
13 Dulio 2008, 52–9.
14 Chitty 1946; Zevi 1957.
15 Zevi 1959.
16 Zevi 1993, 79. See also Dulio 2008, 114–19.
17 Zevi 1950: 316 and 325.
18 Amati and Freestone 2016.
19 Zevi 1944.
20 Forshaw and Abercrombie 1943, 2.
21 Forshaw and Abercrombie 1943, 21 and 28–9.
22 Forshaw and Abercrombie 1943, Plate xxxvi.
23 *Concorso* 1949. See also Scrivano 2000.
24 *Piano* 1947.
25 *Piano* 1947, 28–9.
26 *Concorso* 1949, 36.
27 *Concorso* 1949, 36.
28 Astengo 1955; Rigotti 1955.
29 Lamb 1995.
30 Woolley 1947, 5.
31 National Archives (London), T209/1, Proposals to set up a committee on the protection of cultural monuments and works of art.
32 National Archives (London), War Office 204/2986 and WO 204/2987, Italy: Preservation of historic monuments and fine art: Directives, reports lists and correspondence.
33 National Archives (London), War Office 204/1077, Protection of historic monuments in Italy.
34 The biographies are available on the Monuments Men Foundation for the Preservation of Art website. After the war those men assumed leading roles in the British cultural institutions: Lieutenant Colonel Thomas Brooke was appointed deputy director of the Tate Gallery in 1948, Major Edward Croft-Murray was hired to the print room of the British Museum while Major Roger Ellis was enrolled as a professor at University College London.
35 *The Monuments* 1944; *The Monuments* 1945.
36 The typescripts of the three reports can be found in National Archives (London), T 209/17/1, Reports on damage to monuments. Incorporated in works of art in Italy Part I. Woolley sent the reports to the War Office in London on 4 July, 28 October and 11 November 1944.
37 Woolley 1939.
38 Woolley 1947, 5.
39 *The Monuments* 1944.
40 Woolley 1945.

41 Woolley inserted 27 full-page photographs in his book. Twenty of them related to Italian monuments, buildings and cities, while only two reported North African monuments, three Austrian monuments and individual images of France and Austria. Even in the text, Italy is the only country to which two entire chapters are dedicated.
42 National Archives (London), War Office 220/636: Record of war damage to monuments in Italy; War Office 220/600: List of protected monuments in Italy; and the monthly field reports kept in War Office 220/624, 220/625, 220/626, 220/627, 220/628, 220/629, 220/630, 220/631.
43 Woolley 1947, 69.
44 National Archives (London), War Office 220/638, Italy: Final reports.
45 This biographical information is contained in a Curriculum Vitae written by Enthoven himself, and in newspaper clippings referable to him, contained in three volumes kept at the RIBA Archive (London), ENR/1–3, Three albums of texts, cuttings and illustrations compiled by R.E. Enthoven, Architect and Designer, between 1919 and 1976.
46 National Archives (London), War Office 220/638, Italy: Final reports.
47 RIBA Archives (London), RIBA/MEM, Naturalisation subcommittee papers, 1946–7.
48 *Exhibition* 1949; *Italian* 1949.
49 Deakin's photographs are kept in the homonymous collection at the Robert Elwall photographs collection at the RIBA British Architectural Library.
50 *Exhibition* 1949, 470.
51 Richards 1950.
52 Richards 1950, 166.
53 Rosso 2001; Higgott 2007, 33–56.
54 Erten 2004.
55 'Townscape Revised' 2012.
56 Since this article, and in all subsequent ones, Hubert de Cronin Hastings assumed the pseudonym of Ivor de Wolfe. So De Wolfe 1949; Cullen 1949. See also Goslin 1996.
57 Richards 1958.
58 Hope Reed 1950.
59 Hope Reed 1950, 91.
60 Hope Reed 1950, 91.
61 Hope Reed 1950, 91.
62 Campbell 2018; Pane 2018.
63 Browne 1964.
64 Hope Reed 1950, 103 and 108.
65 Hope Reed 1950, 103.
66 Hope Reed 1950, 104.
67 Hope Reed 1950, 103.
68 As an example, see Mortimer 1950; Masson 1951; Giedion 1952; Whiffen 1953; Masson 1954; Powell 1954; Tomlison 1954; Masson 1955; Masson 1956a; Masson 1956b; Lang 1957.
69 Richards 1953a; Richards 1953b. See also Aldridge 1979.
70 Nairn edited two monographic issues of *The Architectural Review*: the first (702, 1955) entitled *Outrage*; the second (719, 1956) *Counter Attack*. See Darley and McKie 2014.
71 See in particular *Summing Up* at the end of the monographic issue *Outrage*, 451–4.
72 Erten and Powers 2013.
73 Marsoni 1968, 189.
74 Marsoni 1968, 191–4. See also Sacchetti and Zaffangini 1960; 'La nuova' 1963; Lewis and Stead 1963.
75 Copcutt 1963.
76 As an example, Aymonino 1965, 62. For the travels of Italian architects and town planners to Cumbernauld see Ferrari 1977; Imbesi 2004.
77 Dal Co 1997, 11–12.
78 The editorial campaign consisted of eight monographic issues, published from September 1969 to September 1970, and dedicated to the following themes: frustration, transport, industry, education, religion, health and welfare, local government, housing. See Erten 2012.
79 Fourastié 1979.
80 Amery and Cruickshank 1975.
81 'Italy' 1966; 'Urbino' 1972; Loach 1979; 'Carlo' 1973.
82 As an example, Izzo 1979; Nicolin 1979.

References

Aldridge, Meryl. *The British New Towns: A programme without a policy*. London: Routledge and Kegan Paul, 1979.

Amati, Marco and Robert Freestone. 'All of London's a stage: The 1943 County of London Plan Exhibition', *Urban History* 4 (2016): 539–56.

Amery, Colin and Don Cruickshank. *The Rape of Britain*. London: Paul Elek, 1975.

Anichini, Ferdinando and Godfrey Grima. 'Fisionomia del costume architettonico inglese in quattordici opere', *L'Architettura: Cronache e Storia* 54 (1960): 822–43.

Astengo, Giovanni. 'Torino senza Piano', *Urbanistica* 15–16 (1955): 110–17.

Aymonino, Carlo. *Origini e sviluppo della città moderna*. Padua: Marsilio, 1965.

Bello, Francesco (ed.). *Bruno Zevi intellettuale di confine*. Roma: Viella, 2019.

Browne, Kenneth. 'A Latin Quarter for London: A townscape survey of Covent Garden and a plan for its future', *The Architectural Review* 803 (1964): 192–201.

Bullock, Nicholas. *Building the Post-War World*. London: Routledge, 2002.

Campbell, Louise. 'Reconstruction, Englishness and Coventry Cathedral', *Storia Urbana* 158 (2018): 87–110.

'Carlo Scarpa', *The Architectural Review* 922 (1973): 393–6.

Chitty, Anthony. 'Scienza ed edilizia', *Metron* 9 (1946): 2–16.

Ciccarelli, Lorenzo. *Il mito dell'equilibrio: Il dibattito anglo-italiano per il governo del territorio negli anni del dopoguerra*. Milan: Franco Angeli, 2019.

Ciorra, Pippo and Jean-Louis Cohen. *Zevi's Architects*. Macerata: Quodlibet, 2018.

'Concorso per il piano regolatore di Torino', *Urbanistica* 1 (1949): 36–43.

Copcutt, Geoffrey. 'Cumbernauld New Town Central Area', *Architectural Design* 5 (1963): 210–25.

Cullen, Gordon. 'Townscape casebook', *The Architectural Review* 636 (1949): 363–74.

Dal Co, Francesco. 'Introduzione'. In *Storia dell'architettura italiana: Il secondo novecento*, edited by Francesco Dal Co, 11–20. Milan: Electa, 1997.

Darley, Gillian and David McKie (eds). *Ian Nairn: Words in place*. Nottingham: Five Leaves Publications, 2014.

De Wolfe, Ivor. 'Townscape', *The Architectural Review* 636 (1949): 354–62.

Dulio, Roberto. *Introduzione a Bruno Zevi*. Bari: Laterza, 2008.

Enthoven, Roderick. 'An architectural journey in war-time Italy: Describing the work of the monuments and fine art division of the War Office', *Builder* 5 (1946): 328–9.

Enthoven, Roderick. 'Architectural journey in war-time Italy', *The Architectural Association Journal* vol. 61 (May 1946): 73–83.

Erten, Erdem. 'Shaping "The Second Half Century": The Architectural Review 1947–1971'. PhD thesis, Massachusetts Institute of Technology, 2004.

Erten, Erdem. 'I, The World, The Devil and The Flesh: Manplan, Civilia and H. de Cronin Hastings', *The Journal of Architecture* 5 (2012): 709–12.

Erten, Erdem and Alan Powers. 'Introduction'. In *The Italian Townscape*, by Ivor De Wolfe, 5–20. London: Artifice, 2013.

'Exhibition of Italian Architecture', *RIBA Journal* 56/11 (1949): 470.

'Exhibition of Italian Architecture at the R.I.B.A.', *RIBA Journal* 56/12 (1949): 511–16.

Ferrari, Alberto. 'Cumbernauld rivisitato', *Casabella* 422 (1977): 58–61.

Forshaw, John Henry and Patrick Abercrombie. *County of London Plan*. London: Macmillan and Co., 1943.

Fourastié, Jean. *Les Trente Glorieuses ou la révolution invisible de 1946 à 1975*. Paris: Fayard, 1979.

Gentili, Alberto. 'Costume britannico: Facoltà di Tecnologia e Commercio a Sheffield degli architetti Gollins, Melvin, Ward and Partners', *L'Architettura: Cronache e Storia* 55 (1960): 29–31.

Gentili, Giorgio. 'Tre scuole di Frederick Gibberd', *L'Architettura: Cronache e Storia* 58 (1960): 252–8.

Giedion, Sigfried. 'Sixtus V and the planning of Baroque Rome', *The Architectural Review* 664 (1952) 217–26.

Goslin, David. *Gordon Cullen: Visions of urban design*. London: Academy Editions, 1996.

Higgott, Andrew. *Mediating Modernism: Architectural cultures in Britain*. London: Routledge, 2007.

Hope Reed, Henry. 'Rome: The third sack', *The Architectural Review* 638 (1950): 91–110.

Imbesi, Giuseppe. 'Il corsivo: Il Grand Tour degli urbanisti'. In *Reti verdi e disegno della città contemporanea*, edited by Lucia Nucci, 9–12. Rome: Gangemi, 2004.

'Italian Architecture at the RIBA', *The Architects' Journal* No. 2852 (1949): 367.
'Italy, University College, Urbino: Giancarlo De Carlo', *Architectural Design* 12 (1966): 627–8.
Izzo, Alberto. *James Stirling*. Rome: Officina, 1976.
James, John. 'Un centro di case economiche presso Londra dell'architetto Eric Lyons', *L'Architettura: Cronache e Storia* 26 (1957): 530–5.
'La nuova città di Cumbernauld', *Urbanistica* 39 (1963): 129–42.
Lamb, Richard. *War in Italy: 1943–1945*. London: Penguin, 1995.
Lang, Susan. 'Bomarzo', *The Architectural Review* 725 (1957): 427–30.
Larkham, Peter. *The London Regional Reconstruction Committee: Architects, exhibitions and postwar vision for replanning* (Working Paper 16). Birmingham: Centre for Environment and Society Research, 2013.
Lewis, David and Peter Stead. 'La zona centrale di Cumbernauld', *Casabella-Continuità* 280 (1963): 9–17.
Loach, Judy. 'Giancarlo De Carlo in Urbino', *The Architectural Review* 986 (1979): 204–14.
Mace, Angela. *The Royal Institute of British Architects: A guide to its archive and history*. London: Mansell, 1986.
Mack, Joanna and Stephen Humphries. *London at War: The making of modern London 1939–45*. London: Sidgwick and Jackson, 1985.
Marsoni, Lina. '20 anni di new towns: Rilettura di un intervento parametrico', *Zodiac* 18 (1968): 189–200.
Masson, Georgina, 'The Hohenstaufen Castles in Apulia', *The Architectural Review* 651 (1951): 185–9.
Masson, Georgina. 'Venetian gardens', *The Architectural Review* 687 (1954): 199–201.
Masson, Georgina. 'Palladian villas as rural centre', *The Architectural Review* 703 (1955): 17–20.
Masson, Georgina. 'Rococo pharmacy', *The Architectural Review* 710 (1956): 124–6.
Masson, Georgina. 'The Sferisterio of Macerata', *The Architectural Review* 714 (1956): 50–1.
Mortimer, Raymond. 'San Giorgio Maggiore', *The Architectural Review* 646 (1950): 259–62.
Nicolin, Pierluigi. 'Caratteri istituzionali e linguaggio metaforico: Due progetti di James Stirling', *Lotus International* 25 (1979): 4–14.
Pane, Andrea. 'Ruins for remembrance: The debate around the bombed London city churches and its echoes in Italy', *Storia Urbana* 158 (2018): 111–48.
'Piano regionale piemontese', Special Issue of *Metron* 14 (1947).
Pedio, Renato. 'Costume inglese in due opere di Lyons, Israel & Ellis', *L'Architettura: Cronache e Storia* 77 (1962): 750–7.
Powell, Nicholas. 'The Certosa di San Lorenzo at Padula', *The Architectural Review* 688 (1954): 267–9.
Richards, James Maude. 'The next step?', *The Architectural Review* 639 (1950): 165–81.
Richards, James Maude. 'Failure of the new towns', *The Architectural Review* 679 (1953): 28–36.
Richards, James Maude. 'Failure of the new densities', *The Architectural Review* 684 (1953): 355–61.
Richards, James Maude. *The Functional Tradition in Early Industrial Buildings*. London: The Architectural Press, 1958.
Richardson, Margaret. *66 Portland Place: The headquarters of the Royal Institute of British Architects*. London: RIBA Publishing, 2004.
Rigotti, Giorgio. 'Studi in corso per il nuovo piano regolatore di Torino', *Urbanistica* 15–16 (1955): 118–24.
Rosso, Michela, *La storia utile: Patrimonio e modernità nel lavoro di John Summerson e Nikolaus Pevsner: Londra 1928–1955*. Turin: Edizioni di Comunità, 2001.
Sacchetti, Raffaella and Mario Zaffangini. 'Dopo Cumbernauld', *Casabella* 328, 329 (1960): 6–25, 6–15.
Samonà, Giuseppe. *L'urbanistica e l'avvenire della città negli Stati Europei*. Bari: Laterza, 1959.
Scrivano, Paolo. 'The elusive polemics of theory and practice: Giovanni Astengo, Giorgio Rigotti and the post-war debate over the plan for Turin', *Planning Perspectives* 15 (2000): 3–24.
Scrivano, Paolo. *Building Transatlantic Italy: Architectural dialogues with postwar America*. London: Routledge, 2013.
'The monuments of central Italy: Second report from Civil Affairs Department of the War Office', *RIBA Journal* 51/11 (1944): 287–9.
'The monuments of central Italy: Third report from Civil Affairs Department of the War Office', *RIBA Journal* 52/1 (1944): 11–13.

'The monuments of central Italy: Fourth report from Civil Affairs Department of the War Office', *RIBA Journal* 52/4 (1945): 105–8.
Tomlinson, Anna. 'Sacri Monti', *The Architectural Review* 696 (1954): 368–73.
'Townscape Revised', Special Issue of *The Journal of Architecture* 17/5 (2012).
'Urbino Renewal. Law Faculty, University of Urbino. Architect: Giancarlo De Carlo', *The Architectural Review* 908 (1972): 242–6.
Whiffen, Marcus. 'Visitors to Vicenza', *The Architectural Review* 679 (1953): 5–10.
Woolley, Leonard. *Ur Excavations: The Ziggurat and its surroundings*. Oxford: Oxford University Press, 1939.
Woolley, Leonard. 'The preservation of historical architecture in the war zones', *RIBA Journal* 52/2 (1945): 35–42.
Woolley, Leonard. *A Record of the Work Done by the Military Authorities for the Protection of the Treasures of Art and History in the War Areas*. London: HMSO, 1947.
Zevi, Bruno. 'Un esempio di urbanistica organica: Il piano regolatore per la ricostruzione di Londra', *Urbanistica* 3–6 (1944): 31–41.
Zevi, Bruno. *Storia dell'architettura moderna*. Turin: Einaudi, 1950.
Zevi, Bruno. *Towards an Organic Architecture*. London: Faber and Faber, 1950.
Zevi, Bruno. 'John Summerson e una teoria per l'architettura moderna', *L'Architettura: Cronache e Storia* 25 (1957): 436–7.
Zevi, Bruno. 'L'esempio del Royal Institute of British Architects', *L'Architettura: Cronache e Storia* 41 (1959): 728.
Zevi, Bruno. *Zevi su Zevi: Architettura come profezia*. Venice: Marsilio, 1993.

Part I

Personae and Debates

4
Banham's Italy

Davide Spina

Never trust first impressions, they say. The old adage surely rang true for Reyner Banham, the British historian and critic, as he recollected his first encounter with Italian modernism:

> At a Milan bookstall, outside of Brera, I picked up a bound volume of Futurist manifestoes, looked at it, put it down and walked off without even inquiring the price. That was in 1951, and I think I must have been mad. Three years later I was battering on the door of the *Soprintendenza* in order to get to see the Futurist paintings in the Modern Gallery in Milan.[1]

At the time of this door-battering, 32-year-old Banham was a part-time editor at the *Architectural Review* and a part-time PhD student at the Courtauld Institute in London, where he was working under the tutelage of Sir Nikolaus Pevsner. The book that came out of that doctorate, the instantly successful *Theory and Design in the First Machine Age* (1960), turned the futurists from marginal figures to cornerstones of European modernism. In Banham's view, no one better embodied what he called 'the mechanical sensibility' – that is, the real spirit of architectural modernism, which he found lacking in most of the production that then went under the 'modernist' banner – than Antonio Sant'Elia and co.[2] And so, almost overnight, the visions of this Italian avant-garde became something of a normative reference for the British historian to gauge whatever came under his scrutiny. Banham did this, most famously, when in 1959 he took aim at another Italian phenomenon, the so-called 'neoliberty', which he located exactly at the polar opposite of futurism. In short, Italy was important to Banham as it helped him construct his own narrative on modern architecture (what it had been; what it could and should be), and therefore set forth the latter's 'Dos and Don'ts' (futurism good, neoliberty bad).[3] Conversely, I would argue that Banham is equally important to Italy, as his writings help us better understand the trajectory of modernity in this country, and architecture's role in the unfolding of this process.

In the early 1950s, when Banham made his first trips to Italy, a formalist trend was in full-swing across the peninsula. To a visitor from England – especially to a member of the Independent Group, as Banham was – coming to grips with this architectural production proved 'an uneasy exercise'.[4] Consider the sculptural extravaganza and historicism of the two Italian Luigis whose work he examined for the *Architectural Review* (respectively, Moretti and Vagnetti). Both were incompatible with the restrained and forward-looking modernism advocated in Banham's own London circles – 'to those whose aesthetic standards are moral, this is confusing', was his comment on the work of the latter.[5] In Italy, the British historian found no taste for iconographic clarity, structural honesty, and use of materials 'as found'. Instead, over and over again he encountered a penchant for artifice and deception. Under his lens, for instance, Gio Ponti 'successfully pulls off a rather *risqué* aesthetic effect' with the Pirelli building, while Leo Calini and Eugenio Montuori achieve 'the sort of effect that only an Italian … would have the nerve to try and attain by such means' when they make the Termini building look taller by carving two slits across its façade.[6] Now, what matters to us is that Banham framed this Italian liking for effects not as a contingent feature of a few buildings, but as a manifestation of a broader attitude towards modernism in this country, one that gave him grounds to question the moral integrity of Italian architectural production as a whole – 'Italy's contribution to post-war architecture has been equivocal', he declared in 1962.[7]

Italian architects, he believed, seemed to appreciate modernism as yet another style in the history of styles, and not as a new and different way of building, and thus showed little understanding for the movement's *raison d'être* – by 'using traditional craft and pretechnological materials to produce … mechanistic effects of smooth precision', Banham observed in 1975, 'the Italians … undermin[ed] the symbolic values of the machine aesthetic'.[8] In another piece, he wondered whether Italian architecture wasn't '*only*' about 'a brilliant handling of forms'.[9] And so, in the eyes of the British historian, post-war Italy became the site of a collective deviation from modernist orthodoxy – of 'a flight from functionalism', to borrow the definition of his fellow countryman and Liverpool University professor, Robert Gardner-Medwin, who was observing the same phenomenon in the same period.[10] To Banham, however, this phenomenon had long been an Italian prerogative: even 'before the war', one reads in his 'neoliberty' piece, '"modern" was practised as a style, since it could not be practised as a total discipline'.[11] Banham, in short, registered an enduring mismatch between how modern Italian buildings *looked*, and how they were *produced* (between the finished product and the manufacturing process behind it), an obvious inconsistency with the modernist method. The latter was present in most modernist architecture anyway, but in Banham's view seemed particularly pronounced in Italian production.

This leads us to another mismatch detected by Banham, which went surprisingly unnoticed in later commentary: the mismatch between the building's form and its social content, or rather, between what you *see* and what the thing actually *is*. Banham hinted at this problem several times in his career, first with regard to Sant'Elia's drawings. These visualizations provide a wealth of information on the aesthetic experience of the city of the future (on the buildings' external appearance, on pedestrian and car circulation, on its overall atmospheric quality), while they say nothing about the societal and economic forces that would sustain a city of this kind: '[Sant'Elia's] drawings', wrote Banham in 1955, 'reveal a designer whose intentions in the modelling and disposition of forms were of a simplicity and boldness far ahead of those of his older contemporaries … though [one whose] functional and planning intentions remain inscrutable in the complete absence of any plans among these drawings'.[12] We are left to think that in futurism a modern *image* does not necessarily correspond to a modern *programme*. In 1959, Banham came to a similar conclusion upon reviewing Luigi Moretti's Casa Girasole (1950) and Ludovico Quaroni's La Martella estate (1954): in both he acknowledged 'a degree of progressive aspiration, a forward-looking aesthetic, even when structural techniques and social orders seem a millennium behind those for which the modern movement was created'.[13] He made this point most cogently with respect to Moretti's famous apartment block – 'the exterior is unmistakably modern … as modern as the *Pavillion Suisse* [but] what goes on inside it is in no way modern: routine Roman apartments planned along a corridor, and … a basement full of servants and services, as in all Italy back to the Quattrocento';[14] another instance where the aesthetics and ontology of the architectural object simply do not match. Banham doubled down on the issue one year later, in 1960, on the occasion of the XII Milan Triennale, where the British had put on display one of their prefabricated CLASP schools: 'what concerns some

Italians', reads Banham's report on the event, 'was imitating the forms of these school buildings rather than the programme behind them' – quite a lapidary statement.[15] Then, in 1976, after a 15-year hiatus, Gino Valle's Zanussi-Rex building in Pordenone (1961) received the same treatment from the British historian: apparently a megastructure, he observed, 'but not reckoned as [such] because of its single administrative function' – the same thing, a slippage between the building's form and its content, an inconsistency that, in his view, was found also in the oft-celebrated visions of Archizoom and Superstudio, which he reviewed in the same book (*Megastructure*).[16] To Banham, both *No Stop City* (1969) and *Twelve Cautionary Tales* (1971) featured an 'unmistakably megastructural presentation [that] could stand up on [its] own without any such radical programme to support [it]' – once more, a mismatch between 'appearance' and 'substance'.[17] Banham returned to this issue one last time in 1984, as he covered another Italian story, the competition for the repurposing of the Lingotto building in Turin (1923) – 'the building shell, without its social content, is not what they set out to preserve. The building without the life is not the building, merely a travesty',[18] a criticism that he radicalized in his 1988 bumper-sticker definition of postmodernism, the movement that ratified this schizophrenia between outside and inside – 'it is not architecture, but building in drag'.[19] And so, over time Banham came to see the split between the exterior and the interior of a building as more and more problematic. What in the 1950s had seemed to him a property distinguishing the architecture of a single country (Italy), in the 1980s had become the defining characteristic of a global movement (albeit one pioneered in that very country).

But what is architectural postmodernism other than a particular take on architectural representation? Banham took representation seriously, but he, of course, stood on the modernist side of the fence. 'Imageability' was what he really cared for in this department – 'the building should be an immediately apprehensible visual entity … the form grasped by the eye should be confirmed by experience of the building in use … this form should be entirely proper to the functions and materials of the building in their entirety', is how he put it in his essay, 'The New Brutalism'.[20] In Italy, Banham found almost none of this 'imageability', with a few exceptions, like Gio Ponti and Pier Luigi Nervi's Pirelli building, which he praised exactly as 'an immediately comprehended slogan in itself'[21] upon reviewing it in 1961, and as 'an advertising symbol that is not just a gimmick' when he returned to it in 1975.[22] As a whole, though, more than an ethic or a programme of their own, to him modern Italian buildings seemed to represent something other than themselves. In this, he was picking up on an existing strand of British criticism. For instance, in Luigi Moretti's Corso Italia building in Milan, Robert Gardner-Medwin did not see modern architecture, but 'a dramatized abstraction of modern architecture' – abstraction being one form of representation.[23] Banham, however, was concerned with representation in a broader sense. Take his interpretation of the Lingotto building, FIAT's main manufacturing facility in the inter-war period:

> What separates it from American plants ... is sheer rhetoric. The American plants are useful and fairly cheap facilities ... By the time Lingotto and its ramps were finished in 1926, it was already becoming *passé* by American standards, for Henry Ford was getting out of multi-storey Highland Park moving into one-storey thin sheds at the River Rouge. Lingotto was really a monument – a memorial to a myth of modernity, and of America as the home of modernity'.[24]

What Banham is saying here is that the building *represents* modern industrial practice rather than providing the spaces for it, that it is nothing but a grand representation of American modernity. He is also implying that FIAT's Lingotto is a derivative object, an object that owes its existence to another type of object from another place.

The idea of the derivative and the presence of foreign models pervades most of what Banham wrote on modern Italian architecture from the mid-1970s onward. In this literature, the peninsula's architecture lives an utterly vicarious existence: the Lingotto, again, is 'a derivative ... version of a manner of building whose metropolitan heartland was elsewhere'; Archizoom are 'in direct emulation' of Archigram; the megastructure designs by students of Manfredo Tafuri at La Sapienza are 'plainly derivative, from ... foreign sources like Metabolism'.[25] And one could easily include, in this list of *ersatz* items, two Italian buildings that did not fall under the scrutiny of the British historian, but that are still as committed to an idea of modernity as they are derivative in nature: the futuristic ENI building in Rome (a simulation of the American corporate box), and the pioneering Metro Drive-In theatre in Casal Palocco, the first building of its kind in Europe (and a monument to the American drive-in).[26] Late-career Banham seems to be telling us that all that is modern in Italy is either a monument, an emulation or a simulation of something from *somewhere else*.

In so doing, Banham hinted at something of great consequence: Italy's inherently visual relation with the apparatus of modernity. For, given its peripheral position and belated entrée into the scene of international capitalism, Italy has for ever been looking abroad for ideas and practices geared towards the proverbial 'break with the past'. Now more often than not this process has been overwhelmingly reliant on visual information, and therefore favoured the adoption of modern *things* simply as *images*. Nowhere was this more clearly shown than in Italy's post-Second World War embrace of American modernity, which seeped into the country's collective unconscious through the consumption of Hollywood motion *pictures* – a solely *optical* consumption of course, since these films were all dubbed. And so, the visual nature of this process of selecting, translating and incorporating modern things into the Italian everyday brought about a loss in the significance of such objects and practices in their place of origin – in other words, they became appreciated *not* for their use-value, but (almost entirely) for their sign-value. This is the epistemic order that gives you key Italian buildings of the twentieth century such as Giacomo Matte-Trucco's Lingotto and Luigi Moretti's Casa Girasole: objects whose modernity is, as Banham points out, only skin-deep, and that project an image of modernity while nurturing traditional ways of working and living.

Given its penetrating insight into modern Italian architecture, it is unfortunate that Reyner Banham's work has always been received so lukewarmly in this country. To this day, the British historian is scarcely read in Italian schools (speaking about him with a fellow Italian PhD student a few years ago, he thought I was talking about SOM's Gordon Bunshaft all along!). Arguably the main culprit for this all-but-impressive critical fortune is his 1959 'neoliberty' piece, especially the latter's corrosive ending, which offended one too many people along the peninsula. But the knee-jerk criticism of this piece was generally unthinking, poorly articulated, and very much in contrast to Banham's well-grounded and incisive prose (as late as 2007, Paolo Portoghesi still vaguely characterized the latter as 'driven by ideological intolerance').[27] Perhaps what really made people snap was the Kantian overtone of Banham's accusation: to say that 'neoliberty is infantile regression' is to say that the Italian bourgeoisie has failed to live up to the Enlightenment's ideal ('man's emergence from his self-imposed immaturity', as Kant put it) – a statement that was not far from reality then, nor is it today.[28] Likewise, to say that 'any group of architects showing contempt for "the triumph of the machine" condemns itself to permanent infancy', as he did three years after the 'neoliberty' piece, is to say that, in their work, post-war Italian architects have failed to take mechanization, one of the key forces of modernity, into account – a statement that, again, can hardly be argued with (indeed, Banham himself recognized two exceptions to this rule: Franco Albini and Franca Helg's Rinascente building in Rome, and Marco Zanuso's Olivetti plant in Buenos Aires, both designed around their air-conditioning systems).[29] And even when, in the same article, Banham went as far as to say that Italian architects 'bring to mind what is usually said about the intelligence of whales: an enormous brain condemned to perpetual infancy because of the absolute lack of any means to put it to use', he was simply pointing to a truth that everybody knew, but that nobody was ready to admit: i.e., that, for all their abilities, Italian architects had been basically excluded from all strategic decisions on modern architecture and planning in their country – a proposition that goes a long way to explain the depressing character of the average post-war Italian city.[30]

There is no doubt that in his comments on Italy Banham was more outspoken than usual, and, to some extent, we can understand the defensiveness of the locals towards his language; 'polemical broadsides ... he cannot do without them; it is at once the strength and weakness of his criticism', observed Bruno Zevi – not exactly a 'soft' critic himself – in 1970.[31] It is unquestionable, though, that, by overreacting to his argumentative style, Banham's interlocutors completely missed what he had to say. It is as if, like in their designs, the Italians cared more about the *form* than the *content* of what was being said. And among the things that they thus failed to apprehend was Banham's revisionist message, a message based, among other things, on his characteristic privileging of the object over the designer in the analysis of works of architecture (that is, of the *text* over the *author* of a building). For at the root of Italian discourse's nebulous rhetoric and routine monumentalizing of the discipline's sacred cows was (and Banham understood this from very early on) the ambiguous status of its discussants, many of whom were practising architects wearing a second hat, their judgements for that reason clouded by personal and career connections. 'Architecture must be judged for what it shows', observed Banham in 1962, 'if the result is a good building, the critic must say it, even if he cannot stand the architect ... in Milan ... a priori assumptions on Ponti, Rogers, Gregotti and Viganò interfere with an objective assessment of their work'.[32] The comment was an obvious attack on the typically Italian figure of the architect-cum-historian, and might be read as an application of a programmatic statement that Banham himself had made two years prior on the necessity of enforcing clear boundaries between theory and practice in architecture:[33]

> The historian's ... integrity ... must be beyond question, and this ... means that the amateur historian, the historian with architectural

> connections, is out ... The one secure ground on which an architectural historian can stand is outside architecture ... [though his] professional qualification ... proves an objective attitude towards the evidence ... this does not rule out the amateur contribution, particularly in field-work ... but the final drawing of the map [of architecture] ... need[s] the authority of a trained professional mind that the field workers can trust'.[34]

In Italy, things could not be more different from the situation described above, with Ernesto Rogers and Ludovico Quaroni, among others, freely jumping from writing to building with great nonchalance, all to the detriment of Banham's cherished 'integrity'. A rare critique of this system (and of the grotesque distortions that it caused) came from a group of young Milanese architects, all contributors to the (not by chance, pro-Banham) *Superfici* magazine: 'deep down, Italian magazines are bound together by a code of silence (*omertà*) in their treatment of key national themes and figures. Casabella, for instance, is content ... with pontificating and dishing out generic moralisms, when not devoted ... to pathetic, apocalyptic lamentations about the absence of a Messiah under an empty sky'.[35] Rogers, again, is called out as the prime mover in creating and sustaining this atmosphere of mystification – 'his typical exhortation to always seek an accord between parts (his "let us love each other, we honest and just men") sounds more priest-like the more he insists on stressing its secular principles'.[36]

Certainly, class differences might also have been responsible, at least in part, for Banham's aversion to Rogers and his friends, all well-to-do architects with little more than a parlour interest in the revolutionary message of modernism, as the British historian suggested: 'it appears necessary to clarify ... my credentials, as some Italians seem to be questioning my right to speak. I come from a working-class background ... and, admittedly, I did not undergo the standard training of an architectural critic'.[37] And, perhaps, Banham's attack on the architecture of the Italian bourgeoisie really was laced with his own hostility for the English upper class, which seemed to share with Rogers and co. the same deference to 'taste, culture and history', as he gave to understand in a 1960 follow-up report on Milan.[38] After all, it was Banham himself who described Rogers's idea of *preesistenze ambientali*, a key notion in the Milanese toolkit, as nothing more than 'a more subtle version of "in keeping with", the most suffocating of English dogmas'.[39] It would be extremely simplistic, though, to rationalize Banham's disapproval for the Milanese models of design and criticism as a form of psychoanalytic projection. In the economy of the friction between Banham and the Italians, much more determining were different ideas on the respective roles and areas of activity of the architect and the historian.

And it is exactly against this background of systemic mystification and simmering discontent for the Janus-faced figure of the architect/historian that one must read the rise of Manfredo Tafuri, who, although at the antipodes with Banham on many issues (most famously on the liberating potential of technology), shared with him a certain disdain for designers who dabbled with history and criticism in a maze of architectural mumbo-jumbo. The most convincing defence of Banham's Italian writings, however, did not come from his pessimistic Roman colleague, but from the latter's operative (and optimistic) nemesis in the Eternal City, Bruno Zevi, who seconded the Englishman's critique of the Italian way to modernity in his contribution to the neoliberty debate:

> The Modern Movement landed in Italy almost 50 years after its appearance in the rest of Europe. Therefore, [in this country], the "language" of the movement was adopted before an examination of its programme ... The English, who are sensitive to their own idiosyncrasies as they are to those of other peoples, hit the nail on the head.[40]

Could it be that the reason Zevi backed Banham on this key point was that, as someone who had actually *lived* in England and the United States (and not just visited them, like his peers), he was able to see the deep gaps between the Anglo-Saxon and the Italian paths to modernity? It is difficult to say for sure, but the answer seems to be affirmative as, for the most part, Italian architects of the 1950s had only second-hand knowledge of how life was lived beyond the Alps and across the Atlantic. This brings us to the last point: ultimately, why read Banham's writings on Italy? The answer is simple: because, be they casual or deliberate, Banham's remarks on Italian architecture all express the positions of Anglo-Saxon technocratic reason, of which the British historian was a champion (as well as an instrument) *vis-à-vis* the architecture of a country that has for ever struggled to conform to the Northern European model of modernity due to its peripheral position, tortured politics and encumbering history. In other words, by reading Banham we learn more about the ways in which modernity was conceived and pursued in the *Bel Paese*, an endeavour that has not always been undertaken maintaining the necessary critical distance with the subject matter – especially by Italian scholars. A close reading of Banham's writings on Italy, then, encourages us to ask questions that we may have missed: what 'modernity' really means in this country, what role has architecture had in creating and sustaining our own version of it, and what we could and should do to rewrite its history.

Figure 4.1 Reyner Banham, portrait, 1980
RIBA Collections, image number 5808

Notes

1 Banham 1960, 33.
2 Banham 1957, 130.
3 Vidler 2008, 107–55.
4 Banham 1962, 100.
5 For Banham's reviews of Vagnetti's and Moretti's work, see Banham 1952; Banham 1953. Quote from Banham 1952, 213.
6 Banham 1962, 9 and 106.
7 Banham 1962, 100.
8 Banham 1975, 116.
9 Banham 1952, 213.
10 Gardner-Medwin 1958, 413.
11 Banham 1959, 232.
12 Banham 1955, 299.
13 Banham 1959, 232.
14 Banham 1975, 94.
15 Banham 1961, 37.
16 Banham 1976, 45.
17 Banham 1976, 149.
18 Banham 1984, 34.
19 Banham 1990, 23.
20 Banham 1955, 358.
21 Banham 1961, 200.
22 Banham 1975, 116.
23 Gardner-Medwin 1958, 413.
24 Banham 1985, 87.
25 Banham 1986, 47; Banham 1976, 102 and 64.
26 On the ENI Building and the Metro Drive-In, see Spina 2014; Spina 2017.
27 Portoghesi 2007, 7.
28 Kant 2018, 355.
29 Banham 1962, 15. Banham reviews the Rinascente building and the Olivetti plant in Banham 1969.
30 Banham 1962, 15.
31 Zevi 1979, 862.
32 Banham 1962, 16.
33 On the Italian figure of the architect-cum-historian, see Casciato and Fifield 2003.
34 Banham 1960, 332.
35 Bellini *et al.* 1961, 40.
36 Orefice 1961, 44.
37 Banham 1962, 16.
38 Banham 1961, 35.
39 Banham 1961, 36.
40 Zevi 1978, 263.

References

Banham, Reyner. 'Italian eclectic', *The Architectural Review* 112 (October 1952): 213–17.

Banham, Reyner. 'Casa del girasole: Rationalism and eclecticism in Italian architecture', *The Architectural Review* 113 (February 1953): 73–7.

Banham, Reyner. 'Sant'Elia', *The Architectural Review* 117 (May 1955a): 299.

Banham, Reyner. 'The New Brutalism', *The Architectural Review* 118 (December 1955b): 358.

Banham, Reyner. 'Futurism and modern architecture', *RIBA Journal* 64 (February 1957): 129–39.

Banham, Reyner. 'Neoliberty: The Italian retreat from modern architecture', *The Architectural Review* 125 (April 1959): 231–5.

Banham, Reyner. 'Futurism for keeps', *Arts*, 7 January 1960a, 33–9.

Banham, Reyner. 'History and psychiatry', *The Architectural Review* 127, no. 759 (May 1960b): 326–32.

Banham, Reyner. 'Criticism: Pirelli Building Milan', *The Architectural Review* 129, no. 769 (March 1961a): 194–200.

Banham, Reyner. 'Milano: L'orizzonte conteso', *Superfici: Problemi di architettura e tecnologie edili: Rivista dei pavimenti, rivestimenti e coperture* 1 (March 1961b): 35. Translation of Reyner Banham, 'Milan: The polemical skyline', *The Listener*, 1 September 1960, 338–40.

Banham, Reyner. 'Scuole di oggi case di ieri alla XII Triennale', *Superfici: Problemi di architettura e tecnologie edili: Rivista dei pavimenti, rivestimenti e coperture* 1 (March 1961c): 37. Translation of Reyner Banham, 'Schools of today, homes of yesterday', *The Listener*, 18 August 1960, 253–4.

Banham, Reyner. 'Alla ricerca di un'intesa', *Superfici: Problemi di architettura e tecnologie edili: Rivista dei pavimenti, rivestimenti e coperture* 5 (April 1962a): 14–16.

Banham, Reyner. *Guide to Modern Architecture*. London: Architectural Press, 1962b.

Banham, Reyner. *The Architecture of the Well-Tempered Environment*. London: Architectural Press, 1969.

Banham, Reyner. *Age of Masters: A personal view of modern architecture*. London: Architectural Press, 1975.

Banham, Reyner. *Megastructure: Urban futures of the recent past*. London: Thames and Hudson, 1976.

Banham, Reyner. 'Lingotto: Un punto di vista transatlantico', *Casabella* 501 (April 1984): 34–5.

Banham, Reyner. 'Fiat: The phantom of order', *New Society* 72, no. 1164 (18 April 1985): 86–8.

Banham, Reyner. *A Concrete Atlantis: U.S. industrial building and European modern architecture 1900–1925*. Cambridge, MA: MIT Press, 1986.

Banham, Reyner. 'A black box: The secret profession of architecture', *New Statesman and Society*, 12 October 1990, 22–5.

Bellini, Mario, Roberto Orefice and Lucilla Zanon Dal Bo. 'Cavalieri, libertini e frères maçons sulla scena milanese', *Superfici: Problemi di architettura e tecnologie edili: Rivista dei pavimenti, rivestimenti e coperture* 1 (March 1961): 39–40.

Casciato, Maristella and Barry Fifield. 'The Italian mosaic: The architect as historian', *Journal of the Society of Architectural Historians* 62, no. 1 (March 2003): 92–101.

Gardner-Medwin, Robert. 'A flight from functionalism', *RIBA Journal* 65 (October 1958): 408–14.

Kant, Immanuel. 'An answer to the question: What is Enlightenment?'. In *Princeton Readings in Political Thought: Essential texts from Plato to Populism*, edited by Mitchell Cohen, 355–9. Princeton: Princeton University Press, 2018.

Orefice, Roberto. 'Trucchi e galateo di un "Aufklärung" milanese', *Superfici: Problemi di architettura e tecnologie edili: Rivista dei pavimenti, rivestimenti e coperture* 1 (March 1961): 44.

Portoghesi, Paolo. 'Prefazione'. in *Roma città mediterranea*, edited by Antonino Terranova, Alessandra Capuano, Alessandra Criconia, Adriana Feo and Fabrizio Toppetti, 7. Rome: Gangemi, 2007.

Spina, Davide. 'Sign language', *AA Files* 68 (2014): 101–7.

Spina, Davide. 'Il drive in', *AA Files* 74 (2017): 173–82.

Vidler, Anthony. *Histories of the Immediate Present: Inventing architectural modernism*. Cambridge, MA: MIT Press, 2008.

Zevi, Bruno. 'Banham contro l'abdicazione italiana: Elogio del liberty, condanna del Neoliberty'. In *Cronache di Architettura*, vol. 6, edited by Bruno Zevi, 317–19. Bari: Laterza, 1978.

Zevi, Bruno. 'La felicità disurbana delle "freeways"'. In *Cronache di Architettura*, vol. 8, edited by Bruno Zevi, 165–7. Bari: Laterza, 1979.

5

From neoliberty to postmodernism

Benjamin Chavardès

With his editorial entitled 'Continuità o crisi?', Ernesto Rogers introduced issue 215 of *Casabella-Continuità*.[1] He opened a debate that would last two years and exceed the limits of newspaper columns to internationalize.[2] The magazine published a letter addressed to Vittorio Gregotti by Roberto Gabetti (1925–2000) and Aimaro Isola (1928) and intended to be communicated to the public.[3] The two Turin architects developed the characteristics that led to the design of one of their last buildings: the Bottega d'Erasmo (1953–6).[4] The building, built at the foot of the Mole Antonelliana, abandoned the techniques and methods of the so-called Modern Movement, in order to make reference to the architecture of the early twentieth century and Turin's bourgeois architecture of the beginning of the century through the reuse of bow windows. The architects, conscious of the possible controversy they might launch, drew on a recent tradition to reintegrate the present into history. They summarized their vision of architecture: 'we prefer to consider architecture as the conquest of harmony and imagination rather than admire the perfection of a new school'.[5]

The editor Vittorio Gregotti justified his choice to publish this debate because it was for him a meaningful illustration of a moment and a basis for a necessary discussion: 'we chose to publish this work not only for the respect with which we consider you as artists but also for whatever they found most questionable in that work, for defining the limits of a position'.[6]

Clearly, Gregotti uses this project as a typical example of the 'crisis of conscience' and an illustration of 'those moments of revision' that the architects then went through. However, he questions the nature of the use of history. The work of Gabetti and Isola is thus profoundly linked to a

Figure 5.1 Roberto Gabetti and Aimaro Isola, Bottega d'Erasmo, Turin, 1953–7

place. The question refers to the choice of the reference to the late nineteenth-century architecture and the values it embodies:

> If we grant that architects create architecture not only for themselves but also for others, then we must concern ourselves with the

> relationships which spring up between them: face to face with their responsibilities as intellectuals, architects must know how to grasp the civil meaning of our reacquired sense of history or close themselves off in an incommunicable perfection.[7]

Divergences

This publication provoked strong reactions, illustrated by a letter from Eugenio Gentili, and Rogers's reply, headlined 'Ortodossia dell'eterodossia'.[8] Gentili criticized the editorial board for no longer publishing a progressive journal of modern architecture.[9] He objected to the bias towards presenting some works by Mario Ridolfi, which he considered 'brutta'. He denounced work that emphasized a figurative aspect, and was not part of the continuity of the Modern Movement. For the first time, Gentili used the term 'neoliberty' to designate those architectures that referred to late nineteenth-century Italian architecture instead. In response, Rogers justified the continuity of an editorial policy that provided a platform for a diversity of architectural production. He pointed to the historical 'orthodoxy of heterodoxy' of the journal, or in other words, the commitment of *Casabella-Continuità* to presenting contemporary architecture in its full diversity, not from a single ideological viewpoint.[10]

But when Roberto Orefice included in this new research the Torre Velasca in Milan, authored by Rogers and his associates from the BBPR Agency,[11] Rogers reprimanded the young graduate for his impertinence.[12] These exchanges exemplified the questions confronted by a profession that was seeking new directions, conscious of the unsatisfactory answers given by rationalism.

Denunciation

In his article published the following year, Aldo Rossi demonstrated his opposition to the thesis that giving pre-eminence to formal values would be synonymous with abandoning the achievements of the Modern Movement. By contrast, he defended the idea that this formalism would show the way to renewing the link between architecture and society.[13] He justified the reference to nineteenth-century traditions as significant for the development of a new language. The integration in a place means the integration into the history of this place.

In issue 73, *L'Architecture d'Aujourd'hui* published the Stock Exchange project in Turin by Gabetti and Isola, stating that they:

> belong to a movement currently encouraged by the Italian journal *Casabella* and which tends towards the introduction into architecture of a kind of romanticism whose sources of inspiration are very diverse: Wright, neo-Gothic, School of Amsterdam, Gaudí ... It is a violent reaction which questions practically all the assumptions of contemporary architecture ... In the work that we publish, the assertion of a certain doctrinal extravagance is much less pronounced than in the buildings that the same team built in Turin.[14]

The two journals accuse each other of promoting formalism. *L'Architecture d'Aujourd'hui* attacks the new Italian architecture. *Casabella* firmly objects to the retrograde thinking of the French.[15] The latter declares in reaction to the article by *Casabella*: 'A certain gratuity is an acceptable and valid artistic gesture, even necessary. What is not, is the ugliness, the baroque swelling, the emphasis, the false originality, the strange and the unusual'.[16]

In the UK, the debate started with an article by Reyner Banham published in November 1958 in the *Architectural Review* and entitled 'Tornare ai Tempi Felici'.[17] Banham denounced the retrograde design of the architectures of Gae Aulenti, Vittorio Gregotti, Roberto Gabetti and Aimaro Isola. Firstly, he criticized the fact that architectural choices were being guided by consumer tastes without using any double coding. He saw this as an anti-rationalist 're-bourgeoisification' of architecture based on the aesthetic preferences of a pre-Modern Movement middle class. Secondly, he denounced it as a conscious, demagogic and superficial approach that did not respond aesthetically to society.

The following month, Paolo Portoghesi, in his article 'Dal neorealismo al neoliberty', responded to Banham by tracing the genealogy of these new experiences. Putting himself outside the controversy, he turned to history in order to shed light on the new research and place it within a historical continuity. He coined the term 'neoliberty' for these new Italian experiences,[18] drawing on his knowledge of neorealism and his studies on Liberty and more broadly on Art Nouveau. That is why, although Gentili and Rogers had used the term before him, Reyner Banham attributed it to Portoghesi, and it is probably the only thing that Banham retained from Portoghesi's article. Leonardo Benevolo also attributes the first use of the word to Portoghesi.[19]

Banham pursued its analysis in a new, and even more virulent, article published in April 1959. Banham's disappointment was not only roused by the buildings published in *Casabella* but, more importantly, by the fact that *Casabella* was supposed to be the most progressive architectural journal in Italy, having introduced and promoted the so-called Modern Movement in the peninsula since the 1930s. He recognized the quality of Ludovico Quaroni's work at the Martella, and Luigi Moretti's Girasole, in his article for the *Architectural Review*. Furthermore, he strongly denounced the work of the Milan architects.

Banham analyses neoliberty production from a stylistic, economic and social point of view. He makes an aesthetic and cultural criticism and expresses his expectation of a socially acceptable architecture running counter to a bourgeois aesthetic. Nevertheless, he ignores the debate on tradition, avoiding this term, and similarly ignores the question of realism, two themes that are very prevalent in the Italian debates. Banham blames the neoliberty for looking backwards instead of looking into the future. He ends his article with this formula that sounds like a punishment: 'Neoliberty is infantile regression'.[20]

In an article entitled 'Dal neoliberty al neopiacentinismo' (echoing that of Portoghesi, on which he relies in part), Carlo Melograni preferred to focus on the political aspect of the process rather than its recourse to the past.[21] He points out that the neorealist experience, in which he himself participated, had failed to produce a general renewal of the architectural language and remained reduced to the production of low-cost collective housing. According to him, the error of neorealism was to have followed reality rather than proposing any modification to it. In addition, neorealism had mainly focused on the outskirts of the city, not working on the overall coherence with the rest of the city. Melograni makes the same criticism of neoliberty, which he defines as a renunciation of general principles, a return to a bourgeois tradition and an exaggeration of ornamental invention. He thus denounces a 'neopiacentinismo' characterized by the refusal to make a significant contribution to the transformation of society and privileging formalism and irrationality.[22]

Melograni's response to the articles of Banham and Portoghesi was the first of a long series by authors including Ernesto Rogers in June 1959, Bruno Zevi in August 1959 or Gillo Dorfles 1959.[23] Then the debate spread across Europe to reach some of the most important architectural journals of the time: *Casabella*, *L'Architecture d'Aujourd'hui*, the *Architectural Review*, but also *L'Architettura: Cronache e Storia* and *Domus*. Rogers, in his 'Risposta al custode dei frigidaires', accuses Banham of rejecting architectural evolution. He sees the Modern Movement as a continuous revolution and denounces the superficiality of Banham's analysis.[24] Zevi, although partly blamed by Banham, agrees with him by denouncing 'l'andropausa degli architetti moderni italiani'.

Comunità published in the same year a translation of Banham's article, which includes Portoghesi's commentary,[25] denouncing Banham's work as superficial. He disputes the idea that neoliberty is a movement characterized by unity, insisting on the concept of tradition and pointing to the inhibitions of the avant-garde, as well as the problem of communication between architectural culture and the general public.

Sentence

In September 1959, the debate became even more poisonous during the CIAM 11, held in Otterlo. After the controversies staged in the columns of specialist journals, architects exchanged views through the presentation and discussion of their projects. Ernesto Rogers, Ignazio Gardella (the Mensa Olivetti in Ivrea), Giancarlo De Carlo (the edificio per servizi e residenza nel Quartiere Spine Bianche in Matera) and Vico Magistretti (the villa di Arenzano) represented Italy. A divergence emerged between the Team X architects on the one hand, represented by Peter Smithson and Jacob Bakema, and Ernesto Rogers on the other. They all agreed on the necessity of formal revision, continuity with the so-called Modern Movement, attention to context, a humanist attitude and redefinition of the urban structure, but their views reflected different national contexts. Rogers's presentation of Torre Velasca embodied a disagreement in outlook, which, according to Josep Maria Montaner, explains the absence of Italian architects in Team X, except for De Carlo.[26]

To present his project, Rogers tried to demonstrate that the design of the tower followed a rational and functionalist methodology. He justified the architectural form by the need to have more space for the dwellings, which are located in the upper part of the tower to benefit from the air and the view, rather than for the offices located in the lower part. He argued that this distinction was illustrative of the adage 'form follows function', anticipating criticism of the medieval form of the tower, which he presented as 'a casual coincidence'.[27] He highlighted the question of tradition and the particular situation of the building, which required special consideration of its context in Milan's historic centre.[28] But his presentation was mostly devoted to an explanation of the technical and construction choices. His conclusion seems, thus, paradoxical. Indeed, while he seems to distance himself from the question of the relationship

Figure 5.2 BBPR, Torre Velasca, Milan, 1956–8

with history, he also argues that the anti-historical attitude of the fathers of the Modern Movement, which was necessary to initiate an architectural revolution, was no longer necessary. He proposed that a new attitude towards history needed to be developed, and that architects had a responsibility not to perpetuate the aesthetics of the Modern Movement.

As a result, a virulent exchange was initiated by Peter Smithson, arguing that the anti-historical position of the moderns was both moral and aesthetic. He pointed to the BBPR project as a dangerous model that failed to respond to the nature of contemporary society. He assessed its aesthetic as purely formalistic and broken, and the building as incapable of responding to change or anticipating the evolutions of the society. He even condemned the work as irresponsible, and ethically and aesthetically wrong.[29]

Rogers responded with a commentary on the contrast between English and Italian modes of thinking, which would explain the difference of perception between the parties: 'There is one main difficulty that I see and that is that you think in English. Now that is not my way of thinking. But I will try to answer'. He refused the idea that his architecture represented a formal model, circumventing the ethical problematic of his thesis. By contrast, he suggested that the clarity and sincerity of the structure exemplified the morality of the approach.[30] The idea of rationality that Rogers defends is the same as Aldo Rossi's, expressed through the process and not in the form or aesthetics. The same view is expressed at the 1973 Milan Triennale. In this instance, the exhibition directed by Rossi would locate itself within the legacy of Rogers and the Modern Movement masters, to whom were dedicated the first two rooms.[31]

Bakema was more diplomatic in his conclusion to the Torre Velasca debate, emphasizing the need for specificity in an intervention in a historic centre while noting: 'I think that form is a communication about life, and I don't recognize in this building a communication about life in our time. You are resisting contemporary life'.[32] In his summing-up of the CIAM's different presentations, he identifies the positions of the different groups, criticizing the plastic expression of a project group, and qualifying the work as unacceptable:

> But I feel that one of these groups is attempting to find this language in too easy and quick a way. They would like to bring architectural expression to their buildings in a way they can be easily understood by the people.[33]

However, this famous debate on Torre Velasca often overshadows another exchange between Rogers and Peter Smithson, following the Smithsons' presentation during this CIAM meeting. Peter and Alison Smithson gave a lecture on 'Problems Regarded as Central to Architecture in the Present Situation', which focused on methodological and theoretical positions. It is no coincidence that the Smithsons shared Reyner Banham's views on Italian architecture, being part of the Independent Group since the 1950s. Rogers responded by criticizing the projects for their negative relationship with the history of the sites, specifically focusing on their impact on a neighbourhood like Soho, and on the gradual destruction of the historic city.

A decade later, Manfredo Tafuri would offer a synthetic reading of neoliberty.[34] For him, 'the real drama of Neoliberty, [is] the lack of courage'.[35] He considered that neoliberty architecture sought not to be part of the course of history but used it, motivated by emotions and personal nostalgia. Tafuri argued that opposition to the International Style was already outdated, but that neoliberty failed to propose a viable renewal or an alternative. Nevertheless, he recognized its merit in playing a role in exposing the architectural problems of the time, quoting two projects of the neoliberty period: the Bottega d'Erasmo and the casa Baldi, realized between 1959 and 1961 by Paolo Portoghesi.[36]

Recognition or posterity

The casa Baldi is the result of post-war Italian architectural research, extending from neorealism to neoliberty. Moreover, it is also one of the first gems of postmodern architecture. Indeed, in 1977, Charles Jencks begins his chapter 'Postmodern Architecture' with neoliberty, and defines historicism as the beginning of postmodernism[37]. In his geneaology, neoliberty appears as the historicist root of postmodernism, including architects like Luigi Moretti, Ignazio Gardella, Gae Aulenti, Carlo Scarpa, Franco Albini and Paolo Portoghesi. Of Casa Baldi, he writes:

> One of the most convincing historicist buildings of the fifties was Paolo Portoghesi's Casa Baldi, 1959–61, an essay in free-form curves definitely reminiscent of the Borromini he was studying, yet also unmistakably influenced by Le Corbusier. Here is the schizophrenic cross between two codes that is characteristic of Post-Modernism: the enveloping, sweeping curves of the Baroque, the overlap of space, the various foci of space interfering with each other and the Brutalist treatment, the expression of concrete block, rugged joinery and the guitar-shapes of modernism.[38]

It is perhaps ironic, in view of the contrast between Italian and English positions documented in this chapter, that an Italian, in the person of Bruno Zevi, would come out in defence of the Modern Movement, while an Englishman, Charles Jencks, student of Banham, would promote postmodernism. In 1970, Charles Jencks produced a thesis supervised by

Banham at University College London on *Modern Movements in Architecture* (1970), in which he studied the work of the Smithsons, Bakema and Rogers, among others, having attended the Team X meeting at Urbino in 1966, unlike the Smithsons who were exceptionally absent. In 1977 Jencks published *The Language of Postmodern Architecture*,[39] as a direct answer to Zevi's *Il linguaggio moderno dell'architettura* (1973),[40] which was itself conceived as a 'natural and indispensable complement' to Summerson's book, *The Classical Language of Architecture*. Summerson had explained that his 'aim is to speak of architecture as a language; the reader must be able to recognize the Latin of architecture',[41] tracking a history of a classical language from antiquity to the nineteenth century. Ten years later, Bruno Zevi positioned his book as pursuing the goal of structuring the language of modern architecture through the identification of seven invariants, or defined rules and norms. Of his own book, Charles Jencks explained: 'So the term Post-Modern has to be clarified and used more precisely to cover, in general, only those designers who are aware of architecture as a language'.[42] From Leonardo Benevolo's perspective, this was Jencks's primary contribution to the debate:

> The titles of the two works by Charles Jencks (*Modern Movements in Architecture*, 1971, and *The Language of Postmodern Architecture*, 1977) perfectly summarize these positions, where the explicit theses (the modern movement is multiple, non-unitary, and there is a postmodern movement) are less important than their implicit presupposition, that it is a question of promoting architecture as a language, an autonomous system of existing and significant visual values.[43]

Zevi's response to Jencks's publication was one of irony:

> This book shows that post-modernism, as opposed to modernism, returns to pre-modernism, that's academic classicism. Perhaps we should rename my work "the post-post-modern language of architecture".[44]

For Bruno Zevi, considering architecture as a language entailed understanding modern architecture as a system of defined rules and norms. For Charles Jencks, modern architecture was the architecture of the bourgeoisie, an architecture of the elite not the general public. He proposed that the postmodern building was characterized by a system of 'double coding', which allowed it to speak simultaneously on two levels:

'to other architects and a concerned minority who care about specifically architectural meanings, and to the public at large, or the local inhabitants, who care about other issues concerned with comfort, traditional building and a way of life'.[45]

Postmodern architecture is therefore intended to be both savant and popular. However, this distinction created problems.[46] The desire to revalue popular culture was critiqued as an elitist point of view in itself, and the very notion of 'popular culture' a scholarly concept, open to definition. For Robert Venturi, it indicated the culture of mass consumption, with its commercial devices and advertising as it invades the strip of Las Vegas.[47] For the Italian neorealists, like Mario Ridolfi, the popular meant a reclamation of traditional knowledge. For Christopher Alexander, the 'popular' is equated with participatory urban planning, in which future users are involved in the design process.[48]

Conclusion

Finally then, we can identify two postmodern cultures, each of which seeks a popular anchorage and a link between architecture and society. In Italy, this link is sought in the integration with the site and respect for history and traditions. The English do not read much of the Italian context in their analysis, but develop programmes that recognize the realities of everyday life, and are designed to adapt to changes in society.

From both positions, there was a renewed attention to the question of function. In Italy, architects worked on the form, integrating it with a building's evolving use over time, as explained by Rossi in 1966.[49] In the UK, following the position of the Smithsons, anticipating the needs of society was highlighted as a necessity. These exchanges would extend beyond the borders of these two countries, and some personalities like Louis Kahn managed to gain unanimity. However, we can argue that the postmodern debate originated in the exchanges between Italy and the UK, and it was there that the contours of the debate developed most openly.

Notes

1 Rogers 1957a.
2 For the first bibliography of these dialogues, see Cellini 1977a ; Cellini 1977b. See also D'Amato 1977.

3 Gabetti and Isola 1957.
4 Cellini and D'Amato 1993; Olmo 1993.
5 Gabetti and Isola 1957.
6 Gregotti 1957.
7 Gregotti 1957.
8 Gentili 1957; Rogers 1957b.
9 Gentili 1957; Rogers 1957b.
10 Rogers 1957b.
11 Orefice 1957, 99.
12 Rogers 1957c, 99.
13 Rossi 1958, 16.
14 *L'Architecture d'Aujourd'hui* 1957, 55.
15 *Casabella-Continuità* 1958, 53.
16 *L'Architecture d'Aujourd'hui* 1958, xxxiii.
17 Banham 1958.
18 Portoghesi, 1958; Portoghesi, 1963.
19 Benevolo 1960.
20 Banham 1959.
21 Melograni 1959.
22 Melograni 1959, 26.
23 Rogers 1959; Zevi 1959; Dorfles 1959.
24 Rogers 1959.
25 Portoghesi 1959.
26 Montaner 1993.
27 Newmann 1961, 92.
28 Newmann 1961, 93.
29 Newmann 1961, 94–6.
30 Newmann 1961, 95–6.
31 Chavardès 2015.
32 Newmann 1961, 97.
33 Newmann 1961, 218.
34 Tafuri 1968, 84–7.
35 Tafuri 1968, 85.
36 Tafuri 1968, 86.
37 Jencks 1977, 81–2.
38 Jencks 1977, 82.
39 Jencks 1977.
40 Zevi 1973.
41 Summerson 1963.
42 Jencks 1977, 6.
43 Benevolo 1960.
44 Zevi 1973.
45 Jencks 1977, 6.
46 Cohen 2004.
47 Venturi, Scott Brown and Izenour 1972.
48 Alexander 1975.
49 Rossi 1966, 34.

References

Alexander, Christopher. *The Oregon Experiment*. New York: Oxford University Press, 1975.

L'Architecture d'Aujourd'hui 73 (1957): 55.

L'Architecture d'Aujourd'hui 77 (1958): xxxiii.

Banham, Reyner. 'Tornare ai Tempi Felici', *The Architectural Review* 742 (1958): 281.

Banham, Reyner. 'Neoliberty: The Italian retreat from modern architecture', *The Architectural Review* 747 (1959): 285.

Benevolo, Leonardo. *Storia dell'architettura moderna*. Bari: Laterza, 1960.
Cellini, Francesco. 'La polemica sul Neoliberty', *Controspazio* 4–5 (1977a): 52–3.
Cellini, Francesco. 'Elenco cronologico degli scritti relativi alla polemica sul Neoliberty', *Controspazio* 4–5 (1977b): 53.
Cellini, Francesco and Claudio D'Amato. *Gabetti e Isola: Progetti e architettura 1950–1985*. Milan: Electa, 1985.
Chavardès, Benjamin. *Quand le post-modernisme s'expose*. Montpellier: Espérou, 2015.
Cohen, Jean-Louis. 'Promesses et impasses du populisme', *Les Cahiers de la recherche architecturale et urbaine* 15–16 (2004): 167–84.
'Dai giornale e dalle riviste, a cura di Matilde Baffa'. *Casabella-Continuità* 220 (1958): 53.
D'Amato, Claudio. 'Memoria, storia e questioni di stile nell'esperienza del Neoliberty', *Controspazio* 4–5 (1977): 50–1.
Dorfles, Gillo. 'Neobarocco, ma non Neoliberty', *Domus* 358 (1959): 19.
Gabetti, Roberto and Aimaro Isola, 'L'impegno della tradizione, Caro Gregotti ... ', *Casabella-Continuità* 215 (1957): 62–9.
Gentili, Eugenio. 'Ortodossia dell'eterodossia, Caro Ernesto ... ', *Casabella-Continuità* 216 (1957): 2.
Gregotti, Vittorio. 'L'impegno della tradizione, Cari amici ... ', *Casabella-Continuità* 215 (1957): 62–9.
Jencks, Charles. *The Language of Postmodern Architecture*. London: Academy Editions, 1977.
Melograni, Carlo. 'Dal neoliberty al neopiacentinismo?', *Il Contemporaneo* 13 (1959): 17–28.
Montaner, Josep Maria. *Después del Movimiento Moderno: Arquitectura de la segunda mitad del siglo XX*. Barcelona: Gustavo Gili, 1993.
Newmann, Oscar (ed.). *CIAM '59 in Otterlo*. Stuttgart: Krämer, 1961.
Olmo, Carlo. *Gabetti e Isola: Architetture*. Turin: Allemandi, 1993.
Orefice, Roberto. 'Riposte ai giovani, Egregio direttore ... ', *Casabella-Continuità* 217 (1957): 99.
Portoghesi, Paolo. 'Dal neorealismo al neoliberty', *Comunità* 65 (1958): 69–79.
Portoghesi, Paolo. 'Il commento di P. Portoghesi', *Comunità* 72 (1959): 64–9.
Portoghesi, Paolo. 'L'impegno delle nuove generazioni'. In *Aspetti dell'arte contemporanea, Rassegna internazionale, architetture–pittura–scultura–grafica*, 257–63. Roma: Edizioni dell'Ateneo, 1963.
Rogers, Ernesto. 'Continuità o crisi ?', *Casabella-Continuità* 215 (1957a): 3–6.
Rogers, Ernesto. 'Ortodossia dell'eterodossia. Caro Eugenio ... ', *Casabella-Continuità* 216 (1957b): 2.
Rogers, Ernesto. 'Riposte ai giovani. Cari colleghi ... ', *Casabella-Continuità* 217 (1957c): 99.
Rogers, Ernesto. 'L'evoluzione dell'architettura: Risposta al custode dei frigidaires', *Casabella-Continuità* 228 (1959): 2–4.
Rossi, Aldo. 'Il passato e il presente nella nuova architettura', *Casabella-Continuità* 219 (1958): 16.
Rossi, Aldo. *L'architettura della città*. Padua: Marsilio, 1966.
Summerson, John. *The Classical Language of Architecture*. Cambridge, MA: MIT Press, 1963.
Tafuri, Manfredo. *Teoria e storia dell'architettura*. Bari: Laterza, 1968.
Venturi, Robert, Denise Scott Brown and Steven Izenour. *Learning from Las Vegas*. Cambridge, MA: MIT Press, 1972.
Zevi, Bruno. 'L'andropausa degli architetti moderni italiani', *L'Architettura: Cronache e storia* 46 (1959): 222–3.
Zevi, Bruno. *Il linguaggio moderno dell'architettura*. Turin: Einaudi, 1973.

6

Franco Albini and Leslie Martin: 'a parallel working life'

Antonello Alici

Building modern Europe

'Building Modern Britain' was the working title of a research seminar hosted by the Royal Institute of British Architects (RIBA) in September 2016; it emphasized the potential of Sir Leslie Martin's archive for new studies on 'an architectural period that significantly altered the visual language of British housing and changed our understanding of cities and civic institution from the pre-war era to the end of the 1980s'.[1] The so-called 'modernist architectural movement in Britain' – according to the seminar introduction – had started 'the development of radical ideas applied to new housing, universities, civic institutions and city planning'. A younger generation of promising architects, such as Patrick Hodgkinson, Chamberlin Powell and Bon, Ahrends, Burton and Koralek and Powell and Moya, and many others, gathered around the charismatic figure of Leslie Martin (1908–2000). Their archives – avalaible in the RIBA's architectural collections – are strategic sources for a new programme of studies aimed at a deeper undestanding of the British contribution to modern architecture.[2]

In this framework, the chapter aims to focus on the mutual resonances in the British and Italian debate on post-war reconstruction. Complementary sources to the RIBA collections are the architectural archives in Italy, which are organized in a network spread all over the country, related to the place where the single architects were based, a key institution to co-ordinate them being the Italian association of archives of contemporary architecture AAA-Italia.[3] Among the first results of my research in Sir Leslie Martin's archive is the relationship with Franco Albini (1905–1977), revealed in the talk given by Martin at the memorial exhibition on Albini, organized in Milan in December 1980.[4] This aspect of his life and work prompted further exploration from the Italian side, starting with the Franco Albini Foundation in Milan, which revealed no traces of the connection with Leslie Martin, no letters and no records of Albini's several visits to Britain, in London, Cambridge and Oxford at least. So, we have to rely on other archives and on the published sources. The British–Italian dialogue was widely recorded by the main architectural journals, such as the *Architectural Review*, *Architectural Design*, *RIBA Journal* and *Architects' Journal* in Britain and *Casabella*, *Domus*, *Metron* and *L'Architettura: Cronache e storia* in Italy. A common theme was a sensibility to history and tradition, mainly as a consequence of the risk of losing heritage and identity during the war.

According to Nicholas Bullock, the potential loss of valuable heritage brought the question of British identity to the fore: 'Planning the future was inseparably mingled with a desire for continuity with the past … this sense of continuity was linked to the feeling for community … it enabled the country to know what to defend and how to rebuild'.[5] A supplement to the *Architectural Review*, begun in July 1941 and entitled 'Destruction and Reconstruction', stated 'the need for preserving architectural values from subservience to mere expediency and the need for keeping architecture itself in touch with the realities from which it derives its vitality, together form the war-time task of the *Architectural Review*'.[6] In April 1943, a special issue of the magazine dealt with the exhibition 'Rebuilding Britain', organized at the National Gallery in London by the RIBA Reconstruction Committee. It was an attempt to point to the right direction for the future, 'to show how imagination may be applied to the replanning and rebuilding of Britain which will follow the war'.[7] The call for a particularly British modernism, against 'dogmatic and dictatorial' methods, was clear: 'Masons, bricklayers, carpenters and joiners, workers in metals and glass are all anxious to re-create the artistry in craftsmanship which has so largely disappeared'.[8] It noted the need of houses, schools, hospitals of a high quality and standard, far from the current 'Squalor' and claimed that 'England after the war must be England, and not a schematically planned and blue-printed utopia, but it must be not the same England as it was before the war … better, healthier, more harmonious Britain is needed just as badly as victory over Hitler (in fact *is* victory over Hitler)'.[9]

James M. Richards stressed the difference between the *modern movement* (urban sophistication, metropolitan culture, international in style) and a *regional architecture* (a vernacular approach, in harmony with differences in places, climates, building materials, local custom and traditions): 'In a word, the expression of the city culture is intellectual and synthetic. *Regional architecture* uses natural rather than synthetic materials, materials which mellow and sink into the landscape rather than those which shine in the sun and are kept perpetually brand new. The work of C. F. A. Voysey was an attempt to rehabilitate it in recent times. In even more recent times, it is well expressed in modern Scandinavian architecture, and in that of Frank Lloyd Wright as distinct from that of Le Corbusier ... '.[10]

The relevance of heritage and the search for identity, focusing on regional characters, were equally central to the architectural debate in post-war Italy. Much effort was devoted to the search for a continuity with the best products of the inter-war period, which were mainly to be found in the rationalist avant-garde. We should consider two major poles of the Italian cultural scene: Milan with Ernesto Rogers and BBPR studio, acting as a hub of international connections, and Rome with Bruno Zevi and the Associazione per l'Architettura Organica (APAO).[11]

Rationalism and creativity

Franco Albini was very active in the new avant-garde institutions, as the first president of the Movimento di Studi per l'Architettura (MSA) established in Milan in 1945 and the director of the CIAM summer school, which moved from London to Venice in 1952, with Ignazio Gardella, Ernesto Rogers and Giuseppe Samonà (the director of Istituto Universitario di Architettura di Venezia – Iuav).[12] Albini was a professor at Iuav as well.

Rationalism was considered inadequate to face the situation of a country, still largely rural, characterized by fragile social situations and purely artisanal construction techniques. According to Augusto Rossari, the role of history, which had always been considered with suspicion by the avant-garde as a possible bearer of eclectic or academic attitudes, began at that time to be seen as an antidote to the formalist evolution of an undifferentiated International Style.[13] In a meeting of MSA in June 1955, Albini focused on the relevance of 'tradition' as an expression of 'continuity of civilization (spirit and form) – historical continuity – continuous motion of life'.[14] A direct link to the legacy of Giuseppe Pagano and Edoardo Persico was established, firstly in 1945–6 by Albini and Giancarlo Palanti in a new edition of *Costruzioni Casabella*, and in 1953 by Ernesto Rogers as newly appointed editor-in-chief of *Casabella*. Rogers added the word *Continuità* (*Continuity*) to its name: '*Continuità* means historical awareness, awareness of a deep-running tradition ... expressed in the eternal struggle of the creative spirit against every manifestation of formalism, past and present ... '.[15] He underlined the mission of modernity: 'No work is truly modern which is not genuinely rooted in tradition, while no ancient work has a modern meaning which is not capable of somehow reflecting our modern mood ... We stand for a truly international language sprung from mutual understanding, to which every artist can contribute from his inner freedom and the cultural climate he works in ... '.[16]

Back to our case study: in the introduction to his book *Buildings and Ideas 1933–83*, Martin revealed his deep appreciation of 'the distinguished Italian architect Franco Albini' mentioning the evolution of his architecture from the inter-war to post-war years.[17] According to him, Albini's talent lay in finding appropriate solutions to each problem, from the space and light of temporary exhibitions to the architecture of the cave, from the rationalist interpretation of traditional construction rooted in Pagano's 'Architettura rurale' to his highly creative formal achievement in the use of new technologies.[18] The evolution in his architecture is evidence of the capacity of 'many architects whose work has been connected with some of the early ideas of the Modern Movement' to challenge them, widen and deepen their architectural language.[19]

Leslie Martin, who published the book in 1983, refers to the retrospective exhibition on Franco Albini organized in Milan in December 1980.[20] As already mentioned, a manuscript preserved in Leslie Martin's archive contains the text of the lecture that he had been invited to give at a ceremony linked to that exhibition, which is evidently the origin of the above-mentioned introduction.[21] The invitation came from Marco Albini, the son of Franco, who had visited Cambridge in the mid-1960s for a few months' internship in Leslie Martin's practice.[22] The text provides a fascinating chronological narrative of the main steps in the evolution of British and Italian architectural culture from the inter-war years, illustrated by key works of Albini and Martin's personal experience.[23] The main point for Leslie Martin is Albini's ability to enrich the prime requirements of rationalism and of new technologies, which are complemented in his work by 'imaginative and creative thought'.[24]

From the lecture we can follow what Martin labelled 'a parallel working life':

> In the early '30s (Albini) was involved, as I was, in the changing attitude to architecture that was developing generally in Europe.

> It became usual to refer to that changing style as the International Style and to argue that this change was the direct result of new problems, such as low-cost housing which could only be solved by new techniques. And great stress was laid on rational analysis.[25]

Albini showed his capacity for combining 'rational analysis' and 'imaginative and creative transformation':

> … he can take the rational elements: the frame, the cage, the suspension system, the opaque or the transparent plane and he will transform these (as he did at the Milan Triennale Exhibitions of 1934–36) into a world of the imagination: into creative art, into an architecture of endless space and light … In contrast to this he has given us, in the Museum of the Treasury of S. Lorenzo in Genoa, a brilliant enclosure of space: the architecture of the cave.[26]

The other parallels with Albini's work that he referred to were the Pirovano Hotel in Cervinia (1946–8) and 'La Rinascente' department store in Rome (1957–61), which indicated a talent for choosing appropriate materials and technology for very different contexts: stone and timber for the Alps (Roberto Gabetti was later to describe the Pirovano Hotel as 'organicist rationalism' deeply innovative in its connection with the local culture[27]) and the exposed metal structure of a highly creative design for the Roman street scene.

Martin's final comment praised Albini's 'austere, immaculate and always creative work … that has enriched the language of architecture for us all'.[28] In 1962 Fello Atkinson published in the *Architectural Review* an enthusiastic criticism of 'La Rinascente' stressing how 'the exposed frame … (designed with the engineer Gino Covre) is restless, even casual, alive with cantilevers, brackets and section changes and apparently lighter than and independent of the "heavy" walls'.[29]

The second part of the lecture dealt with Martin's own life and practice, which had faced major changes over time. He shared his direct experience of the development of the architectural discourse in the UK from his youth: 'Architecture is a developing process, architecture means to compose and to construct buildings, with a sense of harmony and formal order'.[30] He stressed the need for a relation with the context in the urban environment, as well as the need to recognize and to create a sense of identity that is so vital to certain areas of the city.

Figure 6.1 Franco Albini with Luigi Colombini, Albergo-rifugio per ragazzi, Pirovano, Cervinia, 1948–52

Fondazione Franco Albini, Milan

In his review of the evolution of British architecture, Martin mentioned the role of tradition, the relevance of the vernacular and of the English Free School ('the master craftsman of my youth was Lutyens'). He disagreed with Nikolaus Pevsner's thesis that there was a direct evolution

Figure 6.2 Franco Albini and Franca Helg, Grandi magazzini 'La Rinascente', piazza Fiume, Rome, 1957–61
Fondazione Franco Albini, Milan

from the Arts and Crafts Movement and the English Free School to the Deutsche Werkbund and the International Style:

> I do not believe that it happened like that ... After the war, there was a need to reassess human needs ... but the important things to be

noted are not the common elements … But the differences, of timing, of historical background, in the assumptions within which the architects of each country may be working.[31]

A key passage is on the impossibility of solving the 'new problems that we had to face (in the 1930s) … by an Arts and Crafts tradition of work … so, after the war (which determined a break) we faced a complete change' and 'England was isolated from the Modern Movement abroad'. This is evident in the publication of the 1925 Paris Exhibition of Decoration, Art and Industrial Design in the pages of the *Architectural Review*, which had ignored the only two modern pavilions, the Russian one by Melnikov and Le Corbusier's Pavilion de l'Ésprit Nouveau.[32]

Only after the first years of the 1930s, therefore, did a gradual absorption of the Modern Movement become evident in Britain in a few 'outstanding buildings' such as Owen Williams's Boots Factory at Nottingham, McGrath, Chermayeff and Wells Coates's BBC New Broadcasting House, Tecton's Gorilla House and Penguin Pool at London Zoo, to be followed in 1934 by the foundation of the Mars Group, which finally provided a connection with the International avant-garde of CIAM.

Martin's lecture continued with a detailed review of the development of modern forms and experimental construction systems, which he did not interpret as 'imported from abroad' but as 'the spontaneous growth of a way of designing buildings around new and changing needs'. He mentioned his own contribution to a widening acceptance of modern forms in a revolutionary publication, edited in 1936–7 with Ben Nicholson and Naum Gabo, which consisted of a dialogue between painters, sculptors and architects: *Circle: International Survey of Constructive Art*[33]:

> The work of 22 painters, 10 sculptors and 29 architects. 21 others contributed to the text including a scientist, a choreographer and a typographer. There was no question of trying to establish a new group of style … [rather they wished to demonstrate that] … the work of art (is) a symbol of an attitude of mind. We saw art and architecture as one of the great constructing and unifying forces in our lives.[34]

Marcel Breuer's contribution at the time had confirmed the position he was now outlining: 'The base of the new architecture is not the new materials, not even the new forms; it is the new mentality. Modern architecture would exist even without reinforced concrete. It would exist in stone, wood or brick'. And this provided a 'parallel with Albini's Pirovano Hotel', which similarly demonstrated the relevance of reconsidering vernacular tradition.[35]

It was the contribution of a younger post-war generation in the late 1940s 'to consolidate the earlier ideas and to link them firmly to the new social programmes of building'. Here Martin underlined the key role of the London County Council from the 1950s as a place for meeting and debate between generations: when modern architecture was 'a method, perhaps the method of building ... the architects of the '50s found themselves able to work with remarkable freedom on important projects ...'.[36] Colin St John Wilson (1922–2007), who was close to Martin from the LCC times and followed him to Cambridge, was an active member of this 'young and angry' generation of architects who questioned current architectural thinking.[37] He joined the Independent Group, the 'more cerebral group of avant-garde artists' that were soon identified with *Architectural Design* edited by Monica Pidgeon, as an alternative to the 'conservative' *Architectural Review*.[38]

In his narrative on the post-war evolution of architectural research and practice, Martin stresses – as Albini and the Italian avant-garde did – the inadequacy of the Modern Movement to interpret the new challenges and new sensibilities expressed by the young generation. The dissolution of the Mars Group in 1957 was followed by the end of CIAM and the spontaneous birth of Team X, searching 'for a deeper sense of involvement and a new direction'.[39]

He himself had participated in this delicate process on his arrival in Cambridge as the Professor of Architecture in 1956, when he also established his practice in the King's Mill at Great Shelford.[40] The growing dialogue and the relationship between research, teaching and design practice were concerned with uncovering the 'appropriate meaning and significance' of architecture: 'In 1959 we attacked the thoughtless use of the tower or slab block as a universal solution to the housing problem. We argued that housing problems cannot be solved purely in terms of density', emphasizing the provision for family life and the appropriate balance between private and shared community space.[41] This was the starting point of the research into land use and the form of buildings to show that 'quite high densities could be achieved in low buildings'.[42] In the case of university residential buildings in Cambridge, his research produced the model of the 'Collegiate Community', based on the form of the 'court' traditionally used in the colleges: the first relevant result was published in the *Architectural Review* in 1959 with the title 'The Collegiate Plan', followed in 1960–2 by Harvey Court, new student accommodation for

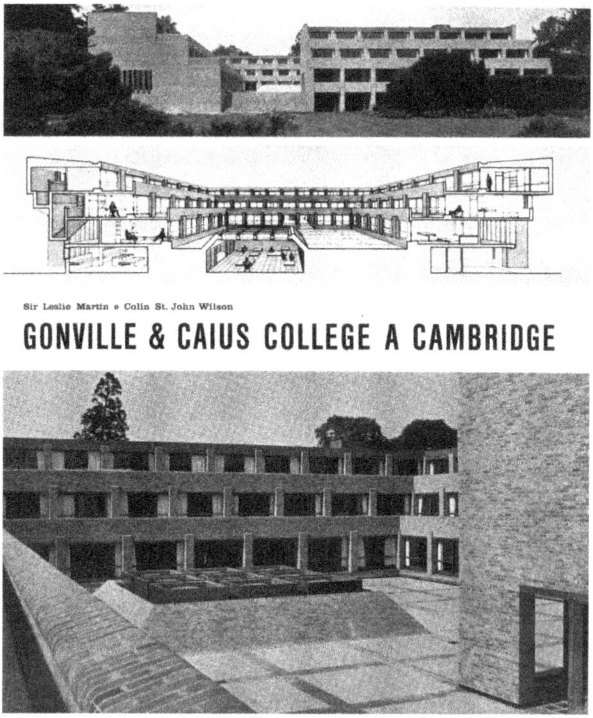

Figure 6.3 Leslie Martin, Patrick Hodgkinson and Colin St John Wilson, Harvey Court, New student accommodation for Gonville and Caius College, Cambridge, 1960–2

Casabella-Continuità, 268, October 1962

Gonville and Caius College designed and realized by Leslie Martin, Patrick Hodgkinson and Colin St John Wilson.[43]

The legacy of Franco Albini

In conclusion, Leslie Martin stated the need for architecture to contribute to a better environment, using 'modest and anonymous scale' in infill sites and 'at the other extreme ... new structure and framework ... where significant public buildings can take their proper place'. According to Martin it was ' ... part of a continuous line of development starting with the new ideas of the '30s and reached by criticism, re-assessment and creative thought about architecture', an approach that clearly states the distance to 'the flood of thoughtless building development that seems to be shaping the form of most of the cities of the western world'.[44] Such a sensibility to the site and the concept of 'modesty' had a parallel in the work of Franco Albini, Giancarlo De Carlo, and also Mario Ridolfi.

The appreciation for Albini in the British context is proved by several articles in the architectural journals.[45] Michael Brawne, who was a Lecturer in Architecture at Cambridge School of Architecture in 1964–78, has published in the *Architectural Review* two key articles on the Italian experience in the design of museums and exhibitions, mentioning the central role of the Milan Triennale and the successful approach by Albini and Franca Helg in Palazzo Rosso, Palazzo Bianco, and the Museum of the Treasury of S. Lorenzo in Genoa.[46]

The high prestige acquired by Albini in the field of museology is, perhaps, the reason for his first co-operation with Leslie Martin at the Calouste Gulbenkian Foundation in Lisbon. In April 1959, in fact, they were both invited to sit on the advisory committee for the new museum.[47] The origin of the project was the establishment in 1956 of the foundation, followed in 1957 by the purchase of one of the largest parks in the city, Santa Gertrudes Park, to host its headquarters and a museum. The curator of the collection, Maria José de Mendonça, was aware of the new frontiers in museum design since she was a member of the International Council of Museums (ICOM). The appointment of Martin and Albini followed her own preliminary proposal. Later the committee has included Carlos Ramos and Francisco Keil do Amaral from Portugal and Georges Henri Rivière from France. Both Martin and Albini were also invited to give public lectures on their work: Albini held a talk on 'Problems of Museology and Museography' on 8 August 1959 at the temporary pavilions of the foundation.[48]

In February 1960 the invited competition was launched, won by Ruy Athougia, Alberto Pessoa and Pedro Cid. Regular visits were undertaken by Albini and Martin from June 1959 and Martin organized some tours in Britain to visit key works. Michael Brawne also joined a trip to Lisbon for a meeting with the team of architects and the advisors. Penelope Curtis, on the occasion of the fiftieth anniversary of the opening of the Lisbon premises, undertook some research, basing her work on the archives of the Gulbenkian Foundation.[49] Her article, significantly named 'The Albini effect', describes the role of Leslie Martin in the interior design of the museum as well as the leading role of Albini as the main representative in view of his relevant museum experience.[50]

In Leslie Martin's archive are several letters mentioning their co-operation, which includes a second relevant case: the invitation to be advisory members of the Master Planning Committee for Kuwait City from July 1968.[51] Leslie Martin and Colin Buchanan, invited by the Prime Minister of Kuwait, suggested a working group including Franco Albini and Franca Helg, Lodovico Barbiano di Belgiojoso and Enrico Peressutti, Raili and Reima Pietilä, George Candilis, Alison and Peter Smithson, and Jørn Utzon.[52] The aim was to propose a new approach to the problem of planning the city. Leslie Martin's archive records several meetings in London and Cambridge, alternating with frequent visits to Kuwait City, and contains several schemes produced by the group. It was an innovative approach, carefully managed by local government staff, interpreting Leslie Martin's experimental method to planning in this context.[53] Among the few realized parts of a project that continued into the mid-1970s, I would mention the way that the design by Raili and Reima Pietilä of the Sief Palace for the Governmental Offices of the Emir, the Council of the Ministers and the Ministry of Foreign Affairs (completed in 1982) successfully adapts to the local character and climate; this has been studied by Aino Niskanen, using the Pietilä's archive and interviewing Raili Pietilä.[54]

The parallel course of the careers of Leslie Martin and Franco Albini, from their earliest design work in the 1930s to their collaboration on planning projects with architects of a younger generation 40 years later, when they had each achieved an international reputation, is representative of the many fruitful interconnections between Italian and British architects in the twentieth century, which promises to provide material for research for some years to come.

The lesson that the younger generation might be expected to absorb from Leslie Martin's address in memory of his friend was how each of them had sought to establish a dialogue with the place, to read its history, character and relationship to local communities, and thereby create an architecture that was modest and understated yet capable of enduring.

Notes

1 Building Modern Britain, Leslie Martin Seminar, Royal Institute of British Architects, London, 12 September 2016. The author gave an address on 'International Perspectives', focusing on the relationships with the Italian post-war avant-garde.

2 RIBA British Architectural Library. See https://www.architecture.com/about/riba-library-and-collections.

3 AAA Italia, Italian Association of Archives of Contemporary Architects is a network of more than 50 public and private institutions, as museums, archives, libraries and universities. See https://www.aaa-italia.org.

4 Martin 1980.
5 Bullock 2002, 34–6.
6 *The Architectural Review* 1941.
7 Ansell 1943.
8 Ansell 1943.
9 *The Architectural Review* 1943.
10 Richards 1941.
11 On the post-war reconstruction in Italy, see Dal Co 1997, 11–20; Irace 1997, 58–81; Conforti 1997, 176–241. On Ernesto Rogers, see Baglione 2012.
12 Baffa 1995.
13 See Rossari 2006, 126–47.
14 Albini 1955, 45–52.
15 Franco Albini and Giancarlo Palanti were appointed editors-in-chief of *Costruzioni Casabella* in 1945. They edited three issues: March 1946, 193, September 1946, 194, December 1946, 195/198, the last being a monograph issue devoted to Giuseppe Pagano. Rogers 1954, 2 ('Continuity', in 'Translation', I).
16 As above.
17 Martin 1983, 10–11.
18 Martin 1983, 10–11.
19 Martin 1983, 10–11.
20 Martin 1983, 10–11.
21 The exhibition 'Franco Albini – architettura e design, 1930–1970' was organized at the Rotonda di Via Besana, in Milan, in December 1979–February 1980. The text of the lecture, drafted by hand and copied with typewriter, is in the Leslie Martin Archive, RIBA Collection, London. The catalogue of the exhibition is in the collection of the library of the School of Architecture in Cambridge, see Helg 1979. On Franco Albini see also Leet 1990; Rossi Prodi 1996; Piva 1998; Bucci *et al.* 2005; Bucci *et al.* 2006; Sherer 2009, 9–38; Kay Jones 2014.
22 From an interview with Marco Albini by the author. In Leslie Martin's archive at the RIBA there is a letter from Franca Helg to Leslie Martin dated January 1980 referring to the invitation to Milan.
23 Martin 1980.
24 Martin 1980.
25 Martin 1980.
26 Martin 1980.
27 See Gabetti 1988, 36; Rossari 2006, 127–47; Conforti 2006, 165–83.
28 Martin 1980.
29 Fello 1962, 268–74.
30 Fello 1962, 268–74.
31 Fello 1962, 268–74.
32 Fello 1962, 268–74.
33 Martin *et al.* [1937] 1971.
34 Martin *et al.* [1937] 1971. See invitation letters to several artists signed by Leslie Martin and Sadie Speight in the Leslie Martin archive section at the Victoria and Albert Museum, London.
35 'At this point we can see the parallel with Albini's Pirovano Hotel and the fact that Breuer once again called attention to the significance of vernacular work', see Martin 1980.
36 Martin 1980.
37 Kite 2010, 55–77.
38 For a portrait of the young generation gathering close to Reyner Banham, see Girouard 1998.
39 Martin 1980.
40 Pevsner 1956.
41 Martin 1980.
42 John McKean suggests considering the contribution of Walter Segal on this matter, already expressed in 1948 in his book *Home and Environment*; see Grahame and McKean 2021, Martin 1980; see Hawkes 2017, 144–57; Martin *et al.* 1972; Carolin *et al.* 1996; Carolin 2000.
43 Martin 1959; Martin 1983, 28–35. The evolution of his studies and research was the foundation in 1967 of the Centre for Land Use and Built Form Studies (since 1973 The Martin Centre for Architectural and Urban Studies), see Hawkes 2017.

44 Martin 1980. Colin St John Wilson was a key figure in the award of the RIBA Gold Medal to Giancarlo De Carlo in 1993. On that occasion he stressed the humanistic approach to architecture and to the historic city by De Carlo; see Wilson 1993, 74–9.
45 Atkinson 1962, 268–74; Obituary: Franco Albini 1978, 192.
46 Brawne 1959a, 314–25; Brawne 1959b, 243–53. On Michael Brawne, see Carolin 2003.
47 In April 1959 President Perdigão asked Albini to be part of the collaboration as an advisor and a week later Albini agreed. See Calouste Gulbenkian Foundation, Lisbon.
48 See Calouste Gulbenkian Foundation, Lisbon.
49 See Curtis 2020, 10–64; Martin 1983, 100–14.
50 Curtis 2020.
51 Sir Leslie Martin Archive, RIBA Collection.
52 BBPR 1969; Smithson 1974, 178–82.
53 Al-Ragam 2015, 1–20.
54 Sir Leslie Martin Archive, RIBA Collection; see Niskanen 2008, 183–94.

References

Albini, Franco. 'Un dibattito sulla tradizione in architettura svoltosi a Milano nella sede del Movimento per gli Studi di Architettura – MSA – la sera del 14 giugno 1955', *Casabella-Continuità* 206 (July–August 1955): 45–52.

Alici, Antonello. 'Peterhouse: Prove di modernità in un college di Cambridge', *Città e Storia*, 12/2 (2017): 287–313.

Al-Ragam, Asseel. 'Critical nostalgia: Kuwait urban modernity and Alison and Peter Smithson's Kuwait urban study and Mat-Building', *The Journal of Architecture*, 2015: 1–20.

Ansell, William Henry. 'Foreword', *The Architectural Review* 556 (April 1943): 85.

Atkinson, Fello. 'Department store 'La Rinascente', Rome, Franco Albini and Franca Helg', *The Architectural Review* 132/788 (October 1962): 268–74.

Baffa, Matilde and Corinna Morandi, Sara Protasoni and Augusto Rossari. *Il Movimento di Studi per l'Architettura 1945–1961*. Rome-Bari: Laterza, 1995.

Baglione, Chiara (ed.). *Ernesto Nathan Rogers: 1909–1969*. Milan: Franco Angeli, 2012.

Banham, Reyner. 'Neoliberty: The Italian retreat from modern architecture', *The Architectural Review* 747 (April 1959): 231–5.

BBPR. 'Architectural Report for the Future Development of Old Kuwait City project'. Milan: Fondazione Franco Albini, 1969.

Brawne, Michael. 'The picture wall', *The Architectural Review* 748 (May 1959): 314–25.

Brawne, Michael. 'Object on view', *The Architectural Review* 753 (November 1959): 243–53.

Bucci, Federico and Fulvio Irace (eds). *Zero Gravity: Franco Albini: Costruire le modernità*. Milan: Triennale Electa, 2006.

Bucci, Federico and Augusto Rossari (eds). *I musei e gli allestimenti di Franco Albini*. Milan: Electa, 2005.

Bullock, Nicholas. *Building the Post-War World: Modern architecture and reconstruction in Britain*. London: Routledge, 2002.

Carolin, Peter. 'Sir Leslie Martin, 1908–2000', *Architects' Journal*, 3 August 2000.

Carolin, Peter and Trevor Dannatt (eds). *Architecture, Education and Research: The work of Leslie Martin: Papers and selected articles*. London: Academy Editions, 1996.

Carolin, Peter, Bob Allies, Charles Correa, Philip Dowson, Peter Clegg, Roger Stonehouse, Spencer de Grey and Dean Hawkes. 'Obituary: Michael Brawne, 1925–2003', *Architectural Research Quarterly*, 7 no. 2, 107–12.

Ciccarelli, Lorenzo. *Il mito dell'equilibrio: Il dibattito anglo-italiano per il governo del territorio negli anni del dopoguerra*. Milan: Franco Angeli, 2019.

Conforti, Claudia. 'Roma, Napoli, La Sicilia'. In *Storia dell'architettura italiana: Il secondo Novecento*, edited by Francesco Dal Co, 176–241. Milan: Electa, 1997.

Conforti, Claudia. 'Franco Albini: Architetture di utilità'. In *Zero Gravity: Franco Albini: Costruire le modernità*, edited by Federico Bucci and Fulvio Irace, 165–183. Milan: Triennale Electa, 2006.

Crinson, Mark and Claire Zimmerman (eds). *Neo-avant-garde and Postmodern: Postwar architecture in Britain and beyond*. New Haven: Yale University Press, 2010.

Curtis, Penelope. 'The Albini effect: The Gulbenkian Museum, its international context and Italian museology'. In *Art on Display 1949–69, 10–64. Lisbon:* Calouste Gulbenkian Museum, 2020.
Dal Co, Francesco (ed.). *Storia dell'architettura italiana: Il secondo Novecento*. Milan: Electa, 1997.
Dal Co, Francesco. 'La ricostruzione: Introduzione alla storia dell'architettura italiana del secondo Novecento'. In *Storia dell'architettura italiana: Il secondo Novecento*, edited by Francesco Dal Co, 11–20. Milan: Electa, 1997.
Editor. 'Destruction and reconstruction', *The Architectural Review* 90 (July 1941): 1–2.
Gabetti, Roberto. 'Elzeviro poltrone', in 'La tensione del fare. Il tema e le sue variazioni', edited by Margherita Petranzan and Umberto Tubini. Special issue of *Quaderni di architettura*, 1, 2, 1988.
Girouard, Mark. *Big Jim: The life and work of James Stirling*. London, Chatto and Windus, 1998.
Grahame, Alice and John McKean. *Walter Segal: Self-Built Architect*. London: Lund Humphries, 2021.
Hawkes, Dean. 'Bridging the cultures: Architecture, models and computers in 1960s Cambridge', *Interdisciplinary Science Reviews* 42, no. 1–2 (2017): 144–57.
Helg, Franca. *Franco Albini: Architettura e design, 1930–1970*. Florence: Centro Di, 1979.
Irace, Fulvio. 'Milano'. In *Storia dell'architettura italiana: Il secondo Novecento*, edited by Francesco Dal Co, 58–81. Milan: Electa, 1997.
Kay Jones, Bea. *Suspending Modernity: The architecture of Franco Albini*. Farnham: Ashgate, 2014.
Kite, Stephen. 'Softs and hards: Colin St John Wilson and the contested visions of 1950s London. In *Neo-avant-garde and Postmodern: Postwar architecture in Britain and beyond*, edited by Mark Crinson and Claire Zimmerman, 55–77. New Haven: Yale University Press, 2010.
Leet, Stephen. *Franco Albini: Architecture and design, 1934–1977*. New York: Princeton Architectural Press, 1990.
Martin, Leslie. 'The Collegiate Plan', *The Architectural Review* 750 (July 1959): 42–8.
Martin, Leslie, Ben Nicholson and Naum Gabo (eds). *Circle: International Survey of Constructive Art*, [1937] London: Faber & Faber [1937] 1971.
Martin, Leslie and Lionel March (eds). *Urban Space and Structures*. London: Cambridge University Press, 1972.
Martin, Leslie. Lecture on Franco Albini in Milan, December 1980. Sir Leslie Martin Archive, RIBA Collection, London.
Martin, Leslie. *Buildings and Ideas 1933–83: From the studio of Leslie Martin and his associates*. Cambridge: Cambridge University Press, 1983.
Moustafa, Amer, Jamal Al-Qawasmi and Kevin Mitchell (eds). *Instant Cities*. American University of Sharjah, 2008.
Niskanen, Aino. 'Contextual architecture for New Delhi, Kuwait and Dubai Deira by Reima and Raili Pietilä'. In *Instant Cities* edited by Amer Moustafa, Jamal Al-Qawasmi and Kevin Mitchell, 183–94. American University of Sharjah, 2008.
'Obituary: Franco Albini (1905–77)', *The Architectural Review* 974 (April 1978): 192.
Pevsner, Nikolaus. 'Welcome to Professor Martin', *The Cambridge Review*, 10 November 1956: 136–7.
Pevsner, Nikolaus. *The Englishness of English Art: An expanded and annotated version of the Reith Lectures broadcast in October and November 1955*. London: Penguin, 1993 [orig. ed.: London: Architectural Press, 1956].
Piva, Antonio and Vittorio Prina. *Franco Albini 1905–1977*. Milan: Electa, 1998.
'Rebuilding Britain: Programme', *The Architectural Review* 556 (April 1943): 86.
Richards, James M. 'Towards a replanning policy: Regionalism re-examined', *The Architectural Review* 90 (July 1941): 38–40.
Rogers, Ernesto. 'Continuità', *Casabella-Continuità* 199 (December 1953–January 1954): 2.
Rogers, Ernesto. 'L'evoluzione dell'architettura: Risposta al custode dei frigidaires', *Casabella-Continuità* 228 (June 1959): 2–4.
Rogers, Ernesto. 'Appunti sull'Inghilterra e l'Italia', *Casabella-Continuità* 250 (April 1961): 1–2.
Rossari, Augusto. 'Un percorso antiformalista tra modernità e tradizione'. In *Zero Gravity: Franco Albini: Costruire le modernità* [exhibition catalogue], edited by Federico Bucci and Fulvio Irace. Milan: Triennale Electa, 2006.
Rossi Prodi, Fabrizio. *Franco Albini*. Rome: Officina, 1996.

Sherer, Daniel and Aldo Colonetti (eds). *Franco Albini and Franca Helg Design*. Milan: FragileMilano, 2009.
Smithson, Alison. 'Proposals for restructuring Kuwait', *The Architectural Review* 156 (1974): 178–82.
Wilson, Colin St John. 'Master of the Resistance', *The Architectural Review* 194/1157 (July 1993): 74–9.

7

Superstudio, the sign and the problem of architectural education

Da Hyung Jeong

'In a capitalistic system, there is no break between production, distribution and consumption. All the intellectual anti-consumer utopias that seek to redress the ethical "distortions" of the technological world by modifying the system of production or the channels of distribution only reveal the complete inadequacy of their theories, in the face of the actual structure of the capitalist economic cycle'.[1]

This is the critique of Superstudio, Archizoom and Gruppo 9999 that Manfredo Tafuri put forth in 'Design and Technological Utopia', his essay for the catalogue of the 1972 MoMA exhibition *Italy: The New Domestic Landscape*. He derogatorily called their hypothetical architecture 'surreal' – that is, decidedly out of touch with the real – and was adamant that their attempt to reverse alienation by means of a Benjaminian shock failed.[2] Their apocalyptic visions, in the final analysis, failed to jolt the viewer out of stupor, simply strengthening the tyranny of spectacle. They were architecture radically flattened into pure imagery and circulating as spectacle, as objects of contemplation and never as instigators of concrete action. There was, to be sure, an operaist 'refusal of work' underpinning them, but the out-landishness of the vocabulary used by the radicals devastatingly meant the preclusion of all meaningful communication with the general public.[3] True subversion, for Tafuri, would have consisted in direct intervention in the system of production, which in the context of post-war Italian architecture was understood primarily as intervention in the design, distribution and consumption of housing – for the radicals to refuse to design, then, was for them to deprive architecture of its substantive dimension, one that was a safeguard against reduction to a commodity.

To a degree, Tafuri was prescient. Superstudio, Archizoom and Gruppo 9999's image-manifestoes are now commodities having fallen prey to the art market. They are now 'a means to the artistic and speculative enjoyment of the collector or the museum' and serve as a grim reminder of what Felicity Scott has called 'the suppression of experimental architecture'.[4]

However, a historical revision may be performed against this backdrop. Tafuri's pessimism may be placed under scrutiny in order to argue that the radicals did intervene, and fruitfully at that, in the system of production. Instead of the system of goods production, which they agreed was hopelessly enthralled to the capitalist logic, they turned to the system of knowledge production and attacked its weak spot, namely the arena of education that the 1968 student uprisings had rendered porous and vulnerable to infiltrations – tellingly, Superstudio identified education as one of the five fundamental acts of human existence and sought to sanctify it in a film project undertaken from 1971 to 1973. Adolfo Natalini, one of the collective's founders, took particular interest in didacticism as a form of resistance and, via Alvin Boyarsky, exerted influence over the development of new pedagogies at London's Architectural Association. He then went on to play a key role in the formation of the internationally oriented Global Tools group. The activities of this group, though short-lived, are significant in that they were characterized by an almost exclusive focus on the problem of education.

In 'The Avant-Garde and the New Architecture (Avanguardia e nuova architettura)', Massimo Scolari suggests that Superstudio's 'particular attention to disciplinary discourse' – that is, the discourse surrounding the state of architectural education – is a special characteristic that distinguishes it from the other 'Florentine groups', criticized for doing nothing more than to use various 'tricks' to 'conceal ... the total inexistence of a doctrine'.[5] The essay appeared in the catalogue for the landmark exhibition *Rational Architecture* (*Architettura razionale*), shown at the fifteenth Milan Triennale in 1973. In Francesco Moschini's words, the catalogue far exceeded the function of a 'guide subordinated to the exhibition', serving, like a manifesto, to articulate a new tendency, a new architectural culture constructed around 'a new truth'.[6] The Neo-Rationalist desideratum was a novel system of knowledge production prioritizing 'clarification' over 'invention', clarification that is perhaps not unrelated to the full revelation of half-hidden principles of spatial organization enabled by the rhetorical device of the hyperbole – Superstudio's *Manhattan, photomontage final* relies on an exaggerated, utopic/dystopic image to shed light on the secret tyranny of the grid.[7]

Figure 7.1 Superstudio, *Manhattan, photomontage final (Monumento Continuo)*, 1969
Centre Pompidou, AM 2000-2-141.

Superstudio was represented at *Rational Architecture*, and Natalini, as its spokesperson, confirmed that the essence of its work lay in the realization that architecture was 'one of the few means by which the cosmic order could be *rendered visible* on earth'.[8] When tasked with performing the act of clarification, of rendering visible a hidden truth, the architectural object is pushed beyond its commodified state and acquires a use value, becoming a didactic instrument.

To render visible is principally to 'render communicable and transmissible', asserted Daniele Vitale, who identified 'the content of an experience of architecture' as the ultimate object of the act of clarification.[9] The inclusion of his essay 'Architecture Schools: Presentation of a few projects (Le scuole di architettura: Presentazione di alcuni progetti)' in the catalogue is evidence of the significance that the Neo-Rationalists attached to the issue of education and what they perceived to be an urgent need for a thoroughgoing educational reform. Vitale held that the architecture school should, in addition to enabling the acquisition of the tools necessary for both the effective conveyance and reception of experiences, give the work of individual students a 'collective basis, one that gestures toward a communal, rational core'.[10] The architecture school, in other words, had now to furnish a system of agreed-upon signs and rhetorical devices that, serving as a shared toolbox, could guarantee a degree of consistency in the various forms of expression and ensure their mutual intelligibility – that is to say, to make architecture 'interpretable with respect to a well-defined system of evaluation'.[11]

Superstudio, Archigram and Louis Althusser

The role that architectural magazines played in the establishment of such a collective basis, or of a common language of agreed-upon signs and expressive means, cannot be overestimated. Mindful of their utility as an indoctrination tool, proponents of the anti-design movement had, early on, made a successful attempt to seize control of *Casabella*, having taken 'power away from Ernesto Nathan Rogers' – it would become a crucial outlet for the radicals, who used it to express views that both corresponded to and departed from the Neo-Rationalist position.[12] Tafuri, characteristically, dismissed the usurpation as an 'astute marketing operation', as a gesture motivated primarily by the prospect of profit.[13] The radicals capitalized on the magazine in circulating their ideas and the signs expressing them, and despite Tafuri's scepticism about their capacity for wide communication, favourable responses came from as far as Japan and, remarkably, the socialist world. As for the British periodical *Architectural Design*, the close attention it paid to Superstudio's activities reflects a special camaraderie that existed between the British and Italian neo-avant-gardes. Its December 1971 issue featured Superstudio on the cover and juxtaposed its *Twelve Ideal Cities* to Archigram's *Instant City*. Later in 1982, Peter Cook would revealingly identify a worldwide resistance to complacency as the context of this camaraderie. There was a 'sense of shared conspiracy between all the members of all the groups that were setting up in Europe and Japan, the United States and even the NER Group in [the Soviet Union], pitched against the common foe: our contemporaries who were content to be safe, aggregate-bound mainstream architects', he remarked.[14] He then offered a striking genealogical account of Italian radicalism. The Florentine groups – that is, Superstudio, Archizoom and Gruppo 9999 – crystallized one day in 1965 when '50 copies of Archigram's funny little magazine were sold in the Centro Di shop in Florence', he recalled.[15]

Several aspects of Superstudio's work, indeed, are evidence of a debt to Archigram. Both used montage and the grid to communicate an experience of monumentality and nomadism. Both celebrated the monumentality of 'technomorphous architecture', which takes 'from industrial processes … methods of composition (assembly, repetition, change of scale) and demonstrates them', or, in other words, renders them visible.[16] However, there is an important difference between the two approaches taken to achieving what seems to have been a common goal. Archigram's compositions are finite, each of their abundant details commanding attention and preventing the imagination from making a leap beyond that which is given. Superstudio, on the other hand, opted for an image of the infinite, utilizing an endlessly expanding grid that symbolizes and renders visible the total, dystopian subsumption of human existence by mathematical reason. 'The technical intellect designs reality not only as an object of domination … like a field that lies before us, fundamentally predictable, manoeuvrable and manipulable, but also as perfectible toward an evil infinity', Czechoslovak philosopher Karel Kosik had warned, and Superstudio offered an almost literal illustration of that evil infinity. Filiberto Menna, a historian-critic and an advocate for the radicals, would cite Kosik in 'A Design for New Behaviors', an essay written for the catalogue of *Italy: The New Domestic Landscape*, revealing a deep familiarity with socialist discourse.

Superstudio and Archigram also understood nomadism, a shared desideratum, differently. Both deemed it to be an ideal, to be the ultimate goal of all attempts to revolutionize human behaviour. However, Superstudio's *Supersurface* (*Supersuperficie*) of 1972 is an infinite grid, and the invisible 'cells' that make it up guarantee liberation from reliance on objects, while Ron Herron's *Free Time Node Trailer Cage* of 1966 demonstrates that Archigram clung to the ultimate capitalist fetish – the automobile. Superstudio, in other words, sought to represent a utopia that is a dystopic 'non-place' (*ou*-topia), a vacuum embodying the radical rejection of all commodities, while Archigram's utopia was a 'good place' (*eu*-topia) saturated with objects affording pleasure. There are two possible explanations for these divergent and oppositional views taken by the two groups. Firstly, Superstudio's work came in the wake of and was inevitably a response to the 1968 student uprisings, to the profound cynicism that sustained the uprisings and persisted long after their conclusion, while Archigram's earlier work preceded these momentous events. Secondly, the context of Archigram's practice was Britain's 'intellectual isolation', while Italy was an epicentre of leftist critical discourse – historian Warren Breckman has revealed that an 'anti-theoretical, empiricist culture' prevailed in Britain at the time and engendered a 'poverty of … intellectual life,' which meant that significant exposure to the ideas of leftist philosophers like Karl Korsch, Georg

Lukács, Theodor Adorno, Max Horkheimer, Jean-Paul Sartre and Louis Althusser became possible only in 1976 with the publication of Perry Anderson's *Considerations on Western Marxism*.[17]

Discussing education, progressive thinkers stressed not the acquisition of knowledge but the transformation of behaviour, the paramount ideological significance of which they sought to emphasize. Althusser, for instance, explained that education serves the promulgation of 'the "rules" of good behaviour', which 'actually mean rules of respect for the socio-technical division of labour and ultimately the rules of the order established by class domination', and argued that it formed a site of 'bitter forms of class struggle'.[18] Exploited classes should 'find means and occasions to express itself' within the various apparatuses sustaining education, 'either by the utilization of their contradictions or by conquering combat positions in them in struggle' – it is not insignificant that the philosopher's 'Ideology and Ideological State Apparatuses' was written 'partly as a result of the events of May 1968 in France'.[19] Importantly, in his essay for the catalogue of *Italy: The New Domestic Landscape*, Filiberto Menna brought Althusser's understanding of education and behaviour to bear on the discussion of recent Italian design. Praising the radicals' deconstruction of the object, he asserted that 'objects must definitely abandon their claim to direct the behaviour of the user in an unvarying fashion' and must suggest 'new possibilities for the independent exercise of the user's own choices' or, what is the same thing, new behavioural possibilities that go beyond the norm perpetuated by conventional education.[20] Advanced capitalism had, disconcertingly, reduced conventional education to an 'ideological state apparatus' promoting perfect acquiescence to existing productive relations, and it seemed that the radicals' deconstruction of the object indicated a way out of this impasse. For the Genoese critic Germano Celant, the way out of the impasse lay in the rediscovery of what he called a 'mystical' architecture, which, being 'by nature concrete and radical in its ideological and behavioural premises', refused 'to be alienated from its own ideas and its own image, with a sacred implacability regarding its own ideas and concepts of architecture and design'.[21] That he mentioned the problem of ideology in the same breath as that of behaviour is unmistakably Althusserian.

Althusser's *For Marx* was translated into Italian in 1967, and a compilation of letters exchanged between Althusser and Maria Antonietta Macciocchi, *L'Unità*'s Paris correspondent, appeared in 1969 – incidentally, London-based New Left Books published an English edition of the compilation in 1973. The journal *Marxist Critique* (*Critica marxista*) was instrumental in shaping Althusser's earliest Italian reception, with 'Marxism and Humanism (Marxismo e umanesimo)' and 'Sketch for a Concept of History (Per un concetto di storia)' appearing, respectively, in the 1964 and 1966 issues. By 1970, Althusserianism had suffused Italian architectural criticism. Roberto Segre's 1970 *Cuba: Architecture of revolution* (*Cuba, l'architettura della rivoluzione*) called for a precise definition of the terms 'man' and 'architecture', which were central to the profession and yet problematically 'universal' and overly 'abstract' – as abstract as the concept of humanism that Althusser had brought under scrutiny and of which he had, in 'Marxism and Humanism', revealed a tendency to 'easily blend into themes of petit-bourgeois inspiration'.[22] The Althusserian architectural critic Carlo Olmo, for his part, contended in his 1971 *Politics and Form* (*Politica e forma*) that 'operative criticism', by 'reducing itself to an instrument of an ideology', failed to 'address the problem of redefining, within the historical context and the social structure, the values in question, the political use that had been made of them and the concrete possibility of an alternative to that use'.[23] Superstudio, on the other hand, achieved the redefinition of the signs and rhetorical devices – in short, the values – that it borrowed from Archigram by bringing them to bear on the specificities of the post-1968 context, in which an *ou*-topia had supplanted the *eu*-topia. As for the left-leaning architectural periodical *Zodiac*, whose pan-European editorial board counted the Britons Maxwell Fry and Joseph Rykwert among its members, it reproduced in its 1971 issue the decidedly Althusserian lecture that Sergio Los delivered at the Istituto di Architettura di Venezia on the necessity of an epistemological rupture and a new science.

In a 28 March, 1968 letter to Althusser, Macciocchi remembers a particular assertiveness witnessed among rebellious students at the University of Rome's Faculty of Architecture during the uprisings:

> I found, on the blackboard of the Main Hall, the first revolutionary message aimed directly at language. I was really moved by it … I copied down the whole phrase, which goes like this: 'All speakers will refrain from pronouncing the following words: at the level of, instrumentalization, demystification, document, sensitize, DISCOURSE, structural moment, it is no accident that, to the extent that.[24]

The students sought to problematize the lack of 'rigor' in the language of the Italian Communist Party, which seemed excessively dependent on terms that, 'like rubber bands', could be 'stretched in any direction' until they signified 'almost anything'– in short, terms as ambiguous as 'man', 'architecture' and 'humanism'.[25] The signification of everything, for them, was equivalent to the signification of nothing. That architecture students should have undertaken such a problematization of language is hardly surprising given the increasing popularity that semiotics, the cross-disciplinary study of signs as the basis of communication, was enjoying among them. Italy was among the places where early attempts at understanding artistic productions in terms of signs were made. Emilio Garroni's *Semiotics and Aesthetics: The heterogeneity of language and cinematographic language* (*Semiotica ed estetica: L'eterogeneità del linguaggio e il linguaggio cinematografico*) was published in 1968, while his extended article 'Semiotics and Architecture: Some problems of theory and application (Semiotica e architettura: Alcuni problemi teorico-applicativi)', pertaining directly to the field of architecture, appeared in the May 1970 issue of *Op. cit.*, a left-leaning periodical had published Roland Barthes's 'Semiology and Urban Planning (Sémiologie et urbanisme)' in 1967.

Figure 7.2 Cover of *Op. cit.* 18 (May 1970)

Image courtesy Renato De Fusco

Garroni underscored that all instances of communication necessarily constitute a complex interplay of 'messages, their senders and receivers' as well as the 'historical conditions' under which these individuals find themselves, and that no sign can be absolutely abstract and exist independently of a 'communicative context'. He implied that the act of identifying and making known the specific communicative context in which a given sign functions is a didactic, exhortative one.[26] For the protesting students, the inadequacy of party discourse was simply the flip side of the same coin as the inadequacy of architectural practice and education. They ascribed both problems to imprecise, irresponsible communication.

The sign and the mystique of architecture

In Florence, the Facoltà di architettura was already sustaining 'advanced discussions of semiotics'.[27] Umberto Eco arrived there in 1966 to succeed Gillo Dorfles and, collaborating with the radical collectives 'from the start', guided their 'research into new written language and formal language'.[28] In 1967, he circulated 'Notes for a Semiology of Visual Communications (Appunti per una semiologia delle comunicazioni visive)' among his students. It defined the signified of the architectural signifier as the function enacted by a building and distinguished between denotative, or primary, function and connotative, or secondary, function. If the former is burdened with a stabilized and 'precise signified', the latter is 'open (*aperta*)' and corresponds to the unknown, forgotten function of 'the *menhir*, the *dolmen* and Stonehenge', in short to the mystique of architecture foregrounded by Celant.[29] What Superstudio attempted, then, is to open up a new, connotative dimension of 'technomorphous architecture' by performing a negation of Archigram's denotative signs – signs confined to the expression of optimism – and in the process transforming them into 'open' signs capable of taking on new meanings.

Eco's *Open Work*, published in 1962, had a great influence on the radicals. In this important text, Eco identified avant-gardism with an 'art that, in order to take a grip on the world, falls into it, from the inside taking on the conditions of crisis, using the same alienated language in which this world expresses itself, to describe it'.[30] Superstudio seized, via Archigram, the alienated language of 'advertisements, comics, ad copy, illustrations and other elements used in mass-circulation magazines', but they did not stop there.[31] If Archigram ultimately failed to go beyond the mere description of the world of capital and remained unable to liberate itself from a false sense of optimism, Superstudio performed a critique through negation, through a *détournement* of the 'motifs and techniques' – in short, signs – of mass culture, turning mass culture against itself.[32] Montage, understood broadly as the juxtaposition of disparate signs, was essential to this operation. By inserting them into new, unforeseen contexts, Superstudio restored the mystique of signs derived from mass culture, precisely when their connotative function seemed totally subsumed by the denotative function of influencing consumer behaviour. Familiar fragments of objective reality were rendered alien and disquieting through juxtaposition with signs derived from a thoroughly subjective apocalyptic imagination, through the enhancement of the real that Eco characterized as a process whereby 'a matter never gets simpler; rather, it becomes ever more complicated as it captures and assimilates all sorts of possible meanings, incorporating aspects or moments of reality'.[33]

There is an important analogy between Superstudio's 1969 *Manhattan, photomontage final*, from the series *Continuous Monument* (*Monumento continuo*), and OMA's 1972 *Exodus, or the Voluntary Prisoners of Architecture*, which was a 'response to a competition launched by *Casabella* on the theme of "the city as a signifying environment"' – Koolhaas would remark in a 1985 interview that, at the time, he found *Continuous Monument* to be 'really fantastic' and reminiscent of 'the rationalism of [the Soviet constructivist architect Ivan] Leonidov'.[34] If fragments of reality, namely the Manhattan gridiron and the Berlin Wall, formed the basis of Superstudio and OMA's imaginative leaps, they underwent such a thorough mystification, such a complete estrangement from their denotative meaning that, in their new contexts, they appear as monstrosities. The gridiron of New York has been transformed into a terrifying, infinitely expanding structure of oppression, and the Berlin Wall has become a giant prison, albeit a paradoxical one that inmates inhabit voluntarily. This sort of 'enhancement of the real' reached its logical extreme with Superstudio's *New York of Brains* of 1971, a grotesque 'cautionary tale' hypothesizing a post-apocalyptic New York City:

> In the most charred, devastated and molten area of that grey space that once was New York, and, more precisely, where Central Park once was, at about 81st, there stands the city. When the others realized that the explosion had irrevocably contaminated all the inhabitants of New York, and that their bodies were rotting without recourse, it was decided to build the city. It is a cube, with

> a length, width and height of 180 ft, covered in quartz tiles measuring 10 x 10 inches, in each of which there is a lens 9 inches in diameter. This covering condenses light onto the photosensitive layer behind, which transforms it into energy necessary for the functioning of the city.[35]

The elimination of the body suggested here, communicated through the striking image of 'bodies rotting without recourse' is simply a paraphrase of the radical elimination of all objects that was Superstudio's ultimate desideratum. The gruesome narrative, along with 11 other similar 'cautionary tales', appeared in the December 1971 issue of *Architectural Design* and would not have gone unnoticed by students at the Architectural Association, including Koolhaas and his friends. They must have already been equipped with tools with which to understand the semiotic operations underpinning the tales thanks to Charles Jencks, who was teaching 'the semiology of building systems' at the school.[36] The sublime terror of the monstrous imagery, however, would have seemed cancelled out by its anticlimactic association with 'Christmas'.

Figure 7.3 Superstudio, *Terza città: New York of Brains*, 1971
Centre Pompidou, AM 2000-2-157

Figure 7.4 Advertisement for the International Institute of Design's 1971 Summer Session. The 'conflicting attitudes ... toward education' had already been underscored at this previous iteration of the event

Image courtesy of AA Print Studio, London

A 'Letter from London' published in the October 1972 issue of *Domus* indicates that Natalini, while helping Alvin Boyarsky conceptualize the newest edition of the International Institute of Design's summer school, had in mind an Italian participation that would be 'something very *scientifico-didactic*, involving Germano Celant's lecture on "radical architecture"', as well as the presentation of the 'the political work of student-architects', like the design collective Gruppo Sturm's '*fotoromanzi*'.[37]

It was Boyarsky's hope that the Institute, which he had founded in 1970, would:

> provide an alternative ambiance to the boredom, frustration, futility and waste of precious time experienced by those associated with the universally isolated, statically based, often intellectually under-nourished seats of learning whose institutional hang-ups, narrow professionalism and provincial lore engender a lack of urgency and contact with prevailing problems and ideas.[38]

Boyarsky was already well acquainted with Natalini. They had met in the spring of 1971, when the latter, at Koolhaas's invitation, visited London to lecture on 'Inventory, Catalogue, Systems of Flux'. The lecture anticipated the 1972 summer school, calling for a politicized abolition of the design object and serious engagement, deemed necessary for the achievement of that goal, with conventional architecture's problematic role as an 'inducement to consume' sustaining 'the bourgeois models of ownership and society' – that is, serious engagement precisely with the issues that the summer school would foreground a year later, making it the subject of the seminars 'Architecture and Politics' and 'Urban Insurrections', led respectively by Stanislaus von Moos and Bernard Tschumi.[39] The lectures 'Architecture and Design in Poland' and 'Architecture in Yugoslavia', for their part, offered a view of what architecture looked like under socialism, under circumstances where 'the bourgeois models of ownership and society' had been discarded. As for the workshop 'Made in Italy', it was advertised as 'a five-week ongoing analysis of the current Italian scene with particular focus on', among other things, the current 'political situation'.[40]

Reporting on the 1972 summer school, Natalini underscored the participating students' anti-institutionalism and rebellious behaviour.[41] These, he maintained, were essential to the overall experience, having a disquieting effect on the complacent viewer and jolting him out of passivity and stupor. Ensuring that 'no one could leave the premises happily and calmly', they were essential to the initial step that Boyarsky, through the summer school, sought to take toward eliminating mind-numbing conventional education and replacing it with an 'international and nomadic non-institution' promoting 'continuous education sufficiently akin to the two-way television that Buckminster Fuller would always talk about' – Fuller had proposed the two-way television, a learning platform permitting 'any student anywhere in the world to select from a vast stockpile of documentaries on any subject and watch it over his own TV set at home', in his prescient 1962 book *Education Automation*.[42] An incipient non-institution, the summer school disregarded traditional hierarchies and gave the students full authority to present their work and ideas. Koolhaas, whose rebellious statement 'Cedric Price is a prince who wants to turn into a frog' was perhaps deliberately highlighted in Natalini's letter from London, showed *Exodus* at the 'Manhattan Workshop' led by Boyarsky. As for the anti-establishment eco-anarchism of the Street Farm collective, Natalini, strikingly, mentioned it in the same breath as the activism of Northern Irish separatists.

Wholly dedicated to thinking about the problem of architecture and politics, the October–December 1972 issue of *Architectural Association Quarterly* picked up where the summer school had left off. The Street Farmers' 'Threatening Letter to All Architects' made its way into the issue, and the use of the montage technique, as well as the speech balloons containing subversive messages, allows parallels to be drawn with Gruppo

Strum's *fotoromanzi*, while the language employed is decidedly Debordian – 'modern urbanism organizes the reaction of all social life to a spectacle, but the only spectacle it can stage is that of our own alienation', they asserted.[43] A biographical note on Street Farm in the *Quarterly* describes it as 'a loose but expanding co-operative of people who among other things put together the magazines *Street Farmer* (incorporating amateur architecture) … and *Community Gardening*', and, amiably calling its members by their first names, points out that, 'at the time of publishing … Heather is holding a squat-together, Graham, Bruce and Roger are building Street Farmhouse, and Peter is involved in the Earth Workshop'.[44]

The collective embodied a desire to keep abreast of and actively respond to the new, often radical points of view crystallizing across the Channel, with Dennis Sharp, the editor of the issue, underlining the impossibility of overlooking the 'events in Paris in 1968', of failing to discern a novel source of dynamism in the 'attack on institutions' that they initiated.[45] 'Spearheading a fight for identity, a younger generation of politically conscious people … has brought about, through the techniques of confrontation, an eruption that seeks to threaten the basic structure of society as we know it today', Sharp remarked, throwing the agency of the youth into relief.[46] To be sure, there were those who expressed hesitation and scepticism toward the interface between architecture and radical politics. Michael Sorkin, in an echo of Tafuri's invective, dubbed Archizoom, Superstudio, Gruppo 9999 and others 'false messiahs' and contended that 'these groups, in militating for the destruction of object-architecture, have chosen to develop and emphasize an alternative set of objects', which increasingly resembled the 'visible production of … an apolitically reactionary representative of the Great Tradition like Archigram'.[47] Expectedly, he omitted all mention of Superstudio's interest in education as a potential site of intervention and the way in which this made the Italian collective's agenda distinct from that of its British counterpart, as well as turned a blind eye to the crucial difference between the sign systems through which Superstudio and Archigram communicated, namely to the fact that the former sought to eliminate the commodity fetishism integral to the imaginary of the latter.

Paola Navone and Bruno Orlandoni's *Radical Architecture* (*Architettura radicale*), published in 1974, embeds Koolhaas's *Exodus* in a genealogical narrative of radical design practices bracketed on the one hand by such early Italian works as Andrea Branzi's *Questa sì che è architettura* of 1964 and Natalini's 1966 *Palazzo dell'arte di Firenze* and, on the other, by the activities of Global Tools, a collective that formed in 1973 and operated 'a system of didactic laboratories (*laboratori didattici*) for the propagation of the use of natural materials and techniques as well as of behaviours related to them, with the aim of fostering the free development of individual creativity' – in short, the culmination of Natalini and his colleagues' decade-long reflection on the problem of education and behaviour.[48] Navone and Orlandoni discerned three stages of transformation of the architectural image. First, there was the image of 'structural and technical significance', one that, taking the form of a drawing or a model, served as a representation of the finished product, the fetish of the object-oriented architect-*progettista*.[49] Then came the 'self-referential image (*di autosignificatività*)', a pure image that marked a significant step toward the elimination of the architectural object, and this in turn gave way to the communicative image serving to convey 'a conceptual datum or theoretical assertions' and thereby functioning didactically.[50] Necessarily, they asserted, any genealogy of this third type would begin with 'the storyboards and photomontages of Superstudio' and 'touch on the thesis projects of students at the Architectural Association, from Diana Jowsey's *Holiday Homes* … to Koolhaas and Zenghelis's *Exodus*'.[51]

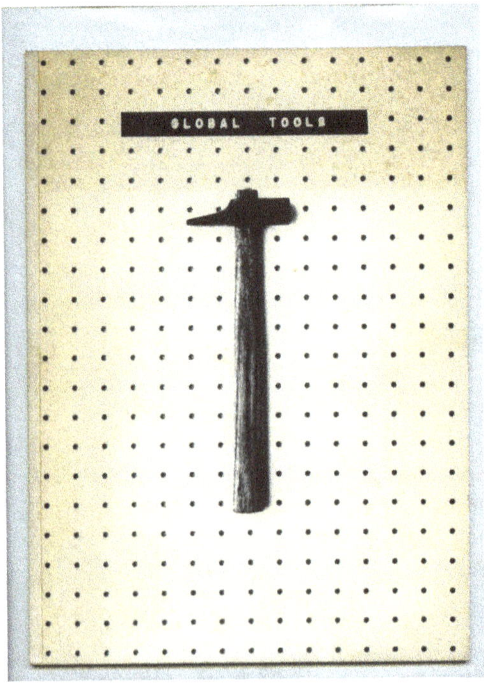

Figure 7.5 Cover of the first issue of the *Global Tools* bulletin, 1974
Image courtesy of Archivio Ugo La Pietra, Milan

The latest chapter in this genealogy of the didactico-communicative architectural image was Global Tools, 'the first Italian counter-school of architecture' only nominally based in Milan, Florence and Naples, having 'no particular site' in reality and being capable of existing, like Fuller's two-way television, wherever 'the courses would take place' – that is, not only in Milan, Florence and Naples but also in 'Wien, Berlin, New York, Toronto, San Francisco, Bergamo, Forlì, etc.'.[52]

The internationalism, the intention to organize 'summer sessions' intended for the presentation of new ideas to be tested during ensuing autumn seminars and the participation of figures like Natalini and Celant are all reminiscent of the precedent set by Boyarsky.[53] In a founding manifesto, Natalini characteristically asserted that there should not be 'any programs for Global Tools, partly because the worldwide scene is ever more confused' and, designating Celant as the 'worker', assigned him the task of exploring the relationship between architecture and magic.[54] As for the Neapolitan Filippo Alison, he was to bring his research on C. R. Mackintosh's 'environments', conducted while studying at the University of Glasgow, to bear on the 'revival of artisanry' throughout the Italian south, 'with the objective of giving back to "culture" the values that are its right'.[55]

'Cosa mentale?'

Among Celant's interlocutors at the time was Bernard Tschumi. The two would, in 1976, organize the conference *Real Space* at the Architectural Association. An aspect of the conference was a happening staged by Tschumi and the experimental musician Brian Eno. Tschumi lectured while Eno played music 'increasingly loudly until [Tschumi's lecture] was drowned out', and the intention was evidently to comment on the obsolescence of lectures as a mode of delivery at institutions.[56] This familiar message, however, was conveyed through a new means. Tschumi rejected printed matter, the medium privileged by Archigram, Superstudio and Global Tools, and opted in favour of events, or signs that are not mediated but performed. A performed sign becomes physical reality and enters an experiential realm activating optical, aural and tactile perception and interpretation. In a special type of environment that Tschumi, borrowing 'the terminology of Germano Celant', called a 'deprived space', the participants 'can only find themselves as the subject, aware only of their own fantasies and pulsations' and able 'only to react to the low-density signals of their own bodies' – in short, all the signs to be interpreted emanate from the body and mind of the participant.[57] For Tschumi, true radicalism resided in such deprived spaces and not on the pages of magazines. He seemed to suggest that, to the extent that Superstudio's utopia remained unperformed and strictly restricted to the domain of visual representations, it simply strengthened the dominion of the eye and, by extension, the dominion of 'the idea over matter' that flattens all real spaces and their occupants, reducing them to a mere '*cosa mentale*'.[58]

Notes

1 Tafuri 1972, 397.
2 Tafuri 1972, 388.
3 Scott 2016, 104.
4 Scott 2001, 115.
5 Scolari 1973, 157.
6 Moschini 1973, 21.
7 Moschini 1973, 22.
8 Bonfanti and Rossi 1973, 116.
9 Vitale 1973, 254.
10 Vitale 1973, 254.
11 Scalvini 1975, 28.
12 Tafuri 1989, 99.
13 Tafuri 1989, 99.
14 Cook 1982.
15 Cook 1982.
16 'Superstudio' 1971, 314.
17 Breckman 2013, 201.
18 Althusser 2006, 88.
19 Althusser 2006, 88; Easthope 1983, 27.
20 Menna 1972, 412–13.
21 Celant 1972, 386.
22 Segre 1970, 18; Althusser 2005, 239.
23 Olmo 1971, 32.
24 Macciocchi 1973, 15.
25 Macciocchi 1973, 15.
26 Garroni 1970, 18.
27 Buckley 2019, 248.
28 Branzi 1984, 155.
29 Eco 1967, 67.
30 Eco 1985, 278.
31 Cook and Nakamura 1987, 7.
32 Cook and Nakamura 1987, 7.
33 Eco 1989, 91.
34 'La deuxième chance de l'architecture moderne' 1985, 2.
35 Superstudio 1971, 738.
36 'January 25–29, 1972 at the Architectural Association' 1972.
37 Natalini 1972, 29.
38 Dunster 2005, 40.
39 Natalini 2003, 167.
40 'Summer Session, International Institute of Design: Preliminary Programme' 1972.
41 Natalini 1972, 29.
42 Natalini 1972, 29; Tomkins 2008, 209.

43 Street Farmers 1972, 17.
44 'Contributors to this Issue' 1972, 2.
45 Sharp 1972, 3.
46 Sharp 1972, 3.
47 Sorkin 1972, 29.
48 La Pietra 1978, 4.
49 Navone and Orlandoni 1974, 37.
50 Navone and Orlandoni 1974, 37.
51 Navone and Orlandoni 1974, 38.
52 Global Tools 1975.
53 Global Tools 1975.
54 Global Tools 1975.
55 Global Tools 1975.
56 Kaji-O'Grady 2005, 388.
57 Tschumi 1994, 42.
58 Tschumi 1994, 42.

References

Althusser, Louis. *For Marx*. London: Verso, 2005.

Althusser, Louis. 'Ideology and ideological state apparatuses: Notes towards an investigation'. In *The Anthropology of the State: A reader*, edited by Aradhana Sharma and Anil Gupta, 86–111. Oxford: Blackwell, 2006.

Branzi, Andrea. *The Hot House: Italian new wave design*. Cambridge, MA: MIT Press, 1984.

Breckman, Warren. *Adventures of the Symbolic: Postmarxism and democratic theory*. New York: Columbia University Press, 2013.

Buckley, Craig. *Graphic Assembly: Montage, media, and experimental architecture in the 1960s*. Minneapolis: University of Minnesota Press, 2019.

Celant, Germano. 'Radical architecture'. In *Italy: The new domestic landscape*, edited by Emilio Ambasz, 380–7. New York: The Museum of Modern Art, 1972.

'Contributors to this Issue', *Architectural Association Quarterly* 4 (1972): 2.

Cook, Peter. 'Archigram's Cook on Superstudio's Natalini'. *The Architectural Review*, 25 March 1982, https://www.architectural-review.com/archive/archigrams-cook-on-superstudios-natalini.

Cook, Peter, and Toshio Nakamura. *Peter Cook, 1961–1989*. Tokyo: A+U, 1987.

Dunster, David. 'Boyarsky and the Architectural Association'. In *An Architect's Guide to Fame*, edited by Paul Davies and Torsten Schmiedeknecht, 33–50. Oxford: Elsevier, 2005.

Easthope, Anthony. *Poetry as Discourse*. New York: Routledge, 1983.

Eco, Umberto. *Opera aperta: Forma e indeterminazione nelle poetiche contemporanee*. Milan: Bompiani, 1962.

Eco, Umberto. 'Proposte per una semiologia dell'architettura', *Marcatré* 34–36 (1967): 58–77.

Garroni, Emilio. 'Semiotica e architettura: Alcuni problemi teorico-applicativi', *Marcatré* 18 (1970): 5–33.

Global Tools. *Global Tools*. Milan: 1975.

'January 25–29 1972 at the Architectural Association'. Natalini Superstudio Collection, Box 1, Folder 36, Beinecke Rare Book and Manuscript Library, Yale University, New Haven, CT.

Kaji-O'Grady, Sandra. 'The London Conceptualists: Architecture and conceptual art in the 1970s'. In *Repenser les limites: L'architecture à travers l'espace, le temps et les disciplines*, edited by Alice Thomine-Berrada and Barry Bergdoll, 386–91. Paris: Publications de l'Institut national d'histoire de l'art, 2005.

'La deuxième chance de l'architecture moderne: Entretien avec Rem Koolhaas', *L'Architecture d'Aujourd'hui* 238 (1985): 2–27.

La Pietra, Ugo. 'Architettura radicale in Italia', *Domus* 580 (1978): 2–7.

Macciocchi, Maria Antonietta. *Letters from Inside the Italian Communist Party to Louis Althusser*. London: New Left Books, 1973.

Menna, Filiberto. 'A design for new behaviors'. In *Italy: The new domestic landscape*, edited by Emilio Ambasz, 405–14. New York: The Museum of Modern Art, 1972.

Moschini, Francesco. 'Triennale (XV) di Milano – Sezione internazionale di architettura', *Bollettino della Biblioteca della Facoltà di Architettura dell'Università di Roma* 4 (1973): 21–3.
Natalini, Adolfo. 'Londra: Lettera dall'IID/SS '72', *Domus* 515 (1972): 29.
Natalini, Adolfo. 'Inventory, catalogue, systems of flux: A statement'. In *Superstudio: Life without objects*, edited by Peter Lang and William Menking, 164–7. Milan: Skira, 2003.
Navone, Paola and Bruno Orlandoni. *Architettura radicale*. Milan: Casabella, 1974.
Olmo, Carlo. *Politica e forma*. Florence: Vallecchi, 1971.
Scalvini, Maria Luisa. *L'architettura come semiotica connotativa*. Milan: Bompiani, 1975.
Scolari, Massimo. 'Avanguardia e nuova architettura'. In *Architettura razionale*, edited by Ezio Bonfanti and Aldo Rossi, 153–87. Milan: Franco Angeli, 1973.
Scott, Felicity. 'Architecture or Techno-Utopia', *Grey Room* 3 (2001): 112–26.
Scott, Felicity. *Outlaw Territories: Environments of insecurity/architecture of counterinsurgency*. New York: Zone Books, 2016.
Segre, Roberto. *Cuba, l'architettura della rivoluzione*. Padua: Marsilio, 1970.
Sharp, Dennis. 'Architecture and politics: Editorial comment', *Architectural Association Quarterly* 4 (1972): 3–5.
Sorkin, Michael. 'Down with false messiahs', *Architectural Association Quarterly* 4 (1972): 26–9.
Street Farmers. 'A threatening letter to all architects', *Architectural Association Quarterly* 4 (1972): 17–20.
'Summer Session, International Institute of Design: Preliminary Programme', *Architectural Association Quarterly* 4 (1972).
'Superstudio', *Perspecta* 13–14 (1971): 303–15.
Superstudio. 'Twelve cautionary tales for Christmas', *Architectural Design* 41 (1971): 737–42.
Tafuri, Manfredo. 'Design and technological utopia'. In *Italy: The new domestic landscape*, edited by Emilio Ambasz, 388–404. New York: The Museum of Modern Art, 1972.
Tafuri, Manfredo. *History of Italian Architecture, 1944–1985*. Cambridge, MA: MIT Press, 1989.
Tomkins, Calvin. 'In the Outlaw Area: Originally published in The New Yorker (January 8, 1966)'. In *Buckminster Fuller: Starting with the universe*, edited by Michael Hays and Dana Miller, 177–211. New York: Whitney Museum of American Art, 2008.
Tschumi, Bernard. *Architecture and Disjunction*. Cambridge, MA: MIT Press, 1994.
Vitale, Daniele. 'Le scuole di architettura: Presentazione di alcuni progetti'. In *Architettura razionale*, edited by Ezio Bonfanti and Aldo Rossi, 227–67. Milan: Franco Angeli, 1973.

Part II
Designing the Post-war City

8

Reweaving the city: the CIAM summer schools from London to Venice (1949–57)

Lorenzo Mingardi

To restart the professional practice of young architects after the Second World War, the seventh CIAM in Bergamo in 1949 concluded with the decision to open professional studies to students and intensify international exchanges among newly graduated architects. This chapter intends to deepen understanding of the relationships between the members of the Italian CIAM group and the UK MARS Group through the organization of the subsequent CIAM summer schools and in the light of the intense relationships and exchanges between the two teams that occurred at the beginning of the 1950s. The First CIAM summer school, co-ordinated by Maxwell Fry, was organized at the Architectural Association, directed by Robert Furneaux Jordan, with other English members of CIAM (the MARS Group) as tutors. Ernesto Rogers was invited to hold a seminar, and the theme proposed by the course was the reconstruction of the city after the bombardments of the Second World War. In 1952, Furneaux Jordan's introductory text for the catalogue to the RIBA exhibition Italian Contemporary Architecture explains the reasons for the English interest in the most recent Italian architecture. The materials found in the archives of Piero Bottoni, Enrico Peressutti (for a brief period also lecturer at the Architectural Association), Pietro Lingeri and Francesco Gnecchi Ruscone, as well as Furneaux Jordan and Patrick Crooke, allow for an investigation of the relations between the two groups and their different approaches to the reconstruction of the cities destroyed by the war, which is clearly demonstrated in the work produced by the students who attended the summer schools.

From 1949 to 1956, five editions of CIAM International summer school were held between the UK and Italy – one in London, and four in Venice. They were first conceived as didactic extensions to the International Congresses of Modern Architecture. In the summer of 1949, the CIAM 7 was held at the Palazzo della Regione (Regional Council) in Bergamo, organized by the representatives of the Gruppo Italiano.[1] The main focus of the congress was the implementation of the Athens Charter through the Grid, a tool that had been studied the previous year by ASCORAL, the French group of the CIAM, under the guidance of Le Corbusier.[2] Two additional themes of the congress were: the interaction between plastic and figurative art and architecture, and the reform of architectural and urban planning education. The work of the CIAM 7 was organized into six thematic committees. Chairman of the committee appointed to research new solutions for architectural education was Ernesto Rogers, member of the CIAM Conseil de direction since 1947.

Vice-chairmen of this international committee were, among others: Jane Drew, English architect (member of MARS, the English group of the CIAM), Alfred Roth (Swiss) and Oscar Singer (English). Gropius, too, should have been there, but was unable to travel to Italy; nevertheless, he wrote a note about architectural and urban planning education, which was read as an introduction to the work of the committee: 'Students

Figure 8.1 Ernesto Rogers at CIAM 7 in Bergamo (1949). From Tentori, Francesco. 'I CIAM per il Cinquecentenario del Congresso di Bergamo: L'architettura, l'arte e l'importanza decisiva della libertà', *La Rivista di Bergamo* 18 (1999), 18

Courtesy of *La Rivista di Bergamo*

should be educated on how to work in a group, so that they can learn how to collaborate with others ... The very essence of group work will lead the students to good architecture'.[3]

During its work, the committee highlighted the fact that schools of architecture were too crowded, the teaching methods did not match the social requirements, and the disciplines were not integrated.[4] At the end of the congress, the report of the committee suggested the establishment of a permanent committee, consisting of a representative of each national group, that was to formulate a *Charte de l'enseignement de l'architecture et de l'urbanisme*: it was suggested that the national groups should examine the specific inadequacies of their own schools and point out the best means to set them right; furthermore, as stated in Gropius's opening note, the plan was to create experimental courses in which students of different nationalities could have the opportunity to interact in groups. It was the first step towards the organization of CIAM international summer schools reserved for students from the countries that were part of the congress.[5] The idea of organizing summer schools had already been outlined at the Conseil de direction held in Paris between 28 and 31 March 1948, and, as a result, in September of the same year, the MARS Group had held a summer school at the Architectural Association School of Architecture, without non-English students and without the denomination CIAM.[6] The first edition of the summer school with the denomination CIAM was organized from 8 August to 2 September 1949, once again in London, once again at the Architectural Association School of Architecture, under the direction of English architect Maxwell Fry. His assistant was Jaqueline Tyrwhitt, and the tutors were members of the MARS Group (C. K. Capon, Arthur Korn, Henry Thomas Cadbury-Brown and Peter Shepheard).[7]

The CIAM summer school in London

In Great Britain, Jaqueline Tyrwhitt had given a major contribution to reactivate the international intellectual exchanges that had been interrupted during the war, setting herself as the one who would put forth the activities of Patrick Geddes: the Scotsman, moreover, even in the late nineteenth century, had already taken part in the summer schools of science, which offered a programme focused on interdisciplinarity and promoted apprenticeship as a way of actively acquiring knowledge. Their structure was similar to that of the CIAM summer schools.[8]

The senior members of the national CIAM groups recommended the participants involved in the summer school: 20 young English graduates and 20 graduates from other Countries: Argentina, Colombia, South Africa, Australia, Italy and elsewhere in Europe.[9] Among the Italians, there were Franco Berlanda and Francesco Gnecchi Ruscone, a student of Ernesto Rogers; in 1949 he had collaborated at the Bergamo CIAM.

The students were to work on four projects: an office building destined for the area between Hyde Park and Knightsbridge, a housing project for 3,000 people in the same area, a national theatre in Park Square, near Regent's Park, and a complex traffic intersection. The four projects had been chosen by members of the MARS Group in co-operation with the London County Council, in order to be confronted with the real problems of the city.[10]

The structure of the school showed the Bergamo suggestions for the new training of the architect: free from any pre-established approach, it

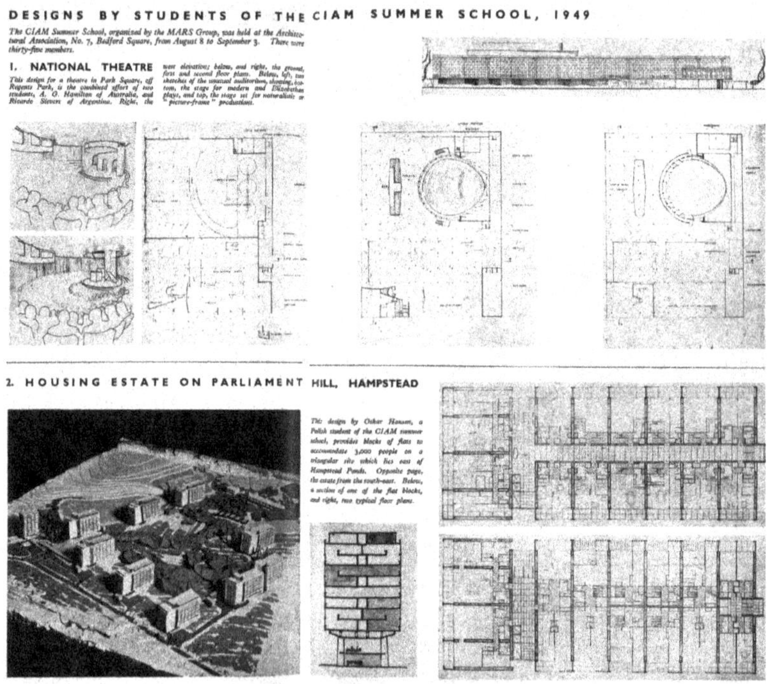

Figure 8.2 Designs by students of the CIAM summer school (1949). From the *Architects' Journal*, 15 September (1949), 276–7

Courtesy of the *Architects' Journal*

tended towards an open didactic experience that students, tutors and experts of various disciplines could share.

On the last day of the school (2 September), many of the architects – J. M. Richards, Ernesto Rogers, José Luis Sert and Sigfried Giedion, Maxwell Fry, Jaqueline Tyrwhitt, Cornelius Van Eesteren and others – held a symposium. They gave reports on the four focuses of the course and on the focus of the Bergamo CIAM, in particular on the interaction between architecture, painting and sculpture.

'In preparation for the symposium on 2 September' – Jaqueline Tyrwhitt wrote to Gnecchi Ruscone – 'I am sending you in confidence, the attached translation of a report on the relation between architecture, painting and sculpture submitted to the CIAM Congress at Bergamo in July of this year by a committee set up there to study this question. Assuming that everybody is agreed that more collaboration between the architect, painter and sculptor is a good thing'.[11]

Rogers gave a lecture entitled 'Towards a unity of plastic arts'.[12] After the conferences, Rogers, Van Eesteren, Robert Furneaux Jordan (principal of the Architectural Association) and Maxwell Fry expressed their final critique on the work of the school.[13]

The students' projects, published by the *Architects' Journal*, are characterized by settlement principles that started to diverge from the Hippodamic structures typical of districts and towns built during the inter-war period and beyond. This feature, too, is a consequence of the CIAM congresses of Bridgewater and Bergamo. During the congresses, the validity of the Athens Charter was reaffirmed. Nevertheless, its results started being questioned: the functionalist urban planning principles should not contribute to producing poor socially qualitative urban inserts and districts.[14] Among the most interesting London projects, that of Oskar Hansen was worthy of attention. He sketched a small-scale *ville radieuse*, where the buildings were a clear homage to the Unité in Marseille, under construction at the time.[15]

After the appreciation for the London projects shown by Principal Jordan, in 1950, Rogers, as well as Belgiojoso and Peressutti, were invited to hold a didactic semester at the Architectural Association School of Architecture.[16]

A proof of the close connection, at that time, between the Italian Group and the MARS Group, and the friendship between their most representative members, Rogers and Fry, is the fact that the very English CIAM representatives, in collaboration with the Istituto Italiano di Cultura in London and the Architectural Association School, suggested an exhibition on Italian contemporary architecture that was to be set up at the RIBA at the end of 1950. After several delays, it was inaugurated only on 21 March 1952.[17] Ernesto Rogers was once again in charge of the selection of the works on display, assisted by Franco Albini and Enrico Peressutti.

In his foreword to the catalogue *Italian Contemporary Architecture*, Graham Henderson (President of the RIBA) wrote: 'All the buildings shown have quality of design and finish, indicating that Italy not only looks forward as well as backward, but also is capable of adding further to the *patrimonio artistico* of which she is so justly proud'.[18] In the introductory note by Furneaux Jordan, the reasons for the English interest in recent Italian architecture emerge more clearly: 'Contemporary Italy is perhaps the most interesting of all countries ... Its building problem has been as intense as any in the world; the solution has been completely Italian'.[19] The rebuilding of a country devastated by the war encouraged a widespread tendency towards research on composition. According to Furneaux Jordan, this kind of focus on the past is not a revival of the 'old battle of modernism versus traditionalism',[20] but 'the more vital, possibly more bitter "civil war" within the Modern Movement'.[21] According to him, the Italian tendency 'to consider contemporary architectural problems in terms of almost pure form' represented a third way between regionalism, that tended towards vernacular Scandinavian Empiricism, and the international style: 'The Italian has in pure architecture found a middle way between the vernacular cosiness of Sweden and the formalism of, say, the Uno Building'.[22]

At the beginning of 1950, for unknown reasons, Well Coates, co-founder of the MARS Group, declared that it would have been impossible to organize the second summer school in London. It was necessary to find a solution: a mobile location, linked to the towns where the congresses were being organized, or a new fixed location. But where? In order to give international visibility to the IUAV, the principal Giuseppe Samonà, member of the Italian CIAM Group, by the time of the Bergamo congress had already shown his interest in establishing summer schools in Venice. The didactic structure of IUAV was freer compared to other Italian universities, therefore it was particularly suitable to the experimentation promoted by the CIAM. The English were very interested in Samonà's didactic project, which was to feature a reform of architectural education and a redefinition of this discipline.[23] In February 1948, Michael Patrick, director of the Architectural Association, had written to him in order to sound out the possibility of students' exchanges between the two institutions:

> The students here are very keen on the idea of going to Venice and so I am naturally anxious to get firm arrangements made. I am also afraid that unless we are able to book fairly well in advance accommodation and travel difficulties may arise both on our side and on yours.[24]

The architecture student, a future architect employed in the rebuilding of the country, had to be educated through new programmes and new teachers. Again in 1948 Pevsner had written to Samonà to ask his permission to publish an insight on the IUAV in the *Architectural Review*.[25] Rogers, urged by his friend Samonà, told his friend Giedion of the Scuola di Venezia's wish to organize in that location a follow-up to that experience:[26] Rogers was therefore the link between the CIAM Conseil, England and Venice. His role was essential: furthermore, Samonà did not hold a prominent position in the CIAM Italian Group,[27] therefore neither did he in the congresses.

Venice was the right place to focus on the relationship between history and modernity, a current debate at the time in the CIAM context. At the CIAM Conseil meeting, on 12 April 1950, the decision was made to organize a Preliminary CIAM summer school in Venice, which would run from 1 to 30 September and would be located at the IUAV main building, Palazzo Giustiniani, in San Trovaso district.[28] The course was to be managed by a school board, whose chairman was Le Corbusier, and by an executive committee whose members were IUAV Professors: Albini, Gardella, Rogers and Samonà.[29] The students had to be chosen from the CIAM Groups: 'Les Groupes CIAM sont responsables du choix des élèves dans chaque Pays et nous bornerons à établir le nombre selon une repartition raisonnable parmi les différents Pays'.[30]

The school seemed to be ready to start; nevertheless, probably due to a lack of funds, or because of the short time compared to the complex organization required, the project didn't come to fruition. The whole matter reached an impasse; it was further discussed at the eighth CIAM in Hoddesdon, England, in July 1951.

The first Italian CIAM summer school

The Hoddesdon meeting was extremely important in CIAM history. The reform of the Athens Charter principles, which had started at the Bridgewater CIAM, began to find a concrete way: the problems of the modern city could not be considered according to the four functionalist categories (dwelling, recreation, transport and work) stated in the 1933 CIAM report. The focus of the congress was The Heart of the City. The 'heart' is no particular place, not necessarily the old town: it was meant as a public area where the community of citizens can meet and can recognize themselves as such. It can be a square or any other place, able to catalyse social life, maybe a place in the old town: thanks to this recognition, every prejudice on the antihistoricism typical of the pre-war CIAM could vanish.

Venice was a recurrent topic of debate in the congress: Piazza San Marco was considered a model of the perfect example of 'heart', to such an extent that it is depicted in a drawing by Saul Steinberg on the back cover of the volume containing the conference proceedings.[31] In general, the importance of the historical urban pattern of Italian cities emerged as a clear example for young architects; this aspect was highlighted in the acclaimed speech by Rogers at the plenary session:

> The squares of Italy, cozy areas, like a large vase, are a wonderful example of "Hearts" ... The heart of the city should be a place suitable for the most relaxed of human connections: conversation, discussion, shopping, "piropeo", "flâneur", and the priceless "dolce far niente" which, in its best meaning, is the most natural expression of contemplation (leisure, in quiet enjoyment of body and soul).[32] (See also chapter 11).

Rogers played a leading role in the Hoddesdon CIAM: he was vice-president of the congress III committee, whose president was Gropius, in which the need for an International CIAM summer school was strongly revived. As part of the committee, Rogers reaffirmed the need for a single location of the school, possibly in Venice. He therefore acted as surety for the initiative and insisted on the alluring power of a city such as Venice for the students: Venice is a city whose squares, churches and palaces could complete the education of young architects and could refine their taste and perception. The Conseil agreed, so that, at the 1952 Paris meeting, the organization of the Venice summer schools was officially approved.[33]

The first Italian CIAM summer course was inaugurated on 10 September 1952, by Giovanni Ponti, president of the Venice Biennial and one of its backers.[34] The participants were 68 young architects and graduating students from several countries: Algeria, Austria, Chile, Cuba, France, Norway, the United States, Switzerland, Peru, Portugal (with Fernando Tavora) and, of course, England (with Joseph Rykwert, Pat

Crooke, who was working at the BBPR studio at the time, and others). The Italians were 10, including Vittorio Gregotti. The assistants of Professors Albini, Gardella, Rogers and Samonà (the executive committee that had formed two years earlier) were Giancarlo De Carlo, Franco Berlanda, Egle Trincanato and other young architects.[35]

During the Hoddesdon congress, James Richards had stated:

> The attitude of the architect towards the pre-existing buildings is increasingly important: we often find the true meaning of a location by analysing its function during history: and in those cases when its meaning has been destroyed during the last Century … the task of the architect might be to recreate it, according to a modern interpretation.[36]

The students were required to work on projects focused on contemporary topics, which nevertheless maintained a perspective on a critical review of the whole urban pattern. In Venice as well as in London, the participants were required to produce projects that had to be strictly linked to the city in which they stayed:

> The Institute of Architecture has decided to offer its collaboration to the city and to the Country. It has decided to undertake and define an urbanistic study of Venice, that can serve as a concrete instrument to formulate the problems of the city in an urbanistic way[37]

Aside from the course, the supplementary interdisciplinary lectures were held by important architects and scholars from other universities, including Lucio Costa, Fausto Franco, Carlo Ludovico Ragghianti and Johannes Hendrik van den Broek. The most decisive lecture was undoubtedly one by Le Corbusier, whose title was 'A propos de Venice':[38]

> When his arrival was announced, on a late Sunday afternoon most of the school went spontaneously to the station to wait for him. The students were rewarded by the joy of the master, who wanted to walk through the city to appreciate it at its best, to discuss and talk to everyone. After dinner, the pilgrimage continued through the squares and on the Schiavoni shore. His lecture was much waited for and the hall was crowded to the brim … Gérard Philipe, with many others, was sitting on the floor. He was in Venice too, those days … The topic of the conversation was Venice; but for Le Corbusier, it was a matter of linking it to his entire work.[39]

Figure 8.3 Le Corbusier at CIAM summer school in Venice (1952)
Source: Università Iuav di Venezia, Archivio Progetti, fondo Egle Renata Trincanato

In his speech, the French architect praised the urban pattern of the city, the same pattern that would inspire him, a few years later, to realize his project for the new Venice hospital.

The didactic structure is the feature that distinguished the CIAM summer course from any other architecture course of the time, apart from the composition of its students, coming from different schools and countries: admittedly, the teaching gave up on any given rule. Just like in the London course, the participants' projects sprang out of the continuous exchange of views with the teachers and out of the repeated discussions in the seminars, together with the work done in groups that were preferably made up of students of different nationalities.[40] If we examine now the projects that were produced in that September 1952, we can see what the didactic aim was: to create, through a great freedom of composition that was granted to the students, a new generation of architects who would be able to think freely about the modern contribution to the context of a historical reality such as Venice. We should not forget that, at that time, Wright was designing the famous house on the Canal Grande for Masieri:[41] the insertion of the modern into the context of the urban historical pattern was a highly current topic that surely filtered in through the lectures and the reviews of the professors.

There were various types of outcome from the projects. One of the most interesting works is that by Gordon Hall and others, in which all the harbour functions were transferred to Marghera and all the arrivals, including cars, were concentrated on the current railway station area. The project involved the Canal Grande, too: modern architectures were inserted between historic buildings. The group of Nani Valle, John Wood and others decided to change the function of the current Santa Lucia station, turning it into a park. Its attention was focused on the bridgehead area, inserting there the disembarking of visitors by train (thanks to the construction of a new station), by sea, and by car.[42]

From 1953 to 1959: The slow dissolution of the CIAM

The following year, from 19 to 26 July 1953, the CIAM 9 took place in Aix-en-Provence, France. The main aim of the congress was to codify a Habitat Charter, a sort of appendix to the Athens Charter. As we already noted, despite the process of review in the context of the CIAM, according to several young architects, the old CIAM institution had not yet proven able to produce convincing plans about the growth of the cities after the Second World War. The disagreement with the older generation and its national groups was expressed clearly and for the first time during this CIAM, mostly by the group of young designers who were about to form the first core of Team X: Allison and Peter Smithson, Aldo Van Eyck, Josep Bakema, Georges Candilis, Shadrach Woods, William Howell and Robert Gutman.[43] According to them, urban growth was a complex matter that could not be resolved with the help of ubiquitous models: according to the young revolutionaries, the rules of growth structure should be strictly linked to context and society.

From 5 September to 4 October 1953, roughly two months after the heated Aix meeting, the second CIAM summer school ran in Venice. The location was the same as the previous year: same professors, several lectures – Carlo Scarpa, Egle Trincanato, Caterina Marcenaro and Ludovico Barbiano di Belgiojoso – and seminar work. The topic of the year was 'Historical city and tourist city through the redesigning of the Biennial Gardens': the aim was to rebuild the central pavilion with its general exhibition services and the rooms devoted to Italy, host special exhibitions, and to accommodate the countries that did not have a dedicated pavilion. The Biennial itself, which was among the financial backers, had suggested the topic, because of its need to receive design input on how to modify a structure that had been unsuitable for its exhibition requirements for many years.[44]

The students' projects clearly reflected what had happened in Aix: first, none of them used the grid when presenting their projects (the grid had been severely criticized at the CIAM 9 by the disagreeing architects); secondly, several solutions for the Biennial pavilion were inspired by coeval projects by Van Eyck, Candilis, Josic and Woods and other architects present in Aix, who were concerned with cultures that were very different from the western world. I refer in particular to African architecture, main topic of some of the conferences at the French CIAM: just consider the Algiers CIAM group that presented the bidonville Mahieddine, that is, a spontaneous gathering of dwelling models, seen as a clear example of the mix of different parts of the social pattern. Apart from the Aix CIAM, the Third World had become at the time a topic of the architectural cultural debate: in the journal *Forum*, Van Eyck published his studies on the mix of ethnography, anthropology and the urban areas; Rogers himself published in the new journal *Casabella-Continuità* some articles on African architecture. Therefore, most of the solutions that had been developed by the students of the Venice school were characterized by mixed volumes that defined, through contemporary forms and materials, the dwelling principles typical of spontaneous urban structures.[45]

Before the start of the third Venice school, on 3 September 1954, during the meeting of the Conseil, held in Paris on 30 June with a view to the organization of the 1956 CIAM in Dubrovnik, the personalities that had strongly disagreed with the old school of the CIAM in Aix emerged with fervour: they had the task of planning the tenth congress.[46]

The international revolutionary wave reached the 1954 summer school. The participants' projects bore traces of the arguments against the Athens Charter even more effectively compared to the previous year. Confronted with social conditions ruled by systems that they considered too old, almost all of the students designed spaces and buildings with the major aim of creating communities. Several groups went further beyond the topic, which was similar to that of 1952: the physical link between island and mainland in Venice. The bridgehead and the problems that occurred in the Venice island urban pattern after inserting a new mechanical dimension into the historical town. The works analysed the historical pattern of Venice as a good example to follow for planning from scratch.[47]

In 1955 the School didn't take place. The reasons were purely financial:

> The international CIAM Architectural course which has run in the autumn of the years 1952, 1953, 1954 has had a great success as for both its participants and its results. The course ... has run every year thanks to the contribution of various city authorities. No matter how generous the contributions from several institutions, every year the annual balance closed with a loss, and the unsolved has always been paid thanks to the financial contributions of the following year. Unfortunately, the 1954 course has closed with a greater loss compared to the previous years, because we relied on funds that have been promised but not paid, so the expenditures exceeded the revenue ... This head office has announced that the VI edition of the CIAM Architectural Summer Course will take place again in the autumn of 1956, but we hope that this executive committee will collaborate for a concrete financial plan that can effectively allow the realisation of this course. The importance and the interest of this international summer school is well known. During its course, it has challenged real and contingent problems of Venice, and it can contribute massively with its ideas and knowledge.[48]

1955 and 1956 were hard times for the relationship between Italy and the CIAM. The organization of the tenth congress signalled a clear detachment of the Italian Group from the international organization. During the Conseil meeting in La Sarraz (8–10 September), the editor of *Casabella-Continuità* also sided against the old school of the CIAM, criticizing the Athens Charter. The partial detachment of the Italian Group from the CIAM went at the same pace as a general crisis of the institution, founded in 1928: the Dubrovnik congress, organized by Alison and Peter Smithson and other members of Team X, was the last episode of a long story that had in Otterlo (1959 congress) its final scene. Despite the CIAM crisis, the school was not affected: moreover, it was never an offshoot of the congress, mostly an autonomous institution, focused on the exchange of young architects from all over the world, who were working on common problems involving the growth of the cities.

Adriano Olivetti was the main sponsor of the 1956 course,[49] which took place from 6 to 30 September (a week later than the Dubrovnik CIAM) in Palazzo Giustiniani. Rogers was not there, so De Carlo was the man who was called to assist Albini, Gardella and Samonà. He was, at the time, a considerably well-known architect, not only in the Venice context but in the national and international cultural debate. The 23 participants were required to design a residential district in Mestre following the usual procedures: the final project was to be just the tip of the iceberg of an analysis that should encompass the problems of the whole city. In his opening speech, Gardella insisted that the commercial and social resources of old Venice were vanishing. It should be remembered that, at the time, Samonà, Trincanato and Piccinato were working on plans for the restoration of the San Giuliano district in Mestre. Therefore, dwelling in Mestre was a rather current topic of debate at the IUAV.

The students' works aimed at understanding the spirit and the structure of the city, and therefore at recreating it in contemporary forms. If we analyse the different projects, we notice that, according to the students, the connection systems were a major theme, one that a new settlement must necessarily refer to.[50] This feature is evident in the projects of the group whose members were Denise Scott Brown and Robert Scott Brown (both students at the Architectural Association). The group of Alan Richards and other English architects analysed in particular the development of social structure in Mestre and Marghera.

The schemes that were suggested by various groups and the focus on the journeys resembled the elaborations of the concepts *identity* and *association* (the relationships between the spaces in the old town and the society that inhabits them). The Smithsons had presented such projects in La Sarraz and Dubrovnik and they were going to be a recurring feature of their theoretical works. After the X Dubrovnik CIAM, the fate of the International Congresses of Modern Architecture was sealed. At the last Otterlo congress in 1959, the architects participated in their own initiative: the CIAM groups dissolved indefinitely. Because of the irreversible crisis of the institution, the 1957 summer school lost the patronage of the CIAM and became simply V International Architectural Summer Seminar. The focus of the year was the critical analysis of the five projects that had won the competition for the local strategic plan in Venice.[51]

Despite the international professors and students among its numerous participants, the CIAM schools never had a repercussion in international debate (there are very few traces of it in international journals and monographs) and they did not make an impression on the local Venetian authorities, despite the initial hopes of Rogers and Samonà, so that they could take into consideration some of the ideas on the growth of Venice that might arise from the seminars of the school.[52] Having said this, the CIAM summer schools represented, for all those who took part, an extraordinary experience of cultural exchange with prominent figures of architecture and urban planning. Moreover, the seeds that had been planted during those five years in Venice have produced fruits that have

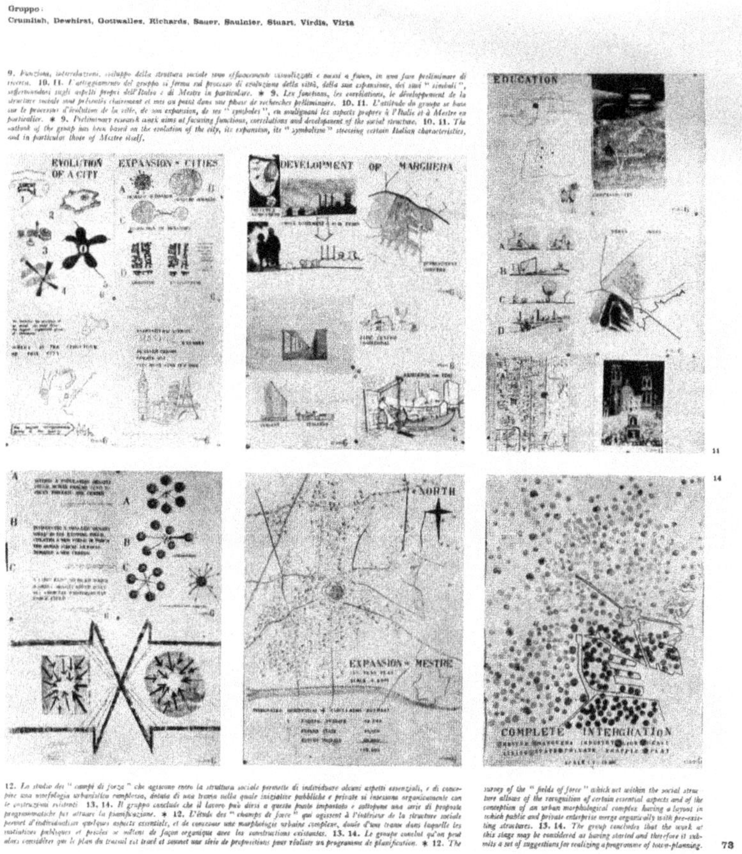

Figure 8.4 Designs by students of the CIAM summer school (1956). From Scimemi, Gabriele. 'La quarta scuola estiva dei CIAM a Venezia', *Casabella-Continuità* 213 (1956), 73

Courtesy of *Casabella*

undoubtedly been seized elsewhere: the school structure, its conferences, seminars and informal, joint project presentations – made by prominent architects, not students – resembles the structure of every meeting of Team X since the Royaumont 1962 meeting. The experience of the International Laboratory of Architecture and Urban Design (ILAUD) that De Carlo had established from 1976 to 1996 in three locations (Urbino, Siena and San Marino) followed faithfully the model of the 1950s summer schools.[53]

The history of the CIAM summer schools shows clearly the tight connections within the representatives of the two countries (Italian Group and MARS Group) between the late 1940s and the early 1950s:

otherwise, the change from London to Venice would never have occurred. At the time, in the context of the cultural architectural debate, the position of the two countries was similar on how to solve the problem of urban growth: at the Hoddesdon CIAM they both agreed on the criticism against the functionalist city and on the need to put a stop to the disorganized growth of the cities in the territory. Nevertheless, there were substantial differences between the two countries with regard to professional practice. In Italy, these positions remained stuck in the intellectual debate: reflection on the development of modern urban planning took place out of the context of the CIAM. The rebuilding of our cities had occurred without any kind of co-ordinated strategic plan, and the launching of the Fanfani Plan was of no help, quite the opposite: probably, it even had bad consequences on the homogeneous development of our territory. In England, on the other hand, the need for control over urban growth was a major topic for government authorities as well; in the UK, even before the 1949 Town and Country Planning Act, the first urban planning instruments dated back to the early twentieth century. The most important legal provisions regarding territory were issued in the 1930s. In Italy, they were never carried out completely.

Notes

1 At that time, the CIAM Italian group consisted of Franco Albini, Lodovico Barbiano di Belgiojoso, Piero Bottoni, Luigi Cosenza, Luigi Carlo Daneri, Luigi Figini, Ignazio Gardella, Gabriele Mucchi, Giovanni Michelucci, Pierluigi Nervi, Pietro Lingeri, Giancarlo Palanti, Enrico Peressutti, Gino Pollini, Mario Pucci, Mario Ridolfi, Ernesto Rogers, Giovanni Romano and Luigi Vietti. Peressutti and Bottoni were in charge of the organization. Protasoni 1992, 32.

2 Nicoloso 2012, 297; Mumford 2000, 179–200.

3 Sacchi 1998, 81.

4 Maffioletti 2011, 160.

5 Centro di Alti Studi sulle Arti Visive, CASVA, Milano, Fondo Gnecchi Ruscone, *VII Congresso CIAM – Bergamo 1949*, PROGR.2. See also Congrès International d'Architecture Moderne 1979.

6 Shoshkes 2013, 112. The researcher affirms: 'Tyrwhitt applied her prodigious energy and efficiency as assistant to Fry in directing the first CIAM summer school, which ran for six weeks beginning mid-July 1948'. Focus of the course was: *Architectural aspects of the central urban replanning*. See also: *The Architects' Journal,* 24 February 1949, 179–80.

7 Centro di Alti Studi sulle Arti Visive, CASVA, Fondo Gnecchi Ruscone, *Ciam Summer School*, B140, fasc 1. See also Zuccaro Marchi, 116–18.

8 Between 1887 and 1889: Edinburgh Summer Meetings, organized by Geddes. Tyrwhitt had taken part in the organization of a summer school in 1944 in London (organized by the TPI, Town Planning Institute). See: Tyrwhitt 1951, 62.

9 Centro di Alti Studi sulle Arti Visive, CASVA, Fondo Gnecchi Ruscone, *Ciam Summer School*, B140, fasc 1.

10 Centro di Alti Studi sulle Arti Visive, CASVA, Fondo Gnecchi Ruscone, *Ciam Summer School*, B140, fasc 1.

11 Centro di Alti Studi sulle Arti Visive, CASVA, Fondo Gnecchi Ruscone, *Ciam Summer School*, B140, fasc 1 Letter by Jaqueline Tyrwhitt to Gnecchi (23 August 1949).

12 Rogers 2010, 421.
13 The output of the school can be found in the *Architects' Journal*, 15 September 1949, 276–8. Centro di Alti Studi sulle Arti Visive, CASVA, Fondo Gnecchi Ruscone, *Ciam Summer School*, B140, fasc 1 Letter by Jaqueline Tyrwhitt to Gnecchi (23 August 1949).
14 For the first time, even in Bridgewater, in the context of the CIAM, the focus was on human emotional needs. Mumford 2000, 168–79.
15 A report of the meeting of the London summer school members states that the subsequent summer schools had to be connected to the CIAM congresses, in order for the output of the schools to be more effective. As a tribute to the Unité d'habitation, Marseille was suggested as location for the subsequent CIAM and summer school; it was also considered to organize a summer school in Belgium. Neither of the two plans came to a realization. Rogers 2010, 421.
16 Centro di Alti Studi sulle Arti Visive, CASVA, Fondo Gnecchi Ruscone, *Ciam Summer School*, B140, fasc 1.
17 Centro di Alti Studi sulle Arti Visive, CASVA, Fondo Gnecchi Ruscone, *Mostra architettura italiana a Londra*, PR_04. See also: 'Italian Contemporary Architecture: Opening of the exhibition at the R.I.B.A., 21st March 1952', *Journal of the Royal Institute of British Architects*, April 1952, 210. The exhibition was at the RIBA until April 1952. It was to be set up in Italy as well, promoted by Carlo Ludovico Ragghianti, at first at the Casa della Cultura in Livorno (14–31 August 1954), then at the Strozzina in Florence (April–May 1955). Massa and Pontelli 2018, 205; Mingardi 2019, 45.
18 Henderson 1952.
19 Furneaux Jordan 1952.
20 Furneaux Jordan 1952.
21 Furneaux Jordan 1952.
22 Furneaux Jordan 1952. The press, too, showed positive reactions. In the *Architects' Journal*, 2 April 1952, we read: 'The Italians have something to say: there's formal and structural clarity, supported, it must be noted, by excellent craftsmanship. Unlike the Swedes, the Italians are not tired of being modern and nevertheless they are not yet inhibited: quite the opposite, they're cutting edge, very busy, very contemporary and very Italian'. Protasoni 1992, 36.
23 Tentori 2006, 249–58.
24 Università Iuav di Venezia, Archivio Progetti, Fondo Giuseppe Samonà, seg. 2.fasc/053. Letter by Michael Patrick to Giuseppe Samonà, London, 7 June 1948. Gordon Brown, too, professor at the Architectural Association, had previously been in touch with Samonà for the same reason. The reply to Brown by Samonà can be found in the archives. It was written by W. Wilson (secretary of the vice-consul in Venice) because the principal of the IUAV did not speak English. Letter by W. Wilson to Gordon Brown, Venice, 2 February 1948. Università Iuav di Venezia, Archivio Progetti, Fondo Giuseppe Samonà, seg. 2.fasc/053.
25 '*The Architectural Review* is preparing a special issue entirely devoted to architectural education outside Britain. I feel sure that from a compilation of information and an attempt at co-ordinating the various methods worked out in different countries much benefit might be derived. I am, of course, only approaching a comparatively small number of individual schools, besides the official professional bodies representing architects in fifteen countries. Your school, however, my colleagues and I felt, should be amongst those whole teaching methods should be included. I should therefore be extremely grateful if you would be so kind as to take the trouble of answering the enclosed questions in as much detail as possible. If you would like to know more of our intentions, or any explanations of some of the questions, will you please write and ask.' Università Iuav di Venezia, Archivio Progetti, Fondo Giuseppe Samonà, seg. 2.fasc/053. Letter by Pevsner to Samonà, London, 18 March 1948.
26 Rogers 2010, 473. Letter by Rogers to Giedion, 3 April 1950. See also Kim 2006, 77–8.
27 Samonà became a member of the CIAM Italian Group only in 1949, after the Bergamo CIAM.
28 Università Iuav di Venezia, Archivio Progetti, Fondo Giuseppe Samonà, seg. 2.fasc/058. For the first year, the school was to be named 'Venice International Architecture Scool – Preliminary CIAM Summer School 1950' and the following year 'Venice International Architecture School – CIAM Summer School 1951' (typewritten document, 13 June 1950). See also 'Scuola internazionale estiva di Architettura a Venezia' 1950, 62.
29 Università Iuav di Venezia, Archivio Progetti, Fondo Giuseppe Samonà, seg. 2.fasc/058. Along with these, another committee was chosen, whose members were local authorities, culture

personalities and financial corporations. 'Un comité de Patronat parmi les Autorités de la ville, les personalités de la culture et les corps financiers. Un conseil de L'Ecole présidé par Le Corbusier comprenant – en plus du Comité de Direction, deux personalités étrangères. Un Comité de Direction formé par les Architectes du CIAM: Albini, Gardella, Rogers, Samonà. Il y aura enfin un sécretariat Administratif et Technique', typewritten document, 13 June 1950.

30 Università Iuav di Venezia, Archivio Progetti, Fondo Giuseppe Samonà, seg. 2.fasc/058. 'The CIAM Groups are responsible for the choice of the students in each Country, and we will limit ourselves to fix the number on the basis of a reasonable distribution among the different Countries', typewritten document, 13 June 1950.

31 Congressi internazionali di Architettura Moderna 1954.

32 Congressi internazionali di Architettura Moderna 1954, 73. A whole part of the congress was dedicated to Italian squares. See 'Discussione sulle piazze italiane', Congressi internazionali di Architettura Moderna 1954, 74–80.

33 *The Architects' Journal* 1952, 661–2 ; Bosman 1992, 14.

34 Lanzarini 2007, 52.

35 Università Iuav di Venezia, Archivio Progetti, Fondo Giuseppe Samonà, seg. 2.fasc/058. Typewritten document, undated.

36 Richards 1954, 61.

37 Samonà's opening speech of the Academic Year 1953/4. Samonà 1975, 248.

38 Lanzarini 2007, 51.

39 Berlanda 2007, 83.

40 Berlanda 1953, 83.

41 Martinis 2016, 17–31.

42 Berlanda 1953, 83–6; Kim 2006, 79; Zuccaro Marchi 2018, 118–19.

43 Mumford 2000, 225–38; Risselada and van den Heuvel 2006, 20–41.

44 Lanzarini 2007, 51.

45 Several projects were published in *Casabella-Continuità*. Guarda 1953, v–vi.

46 Risselada and van den Heuvel 2006, 20–45.

47 Some of the projects are published in *Casabella-Continuità*. Buzzi Ceriani and Crooke, 1954, 83–5. See also: Zuccaro Marchi 2018, 121–9.

48 Università Iuav di Venezia, Archivio Progetti, Fondo Giuseppe Samonà, seg. 2.fasc/058. Typewritten document, undated.

49 Università Iuav di Venezia, Archivio Progetti, Fondo Giuseppe Samonà, seg. 2.fasc/058. Nani Valle, *Preparazione Corso Estivo CIAM 1956*. Typewritten document.

50 Scimemi 1956, 69–73.

51 The prize had been awarded to the group whose members were Giorgio Amati, Mario Bernardo Valeriano Pastor, Antonio Pastorini, Eugenio Salvarini, Vittorio Clauser and Francesco Tentori.
Università Iuav di Venezia, Archivio Progetti, Fondo Egle Trincanato, seg. 2.Attività scientifica/2/014. See also: Zuccaro Marchi 2018, 138–40.

52 'This international course has been very important for us. It has helped our technical activities being more widely known, by making them being part of the concrete affairs of the city'. Samonà 2010, 474.

53 Zardini 2006, 216–17.

References

Berlanda, Franco. 'La scuola del C.I.A.M. a Venezia', *Urbanistica* 13 (1953): 83–6.

Berlanda, Franco. 'La scuola estiva del CIAM'. In *Lo Iuav di Giuseppe Samonà e l'insegnamento dell'architettura*, edited by Franco Mancuso and Adachiara Zevi, 79–85. Rome: Fondazione Bruno Zevi, 2007.

Bosman, Jos. 'I CIAM del dopoguerra: Un bilancio del Movimento Moderno', *Rassegna* 52 (1992): 6–21.

Buzzi Ceriani, Franco and Pat Crooke. 'La terza scuola estiva dei CIAM a Venezia', *Casabella-Continuità* 203 (1954): 83–5.

Congrès International d'Architecture Moderne. (ed.). *Documents: 7 ciam, Bergamo, 1949*. Nendeln: Kraus Reprint, 1979.
Congressi internazionali di Architettura Moderna. (ed.). *Il Cuore della Città: Per una vita più umana delle comunità*. Milan: Hoepli, 1954.
Furneaux Jordan, Robert. 'An English comment'. In *Italian Contemporary Architecture*, edited by the Royal Institute of British Architects, 7–12. London: RIBA, 1952.
Guarda, Giancarlo. 'Attualità di una scuola', *Casabella-Continuità* 199 (1953): 5–6.
Henderson, Graham. 'Foreword'. In *Italian Contemporary Architecture*, edited by the Royal Institute of British Architects, 5. London: RIBA, 1952.
'Italian Contemporary Architecture: Opening of the exhibition at the R.I.B.A., 21st March 1952'. *Journal of the Royal Institute of British Architects*, April 1952, 210–11.
Kim, Ilhyun. 'Alcuni episodi della biografia intellettuale di Samonà: Dai rapporti con la scuola romana alla scuola estiva dei CIAM'. In *Giuseppe Samonà e la scuola di architettura a Venezia*, edited by Giuseppe Marras and Marco Pogačnik, 61–92. Padua–Venezia: Il Poligrafo – Archivio Progetti Iuav, 2006.
Lanzarini, Orietta. 'Lo IUAV e i maestri del Movimento Moderno'. In *Lo Iuav di Giuseppe Samonà e l'insegnamento dell'architettura*, edited by Franco Mancuso and Adachiara Zevi, 39–64. Rome: Fondazione Bruno Zevi, 2007.
Maffioletti, Serena. 'Sguardi contemporanei su una didattica diversa: Alcune indicazioni CIAM'. In *Ricerca didattica e prassi urbanistica nelle città del Mediterraneo: Scritti in onore di Giuseppe Dato*, 159–65. Rome: Gangemi, 2011.
Marras, Giuseppe and Marco Pogačnik. *Giuseppe Samonà e la scuola di architettura a Venezia*. Padova–Venezia: Il Poligrafo – Archivio Progetti Iuav, 2006.
Martinis, Roberta. 'Un americano in volta di Canal: Frank Lloyd Wright e il Masieri Memorial'. In *Venezia e il moderno: Un laboratorio per il novecento*, edited by Maria Bonaiti and Cecilia Rostagni, 17–31. Macerata: Quodlibet, 2016.
Massa, Silvia and Elena Pontelli (eds). *Mostre permanenti: Carlo Ludovico Ragghianti in un secolo di esposizioni*. Lucca: Fondazione Ragghianti, 2018.
Mingardi, Lorenzo. 'Carlo Ludovico Ragghianti "architetto": Dal dibattito al museo', *Op.cit.* 165 (2019): 41–50.
Mumford, Eric. *The CIAM Discourse on Urbanism, 1928–1960*. Cambridge, MA: MIT Press, 2000.
Nicoloso, Paolo. 'Il Ciam di Bergamo, Le Corbusier e le "verità" discutibili della Carta d'Atene'. In *L'Italia di Le Corbusier*, edited by Marida Talamona, 297–312. Milan: Electa, 2012.
Protasoni, Sara. 'Il Gruppo Italiano e la tradizione del moderno', *Rassegna* 52 (1992): 28–39.
Richards, James. 'Elementi vecchi e nuovi nel Cuore della città'. In *Il Cuore della Città: Per una vita più umana delle comunità*, edited by Congressi internazionali di Architettura Moderna, 60–3. Milan: Hoepli, 1954.
Risselada, Max and Dirk van den Heuvel (eds). *Team 10, 1953–1981: In search of a utopia of the present*. Rotterdam: Nai Publishers, 2006.
Rogers, Ernesto. *Architettura, misura e grandezza dell'uomo: Scritti 1930–1969*. Edited by Serena Maffioletti. Padua: Il Poligrafo, 2010.
Sacchi, Nestorio. *I Congressi internazionali di architettura moderna: CIAM 1928–1959*. Milan: Consulta regionale lombarda degli Ordini degli Architetti, 1998.
Samonà, Giuseppe. *L'unità, Architettura-Urbanistica, Scritti e progetti: 1929–1973*, edited by Pasquale Lovero. Milan: Francoangeli, 1975.
Scimemi, Gabriele. 'La quarta scuola estiva dei CIAM a Venezia', *Casabella-Continuità* 213 (1956): 69–73.
'Scuola internazionale estiva di Architettura a Venezia', *Metron* 37 (1950): 62.
Shoshkes, Ellen. *Jaqueline Tyrwhitt: A transnational life in urban planning and design*. Farnham: Ashgate, 2013.
Tentori, Francesco. 'I CIAM per il Cinquecentenario del Congresso di Bergamo: L'architettura, l'arte e l'importanza decisiva della libertà', *La Rivista di Bergamo* 18 (1999): 10–21.
Tentori, Francesco. 'Metodo e progetto: I diversi approcci nello IUAV del secondo dopoguerra'. In *Giuseppe Samonà e la scuola di architettura a Venezia*, edited by Giuseppe Marras and Marco Pogačnik, 249–58. Padova–Venezia: Il Poligrafo–Archivio Progetti Iuav, 2006.
The Architects' Journal, 24 February (1949): 179–80.
The Architects' Journal, 15 September (1949): 276–8.

The Architects' Journal, 29 May (1952): 661–2.

Tyrwhitt, Jaqueline. 'The Valley Section: Patrick Geddes' world image', *Journal of the Town Planning Institute* 37 (1951): 61–6.

Zardini, Mirko. 'ILAUD 1974–2004: Giancarlo De Carlo and the International Laboratory of Architecture and Urban Design'. In *Team 10, 1953–1981: In search of a utopia of the present,* edited by Max Risselada and Dirk van den Heuvel, 216–17. Rotterdam: Nai Publishers, 2006.

Zuccaro Marchi, Leonardo. *The Heart of the City: Legacy and complexity of a modern design idea.* London: Routledge, 2018.

9

The influence of Patrick Geddes in post-war Italy through Jaqueline Tyrwhitt and Giancarlo De Carlo

Maria Clara Ghia

Patrick Geddes, an introduction

> *The City Beautiful must be the result of its own life and labour; it is the expression of the soul and mood of its people.*[1]

It is undeniable that minor currents flowed through the Modern Movement undermining the dominant thinking conveyed in the Athens Charter. One of these streams, probably the stronger, resulted from the ideas formulated by Patrick Geddes (1854–1932) at the beginning of the twentieth century.

Geddes's particular interest was in the interaction of human life with the surrounding environment. But he was also deeply committed to the reconciliation of science, morality and art, the three main areas of human thinking according to Max Weber, divided by the separatist culture of the period: 'value spheres of the world stand in irreconcilable conflict with each other'.[2]

As a botanist, sociologist, educator, artist and town planner, from the 1880s Geddes began to follow his vocation to classify and synthesize knowledge towards the improvement of human living conditions. In 1892 he purchased a tower at the upper end of Edinburgh's Royal Mile, which already had the function of public observatory: the building was topped by a roof platform with an octagonal domed cap house, where a camera obscura was installed. From 1895, after giving the building the name of Outlook Tower, Geddes continued to use it for analysing the social and physical phenomena of the city. The laboratory implemented a taxonomic process, typical of the methods of biology, leading to a far more interesting vision than simply comparing architecture to a living organism, or evoking biological and natural shapes in urban design.

For Geddes, the city is the form that human life assumes when reaching its maximum level of evolution, representing the ultimate effort to safeguard the freedom of the individual and the continuity of species: 'the city is ... the most distinct form that human life can take; even more, it is the form that human life *should* take, especially in its highest development as a co-operative and communal life'.[3]

Geddes's analytic triad, place – work – folk, derived from the trio *lieu – travail – famille* indicated by Frédéric Le Play, led to the investigation of geographical, historical and psychic aspects, providing the basic tools to examine his urban theory.

At the centre of his theory were two well-known diagrams. The Valley Section was a drawing representing a river from its source in the mountains to its estuary. The physical conditions of the territory, represented with the greenery, were combined with human activity, symbolized by work tools and connected, in turn, with various types of settlements.

The city was located on the coast, the village on the hill, then isolated houses were placed on the slope of the mountain, to endorse that social organization emerged according to the integration between the occupations of man and the surrounding ecosystem.

The Notation of Life consisted of a table that again featured the interaction between man and the milieu, this time starting from the conceptions of psychology, politics and contemporary sociology. One method was crucial in Geddes's work: everything was analysed separately, but every disciplinary approach was intertwined with all the others, in a cross-curricular project *ante litteram*. In Geddes's model, the basic division of all forms of human life was that between an out-world and an in-world, and the objective world was to be considered in relation with the world we perceive subjectively. Consequently, the table was divided into four sections: activities, duties, facts and thoughts (dreams), expressing the 'mental part' of social life.

Along the sections, following a spiral, life evolved towards superior levels of consciousness. In the upper left quadrant, life was represented simply through the nine combinations of the three main categories: place – work – folk. Continuing forward, on the opposite level and in the highest quadrant, life was no longer considered as an instinctive interaction with the environment but as the conscious, scientific and artistic expression of this interaction. The ultimate level was that of the 'cloister', a term with which Geddes indicated the site for universities, artist studios, art schools and public spaces: a place of 'contemplation, meditation, imagination'.[4]

By choosing such a problematic and psychologically focused model to explain how a city takes shape, Geddes excluded the dominant vision based on the Marxist notion of class, in favour of an idea of co-operation influenced by the anarchist principles of Peter Kropotkin, who was teaching at Geddes's school at the end of the nineteenth century.[5] Thus, the shape of the city was not to be established by the competing interests of the different classes, but by the interaction between men and the environment: 'the consonance between an individual's action and that of a larger social group would cut across social classes, even going beyond them'.[6]

When Geddes started his large-scale renewal project for Edinburgh at the end of the nineteenth century, his aim was to transform the Old Town, or 'the heart of the city' as we will name it later on, into a sort of contemporary Acropolis.

There were two main purposes: the realization of a cultural, educational, spiritual core and the project for a city that was not divided into different functional areas. Furthermore, a new concept was introduced, the notion of the region, since Geddes felt that a town and its geographical surroundings were strongly related and must be considered together. Of course regionalism opened up a theoretic problem, the question of boundaries. Geddes never felt the need to attain a well-defined answer: regions as biology models do not necessarily have defined borders; they can generate zones of transition and can overlap one another without creating a problem for the conception as a whole.

Bringing to fruition this unconventional vision, where frontiers were considered as unnecessary limitations chiefly derived from war conventions, probably sprang from the transnationalism Geddes developed during his travels. In acquiring a way to investigate the conditions of people starting from local geography and including considerations of language, culture, economics and history, concepts such as the State or the Nation became completely meaningless to him.

Geddes's works and studies in India were critically important: in 1914 he received an invitation from the Governor of Madras to present an exhibition on his survey on cities. He embarked for the Indies, which he reached in September 1915. He was then 60 years old and, although he returned frequently to Europe, his Indian endeavours absorbed much of his energy. His projects unfortunately were never realized except for a

Figure 9.1 The urban-geographical structures of Athens and Edinburgh, as represented by Patrick Geddes in 1911. Published in Welter, Volker. *Biopolis: Patrick Geddes and the city of life.* Cambridge, MA: MIT Press, 2002, 67

Courtesy of MIT Press

minor plan in Indore, but between 1915 and 1917 he published nine reports on the major Hindi cities.

From 1919 he was often in Palestine to accomplish urban and regional analyses for colonial administration. He was responsible for the World Zionist Organization and started planning for the Hebrew University in Jerusalem. When the project was deserted, he went back to India where he was appointed Professor at the University of Bombay and Director of the Department of Sociology. He had excellent relationships with the Hindus, who comprehended and appreciated his cultural relativism, his inclusive way of thinking, his concern regarding history and the local geography even better than his compatriots.[7]

Geddes moved back to Europe permanently in 1924, landing in Marseille and then moving to Montpellier, where he spent the rest of his life pursuing his ultimate dream. He bought a piece of land located three kilometres north of the city, in a perfect rural–urban position, close enough to the centre to integrate with it but sufficiently far from it to enjoy the benefits of the countryside, and decided to build his own house and his Acropolis, the Collège des Ecossais.

The Collège was located on one of the hills dominating the city and was conceived as a centre for international studies. The research community was animated by Geddes, and after his death by his friend Paul Reclus, Élisée's nephew. In addition to lectures, students participated in debates and in the *enquêtes sur le terrain,* on the basis of the Geddesian programme of regional survey.

A tower, as a new version of Edinburgh's Outlook Tower, served as an observatory and public laboratory. From its summit, one can see the south of the city, with the Mediterranean Sea in the background, and the north with the Cévennes block. Unfortunately, a lack of financial resources caused the failure of the project. The connection between the university and the city was never really established, as academics and politicians struggled to appreciate Geddes's eccentricities.

Although reduced and neglected, the Collège continues to dominate what is now the Montpellier campus. The botanical garden, the Celtic enclosure, the enclosure of Greek gods, the Roman patio, the 'golden ratio' terrace and the 'alley of philosophers' are a sublime representation of Geddes's idea of the 'cloister', a core for a region-city to expand. Anyhow, leaving a lasting mark on history was not a main concern for him. His search for new ideas was more important than the accomplishment of a particular project. He did not pursue academic, nor pure intellectual success. At a time when scientific progress was driven by a process of specialization, he defended interdisciplinarity.

We will consider, at least to a small extent, how Geddes's inquiry into the inescapable relationships between nature, culture, territory, people and structures largely influenced post-war architectural thinking, first within the CIAM congresses and consequently influencing Team X and specifically Giancarlo De Carlo's beliefs.

The legacy of Geddes in Italy and Adriano Olivetti

> *Our Community must be concrete, visible, tangible, a Community neither too large nor too small, territorially defined, with vast powers, giving to all activities that indispensable co-ordination, that efficiency, that respect for the human personality, that culture and that art which were created by human civilization at its best.*[8]

Patrick Geddes's ideas first appeared in Italy during that stimulating moment of optimism immediately following Second World War when, despite the shocking economic and social crisis, idealistic architects, planners, artists and scientists believed in realizing their vision for a better world.

Geddes mainly exerted guidance through personal contact. His publications were difficult to obtain, his essential book, *City in Evolution*, first issued in 1915, was simply an assemblage of published papers, presented in a disorderly manner and therefore difficult to understand. His legacy was far from established at the time of his death, and it is common knowledge that Lewis Mumford (1895–1990) had a key role in assuring the enduring impact of his thinking, thanks to the circulation of *The Culture of Cities*. Unmistakably, Mumford's account in the introduction is that he started to collect the materials merged into the essay 'as far back as 1915, under the stimulus of Patrick Geddes'.[9]

First published in 1938, *The Culture of Cities* was a visionary survey on urbanism from the Middle Ages to the late 1930s, from the worker-friendly streets of medieval homesteads to the symmetrical neoclassical avenues of renaissance cities, up to the shabbiness of nineteenth-century factory towns. It reasoned about the outcome of the twentieth-century Megalopolis, whose irrational scale, Mumford believed, could only result in its breakdown into the 'Nekropolis', an enormity of living death. Mumford wished for communal action to re-establish the urban world on a healthier human foundation, stressing the importance of a specific notion he acquired from his mentor: the idea of 'livability', a vision of cities designed around the nature of human bodies, a demand for ecological urban planning and a suitable use of technology, to conceive well-balanced living environments.

It is no wonder, then, in discovering that Adriano Olivetti (1901–1960) had *The Culture of Cities* as a *livre de chevet.*[10] The book was translated in Italy in 1953, a time when the Olivetti movement was committed to the spreading of contemporary international culture through the Edizioni di Comunità.

Of course, in Italy, the aforementioned enlightened *entourage* of idealistic architects, planners and artists gathered around the figure of Olivetti. That is why the thinking of Geddes, disseminated through Mumford's ideas, had great influence on urban planning in the country.

On the enthusiastic wave of the Liberation, the role of the cultural elite was renewed. It now acted within and from within the society, with a direct participation that also involved the classes hitherto excluded from the debate. It was finally possible to look at better organized societies, both in Europe and America, and to import foreign philosophical and social theories, adapting them to the Italian reality. Ideas flowed and grew, such as the pragmatist beliefs of the American philosopher John Dewey, translated by Einaudi in 1949, and Jean-Paul Sartre's existentialism, taken up by the positive conception of Nicola Abbagnano. What is even more crucial to grasping Olivetti's cultural background is the new Catholic belief inspired by the 'integral humanism' of Jacques Maritain, the 'personalism' of Emmanuel Mounier and the radical orientation of Simone Weil. These new concepts affirmed the absolute value of the human personality as an explanatory principle, and they supported a personal conception of God versus a pantheistic 'impersonal' notion. Hence, through his 'personalistic socialism', Olivetti envisioned a society that, looking at the experiences of state socialism and those of liberalism, could take inspiration but surpass both models. The mission was to never ignore the primary foundation on which society itself is based: individual freedom. In this overcoming of the socialist models, references to the concepts expressed by Geddes and the 'anarchist prince' Peter Kropotkin were straightforward.

As a Geddes scholar, Lewis Mumford understandably formulated a new interpretation of the industrial city and its crisis, proposing the recovery of community values within a balanced planning process: 'In this perspective, urban science takes on a new and predominant role, ending up as a guarantor ... of new thresholds of social balance'.[11] In the *Città dell'uomo* by Olivetti, published in 1960 as a summary of the most important speeches of the last decade of his life, many Geddesian and then Mumfordian echoes are indisputable.

But setting aside Mumford's results, already deeply investigated, and thoroughly exploring the spreading of Geddes's legacy, the role of another figure arises; a figure whose importance has been almost neglected and therefore whose position is much more relevant to investigate; a female figure, too often described as 'the woman behind the man': Mary Jaqueline Tyrwhitt.

Jaqueline Tyrwhitt: *The pearl of cardinal virtues*

> *Theirs was the future; ours to clear*
> *Away the dross of yesteryear.*
> *Till that the torch of their bright lives released from strife*
> *Should warm and quicken our chill plans to a new life.*[12]

In July 1951 Le Corbusier gave to Mary Jaqueline Tyrwhitt (1905–1983) a sketch with a dedication, in which he called her 'la perle des vertus cardinales'.[13]

Digging in the history of the post-war period and the years that followed, we discover that Tyrwhitt, with her 'cardinal virtues', had a key role in redefining urban planning during the reconstruction. Her presence was very influential, and considering her merely as a secondary character acting behind Geddes, or later Sigfried Giedion, Josep Lluis Sert or Konstantinos Doxiadis, would no longer be acceptable.

Born in Pretoria in 1924, she was among the eight women admitted to the Architectural Association in London. Her main interest at the time was landscape architecture.

In 1936, with Leonard and Dorothy Elmhirst, she worked at the Dartington Hall School. The attempt of the college, marked by an interdisciplinary approach, was to integrate the effects of agriculture and industry into design thinking. Here she discovered *Cities in Evolution*, a book destined to have a great impact on her future work. In 1949 she decided to re-publish it in an abridged version. Part of the text and some images were cut or re-edited and significantly she included excerpts from a lecture by Geddes at the New School in 1923, clarifying some concepts of the Valley Section that were omitted in the book.

From 1937 Tyrwhitt was director of research and director of studies at the School of Planning and Research for National Development of the Architectural Association, under the direction of Eric Anthony Ambrose Rowse, another Geddes scholar. During the war she replaced Rowse and in 1945 she codified the Geddesian method in order to disseminate it through a correspondence course, after which a three-month seminar in London was to be attended to receive the diploma. Engineers, architects, sociologists and other professionals were educated thanks to this programme during the war period. About 2,000 students enrolled; 172 students completed the course in London between 1945 and 1947. One can almost certainly say that many architects and planners involved in the reconstruction were aware of the Geddesian method thanks to Tyrwhitt's efforts.

She also travelled to North America to lecture on city planning in England and her new perspectives about transnationalism led her to publish another book, *Patrick Geddes in India*, a collection of Geddes's reports on Indian cities. The book stressed two fundamental concepts: first of all the idea of 'conservative surgery' as an intervention to restore an urban area by minimizing the destruction of existing buildings, precisely the methodology applied by Geddes in his Indian projects;[14]

then the notion of 'bioregionalism', underscoring that environments and organisms are conjoined, just like places and people. In the introduction, Mumford affirmed that Geddes's thoughts on political decentralization, civic responsibility, co-operation and personal development sounded indeed like wise and clever considerations in the post-war period. Tyrwhitt urged the West to import the fundamental wisdom of the Eastern peoples in looking at life as a whole.

Moreover, from 1952, she worked at the University of Toronto, where she founded the Ford Foundation Seminar on Culture and Communication with a group of colleagues including Marshall McLuhan, an 'exploration group' with a manifest interdisciplinary approach and with the wide-ranging influence of Giedion's methodology. Her teaching years ended at Harvard in 1969, when Tyrwhitt moved definitively to

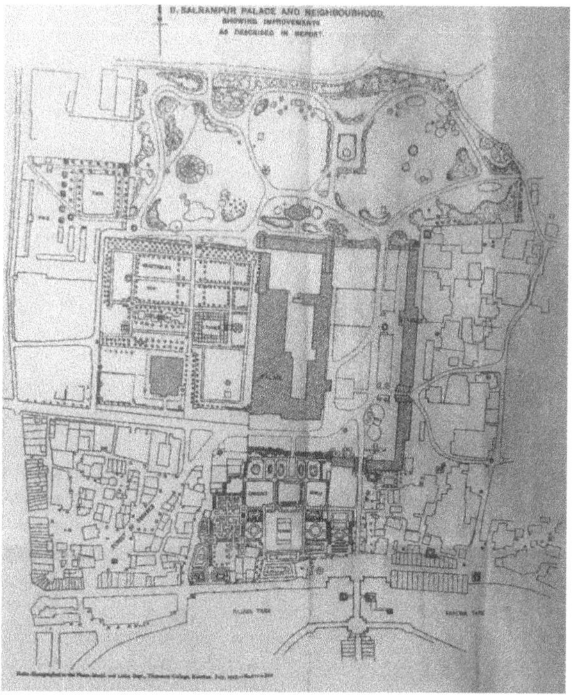

Figure 9.2 Balrampur, an example of conservative surgery applied by Patrick Geddes to a city quarter, 1917 (at lower left). Published in Welter, Volker. *Biopolis: Patrick Geddes and the city of life.* Cambridge, MA: MIT Press, 2002, 117

Courtesy of MIT Press

Greece to work with Konstantinos A. Doxiadis after more than 10 years of contributing to his journal *Ekistics and the New Habitat* which she edited from 1957.[15]

But what is most interesting is of course Tyrwhitt's role within the CIAM congresses: it is precisely during these meetings, where she introduced the Geddesian methods, that a new vision of urban planning arose and affected Giancarlo De Carlo among others.

In 1947 she was one of the key organizers of CIAM 6 hosted by the MARS group at Bridgewater Arts Centre, England. Straight away, the triad 'work, transportation and recreation', predominant in the congresses until the war, was amended into the trio 'work, transportation and cultivation of mind and body'.[16] The aim was now reasoning about 'the creation of a physical environment that will satisfy man's emotional and material needs and stimulate his spiritual growth'.[17] No need to indicate how this shift can be associated with the presence of Tyrwhitt among the supervisors. She contributed to Giedion's essay 'A Decade of New Architecture' and from then on she became intimately involved in his works as translator, rewriter and editor.

Henceforth, a seed began to grow into the heart of the CIAM, cultivated through the analysis of Geddesian methodology as opposed to the principles of the Athens Charter. As is widely known, it was in 1951, during the CIAM 8 in Hoddesdon, England, that this methodology gained the upper hand. The President of this CIAM session was José Luis Sert, and Tyrwhitt was secretary of the board of directors. The intent of defining a so-called fifth space in addition to housing, work, leisure and mobility, veering toward a 'new humanism' in urban planning was crucial in this congress. This space was 'the heart of the city'. The leap undertaken during CIAM 8, that would lead from the Athens Charter to the Habitat Charter, was from the old to the new generation. The basic principle motivating this transition was the interdisciplinary approach, intertwining architectural and urban design with social needs for a different quality of spaces.

The 'heart' was considered as a man-made essential element of city planning. It was the expression of the collective mind and spirit of the community, which humanized and gave form to the city itself.[18] According to Giedion, it was the element that made the 'community a community and not merely an aggregate of individuals',[19] meaning that in it was stimulated the passage from a passive behaviour to an active citizenship. The 'heart' was a re-interpretation of the 'cloister', Geddes's cultural Acropolis, and also of Taut's *Stadtkrone*. It was Tyrwhitt who suggested the use of the term 'heart' instead of 'core', which had been previously taken into consideration: the word, with a convincing organic meaning, was used by Elisée Reclus, Geddes's close friend and collaborator, to describe the communal centre of the expanding city, inspiring the idea of region-city with the Acropolis at its centre.[20]

The book entitled *Il cuore della città: Per una vita più umana della comunità*, published in 1954 by the Italian editor Hoepli and edited by Tyrwhitt with Josep Lluis Sert and Ernesto Rogers, was a significant publication in Italy. Many photographs of 'urban hearts' were included, mostly Italian. Le Corbusier still wrote about 'specific forms, relevant positions, architectural programs', as *a priori* decisions. But an evident divergence now emerged: Giedion explained that the 'heart' was the only element that makes the city a city; Philip Johnson described the 'heart' as a background for spontaneous 'processional' movement through the city.

The subsequent step was the shift from the concept of 'heart' to that of 'habitat', a trans-national and trans-institutional notion that contained the so-called 'organic' value of the 'heart', reiterated its multidisciplinary approach, its anthropological definition, its criticism of the functionalistic division in urban planning. It was consequential that the grid defined by Le Corbusier and utilized till then to study urban phenomena was to be substituted by another scheme of representation, and this scheme was properly derived by Geddes's Valley Section as redesigned by Alison and Peter Smithson, emphasizing the fact that architecture must reflect and respond to the surrounding environment.

Giancarlo De Carlo: Turning the telescope around

> *We believe in the heteronomy of architecture, in its necessary dependence on the circumstances that produce it, in its intrinsic need to be in tune with history, with the events and expectations of individuals and social groups, with the secret rhythms of nature.*
>
> *We deny that the purpose of architecture is to produce objects and we affirm that its fundamental task is to give birth to processes of transformation of the natural environment, contributing to the improvement of the human condition.*[21]

Even before Mumford's *The Culture of Cities* was published in Italy, Giancarlo De Carlo (1919–2005) had the opportunity to read it. Immediately after the war, he and his wife Giuliana Baracco shared an apartment with Carlo Doglio, and since Giuliana was fluent in English, she handwrote a translation of the essay for her husband and friend, so that they could all be well informed of Geddesian principles at the beginning of the reconstruction.[22]

That is why both Tyrwhitt and De Carlo were familiar with the Valley Section schemes later used by Alison and Peter Smithson almost as an assault flag against the dominance of Le Corbusier's thought in CIAM congresses. The first meeting between Tyrwhitt and De Carlo probably occurred in 1955 in La Sarraz, when Giancarlo was invited by Ernesto Rogers at the preparatory meeting for CIAM 10. Tyrwhitt was, once again, on the board of directors of the meeting.

The year before De Carlo curated, with Doglio and Ludovico Quaroni, an exhibition at the X Triennale of Milan. De Carlo was responsible for the urban planning section, and among other materials he displayed three short films: the first, by Doglio, presented La Martella village in Matera; the second, entitled *The City of Men,* had a remarkable script by De Carlo and his friend Elio Vittorini; the third, *A Lesson in Urban Planning,* was realized by De Carlo and Billa Pedroni Zanuso.[23] This last film caught the attention with its ironic and significant message. It represented a critique of the Athens Charter principles and the *existenzminimum*.

In the film a citizen is filmed while moving in the minimal space of his house, banging here and there against its furnishings. Once out, he is crushed by the crowd on a bus. Shortly after, he is lying down on the edge of a road covered by grass, as if to recover the relationship with nature, but he must immediately get up because he is surrounded by a traffic jam. Then, the model of a city is presented. Three urban planners are working on it. The first one is an aesthete: he designs alignments, green places and elegant building. The second one is some kind of a technical designer or engineer, who thinks the most relevant problem is that of mobility: the city must be built for the road network to function. He even drills holes in the central monument to make space for a road passing through it. The last one bases his project on data: with a stethoscope, he auscultates buildings and trees, he takes measurements, counts inhabitants, cars and houses. His aim is to create a space commensurate with the 'average man as deduced statistically'. The voiceover comments that urban science has finally found the ideal space for man. Only one thing is still missing: the man himself. When the citizen enters the scene, he finds an infinite series of prescriptions that prevent him from moving freely in the city. But data cannot be wrong, the voiceover continues. If anything, it is the man himself who is wrong. The city built with statistical calculations must function at any cost, in extreme cases even with the use of power. Eventually, the citizen stands free in the countryside, and the real city is in front of him. It is a space of complexity and problems to be fixed, but one can live in it. The voiceover concludes: 'go to your city and collaborate with those who want to make it more human, more suitable for you'.

In that period De Carlo was just thinking and working on a city corresponding to the human scale and needs. From 1952, after his encounter with Carlo Bo, De Carlo's main occupation were his projects in Urbino, in particular his design for the University and for the houses of the university employees (1952–4). Here, in the fortunate circumstance of a unity of purposes with the client and a particular consonance with the landscape, he began an experiment. The intentions of this investigation are traceable in many subsequent works, based on two purposes: to define urban spaces that were consistent with the historical essence of the city while maintaining a contemporary language, and to articulate the project by relating it to the territory, implementing its specific geography.

Among the drawings conserved at the IUAV Archive, there is a significant 'view from the Palazzo Ducale'. Analysing it, one can read a clear methodology: the long-distance observation in planning. De Carlo's method will be later stated clearly: he wrote about the need for 'turning around the telescope with which we have observed environmental phenomena up to now',[24] discerning all spaces from a distant point of view to continuously remember the connections with the territory all around.

As if this were not enough, at the end of the 1970s he decided to buy the Ca' Guerla, an ancient watchtower of the fifteenth century. His main residence was in Milan, but he spent short stays in Urbino, observing at the right distance the city, just like Geddes used to watch the Collège des Ecossais from his house in Montpellier. Twenty years later, in 1998, he still had in mind the operation Geddes carried out with the Outlook Tower as a place for researching urban society, so he proposed to recover the old stables of the Palazzo Ducale and dedicate their space to an 'observatory on the city'.[25] It was in Urbino that De Carlo's passionate study of the small Italian urban centres in relation to the surrounding landscape originated. Other works on this central theme were to follow, such as the masterplan for Urbino itself (1958–64), the proposal for the urban renewal of Lastra a Signa (1988–9) and the urban regeneration of Colletta di Castelbianco (1994). In this last project the entire historic centre was considered as a whole within which all the voids were interconnected to create a single spatial traversable chain. Experienced space was the scene of variety: a multiplicity of stairs, buildings, streets, alleys, squares, whereby each individual could find his own place and identity in a possibility of unstandardized expressions; a unique and meticulous inquiry into an inclusive design, centred on the enhancement of spatial diversity. Urban space can offer multiple, stimulating and libertarian housing methods.[26]

The theme of freedom, central in De Carlo's work, finds perhaps its highest expression in Colletta di Castelbianco; a theme certainly related to the anarchist movement De Carlo joined under the guiding light of Doglio.[27] Geddes's place in the anarchist pantheon has since been proved, first of all by Colin Ward, and other authors are catching up. Peter Hall writes how 'From Reclus and Kropotkin, and beyond them from Proudhon, Geddes also took his position that society had to be reconstructed not by sweeping governmental measures ... but through the efforts of millions of individuals'.[28]

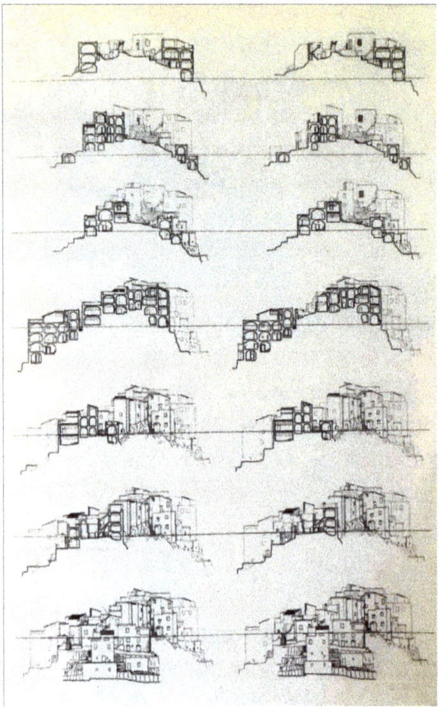

Figure 9.3 Giancarlo De Carlo, the urban regeneration of Colletta di Castelbianco, elevations and sections, Indian ink on tracing paper, 1994. The drawings underline De Carlo's attention towards certain Geddesian key principles, such as the conservative surgery and the unfruitfulness of city–country opposition.

Università Iuav di Venezia, Archivio Progetti, Fondo Giancarlo De Carlo

Beside the anarchist attitude, Geddes and De Carlo shared their operational eclecticism mainly in three directions: the opinions on the unfruitfulness of city–country opposition, the practice of 'reading' to decode the context, and the interdisciplinarity as a criterion to move from urban planning studies to realizations.

'To read' meant to explore the context and understand it with a planning mind, and in this exploration the relationship with history also occurred, as a more direct, reciprocal, connection with the background in which human beings existed and operated. This affirmation had been harshly accepted in the CIAM entourage, but it became one of Team X's essential topics: history as a tool for deciphering social and environmental context and as a foresight of the future.

Interdisciplinarity, more correctly defined by De Carlo 'trans-disciplinary research', consisted in an investigation conducted without specializing the human milieu, but studying it with a comprehensive and inclusive methodology: 'Urban planners who over the years have interested me most, and in whom I still have an interest today, are those who share *transdisciplinarity,* for example Peter Kropotkin and Patrick Geddes. Kropotkin can somehow be defined as an urban planner, but also a sociologist, topographer, writer, traveller, revolutionary. What was he ultimately? He was all of these things at the same time; he had a global vision of the world and he committed himself globally to the world'.[29]

In the same way, De Carlo can be described as an urban planner, an architect, a sociologist, an anthropologist, a traveller, an anarchist, a writer and also an editor.

Thanks to him, in 1970 *City in Evolution* was finally published in Italian in the series *Struttura e forma urbana* by Il Saggiatore, of which he was the director from 1967.[30] And of course he was the editor of the magazine *Spazio e società*, which since 1978 had been published as the Italian version of *Espace et Sociétés* by Henri Lefebvre and Anatole Kopp, focusing on the concept of space intended as a system of multiple physical, economic, political, philosophical and behavioural interrelationships.[31] In 2000, De Carlo wrote in his journal:

> All modern urban planning, from the Camillo Sitte's visibilism, to that of the sanitary and municipal engineers, to the Cerdà's modernistic one, to the rationalist one of the Athens Charter, is based on principles of separation, selection, hierarchy, specialization and – in terms of form – symmetry, programmatic asymmetry, stereometry, etc. etc.: essentially, on principles of authoritarianism or, in other words, military discipline.

It should not be forgotten, however, that urban planning was not a monolithic theory at the time of the Athens Charter. The authoritarian current that triumphed on that occasion was opposed by other non-aggressive, basically libertarian currents …. For example, the one starting from Peter Kropotkin and passing through Patrick Geddes, Olmstedt, somehow Sullivan and F.L. Wright, some of the American New Deal urban planners, Louis Mumford, Kevin Lynch and the group from Cambridge, USA, working with interdisciplinary and participatory methods ….

These are currents considered archaic nowadays, since they have been marginalized. And it is a mistake because today, if we think about it, they would help to understand and to face the period of great contradictions we are going through.[32]

Notes

1 Geddes 1913, 199.
2 Weber 1948, 147.
3 Welter 2002, 11.
4 Geddes 1906, 83–4.
5 See Geddes 1886.
6 Welter 2002, 44.
7 Penin 1993, 10. In India Geddes exchanged a correspondence with Gandhi, recommending him to free himself from the British influence and offering his services. Despite a very kind response from Gandhi, the meeting did not take place.
8 Olivetti 1960, 26 (translated by the author).
9 Mumford 1938, ix.
10 Fabbri and Greco 1988, 44–7.
11 Tafuri and Dal Co 1976, 46 (translated by the author).
12 Tyrwhitt, Jaqueline, *C.T. birthday II.IV.43 & J.F. brother killed,* a poems on a memoranda page in her 1943 diary. See Shoshkes 2013, 76.
13 Shoshkes 2013, 127.
14 Probably, *Patrick Geddes in India* was the publication by which Tyrwhitt made Geddes's words comprehensible to a broad audience, editing many passages. Arthur Geddes wrote to her: 'PG would be grateful, I'm sure, to you for pulling this off'. Patrick Geddes Centre for Planning Studies, Edinburgh University Library Special Collection, Edinburgh, reference n. 31 in Shoshkes 2013, 101.
15 Ekistics had the goals of studying the whole subject of human settlements, conceiving their future, acting to shape the physical habitat, its nature, its functions and its shells and analysing the whole spectrum, from the first settlements of man to the megalopolis and beyond it. Of course Tyrwhitt found a deep consonance with Doxiadis's method.
16 Giedion 1951, 25.
17 Giedion 1951, 6. For a further investigation on this passage see Mumford 1992, 391–417.
18 Tyrwhitt, Sert and Rogers 1952, 168.
19 Tyrwhitt, Sert and Rogers 1952, 160.
20 Welter 2002, 54.
21 De Carlo 2000a, 153–4.
22 Fabbri and Greco 1988, 44.
23 In the years 1955–65 Doglio had the three short films projected at the universities of Manchester, Liverpool and Newcastle and he also presented the Piedmont regional plan and

the Turin plan. With the same materials he organized in 1956 an exhibition at the Italian Cultural Institute in London to display the most advanced Italian planning experiences. See Ciccarelli 2019, 39. Doglio lived in London as a correspondent of the magazine *Comunità*, conducting fundamental researches into English urban-planning culture.

24 De Carlo 1991, 4.

25 The project included a library, an exhibition area, a multimedia study centre and areas for debating on social and urban issues. De Carlo 2000a, 281.

26 For further investigation see: Bilò 2014, 101–2.

27 Colin Ward wrote that 'there were few links between the anarchists and the architects. One was the architect Giancarlo De Carlo': Ward 2000, 46.

28 Hall 1996, 145. For an interesting investigation into anarchist positions existing in Britain towards the end of the nineteenth century see Ryley 2013, 155–88.

29 De Carlo 1998 (translated by the author).

30 The book still circulated in Italy in Tyrwhitt's edition of 1949. Strangely Adriano Olivetti had not deemed it necessary to translate it in its series for the Edizioni di Comunità, so that the diffusion of Geddes's theories had been entrusted only to Mumford's *The Culture of Cities.*

31 The magazine arrived in Italy thanks to Doglio in 1975, with Riccardo Mariani as chief editor. Among other things a column edited by Doglio was included, entitled 'City and surroundings', with a report on legislation and planning in England from the early twentieth century to 1968.

32 De Carlo 2000b, 2 (translated by the author).

References

Bilò, Federico. *Tessiture dello spazio.* Macerata: Quodlibet, 2014.

Ciccarelli, Lorenzo. *Il mito dell'equilibrio: Il dibattito anglo-italiano per il governo del territorio negli anni del dopoguerra.* Milan: Franco Angeli, 2019.

De Carlo, Giancarlo. 'È tempo di girare il cannocchiale', *Spazio e Società* 54 (1991), 4.

De Carlo, Giancarlo. 'Il coraggio della tabula rasa'. In *La carta di Atene: Manifesto e frammento dell'urbanistica moderna*, edited by Paola Di Biagi, 351–60. Rome: Officina, 1998.

De Carlo, Giancarlo. *Architettura e libertà*. Milan: Eleuthera, 2000a.

De Carlo, Giancarlo. 'Arriverderci', *Spazio e Società* 92 (2000b), 2.

Fabbri, Marcello and Antonella Greco. *La comunità concreta: Progetto e immagine.* Milan: Quaderni della Fondazione Comunità, 1988.

Geddes, Patrick. 'On the condition of progress of the capitalist and the labourer'. In *The Claims of Labour,* edited byJames Oliphant, 73–111, Edinburgh: Co-operative Printing Co., 1886.

Geddes, Patrick. 'Civics: As concrete and applied sociology: Part II'. In *Sociological Papers: Vol. II, for 1905,* edited by Francis Galton, Edgar Schuster, Patrick Geddes, M.E. Sadler, E. Westermarck, Harold Hoffding, J.H. Bridges and J.S. Stuart-Glennie, 57–111, London: Macmillan, 1906.

Geddes, Patrick. 'The city beautiful – in theory and practice', *Garden Cities and Planning Magazine* 3 (1913).

Geddes, Patrick. *Cities in Evolution: An introduction to the town planning movement and to the study of civics.* London: Williams and Norgate, 1915.

Geddes, Patrick. *Cities in Evolution*. 2nd edition, abridged, edited by Jaqueline Tyrwhitt London: Williams and Norgate, 1949.

Geddes, Patrick. *Città in evoluzione*. Edited by Giancarlo De Carlo. Milan: Il Saggiatore, 1970.

Giedion, Sigfried. *Congrès Internationaux d'Architecture Moderne (CIAM), Dix ans d'architecture contemporaine: A decade of new architecture.* Zurich: Editions Girsberger, 1951.

Guccione, Margherita and Alessandra Vittorini (eds). *Giancarlo De Carlo: Le ragioni dell'architettura.* Milan: Electa Opera DARC, 2005.

Hall, Peter. *Cities of Tomorrow: An intellectual history of urban planning and design in the twentieth century*. Oxford: Blackwell, 1996.

McKean, John. 'Giancarlo De Carlo et l'experience politique de la participation'. In *La Modernité Critique, autour du CIAM 9, d'Aix-en-Provence – 1953*, edited by Jean Lucien Bonillo, Claude Massu and Daniel Pinson, 191–203. Marseille: Editions Imberton, 2006.

McKean, John, Bruno Racine and Bruno Pacquement (eds). *Giancarlo De Carlo: Des lieux, Des hommes*. Paris: Centre Pompidou, Edition Axel Menges, 2004.

Mingardi, Lorenzo. *Sono geloso di questa città: Giancarlo De Carlo e Urbino*. Macerata: Quodlibet, 2018.

Mumford, Eric. 'CIAM urbanism after the Athens Charter', *Planning Perspectives* 7 (1992), 391–417.

Mumford, Eric. *The CIAM Discourse on Urbanism 1928–1960*. Cambridge, MA: MIT Press, 2000.

Mumford, Lewis. *The Culture of Cities*. New York: Harcourt Brace Jovanovich, 1938 (Italian edition: *La cultura delle città*. Milan: Edizioni di Comunità, 1953).

Olivetti, Adriano. *Città dell'Uomo*. Milan: Edizioni di Comunità, 1960.

Olmo, Carlo (ed.). *Costruire la città dell'uomo: Adriano Olivetti e l'urbanistica*. Milan: Einaudi, 2001.

Penin, Marc. 'D'Edimbourg à Montpellier en passant par Bombay: Patrick Geddes (1854–1932)', *Le Carré Bleu* 2 (1993), 3–20.

Romano, Antonella. *Giancarlo De Carlo: Lo spazio, realtà del vivere insieme*. Rome: Testo e Immagine, 2001.

Ryley, Peter. *The Rise of Ecological Anarchism: Elisée Reclus and Patrick Geddes*. New York: Bloomsbury Academic, 2013.

Shoshkes, Ellen. *Jaqueline Tyrwhitt: A transnational life in urban planning and design*. Farnham: Ashgate, 2013.

Tafuri, Manfredo and Francesco Dal Co. *Architettura Contemporanea*. Milan: Electa, 1976.

Tyrwhitt, Jaqueline. *Patrick Geddes in India*. London: Lund Humphries, 1947.

Tyrwhitt, Jaqueline. 'The Valley Section: Patrick Geddes' world image', *Journal of the Town Planning Institute* 38 (1951), 61–6.

Tyrwhitt, Jaqueline. 'The city unseen', *Explorations* 5 (1955a), 88–96.

Tyrwhitt, Jaqueline. 'The moving eye', *Explorations* 4 (1955b), 115–19.

Tyrwhitt, Jaqueline and Gwen Bell. *Human Identity in the Urban Environment*. London: Pelican Books, 1971.

Tyrwhitt, Jaqueline, José Luis Sert and Ernesto Rogers. *The Heart of the City: Towards the humanisation of urban life*. London: Lund Humphries, 1952 (Italian edition: *Il cuore della città: Per una vita più umana della comunità*. Milan: Hoepli, 1954).

Ward, Colin. *Housing: An anarchist approach*. London: Freedom Press, 1976.

Ward, Colin. 'Anarchy and architecture: A personal record'. In *Non-plan: Essays on freedom participation and change in modern architecture and urbanism*, edited by Jonathan Hughes and Simon Sadler, 44–51. Oxford: Architectural Press, 2000.

Weber, Max. 'Science as a vocation'. In *From Max Weber: Essays in sociology*, edited by Hans Heirich Gerth and C. Wright Mills, 129–57. London: Routledge, 1948.

Welter, Volker. *Biopolis: Patrick Geddes and the city of life*. Cambridge, MA: MIT Press, 2002.

10
Domenico Andriello and the 'città dell'uomo'

Gemma Belli

Reflecting today on the exchange between Italian and British culture after the Second World War is of particular interest, because it allows us to reason about the position that Italian urban planning had in the world during the twentieth century, with regard to its specificity, its debts and its ability to engage in dialogue. In fact, until recently, studies of the circulation of ideas have reserved modest attention for Italy, both from a cross-fertilization point of view and from that of dissemination.[1] The first direction has primarily been investigated in the fields of philosophy and sociology, with reference to the mutual exchange established between Europe and America, with changing origins and destinations; the second direction, on the other hand, was widely followed in planning studies in the second half of the twentieth century, especially in the relationship with the United States. In the latter case, with the emergence of the imperial role of the US, the issue of the transmission of ideas and practices was interpreted – according to the reading suggested by Stephen V. Ward – as a 'loan' or as 'imposition', depending on the order of the relationship between the 'transmitter' and the 'receiving' subject.[2] But, in any case, within these studies, the Italian position and contribution has generally been recognized as marginal.[3]

In this context, the recent research of Lorenzo Ciccarelli certainly composes an interesting picture, because it reconstructs the exchanges and mutual influences between Italian and British urban culture from 1945 to the early 1960s, and highlights how in that period, in the urban planning field, Great Britain exercised an incisive and lasting attraction and influence for Italian authors.[4]

Within this discourse, it is important to shine a light on the role played by urban planner Domenico Andriello. Calabrian by birth but Neapolitan by adoption, he was significantly active from the late 1940s for over two decades, but his contribution was often underestimated, or deliberately neglected, partly because of the general hostility reserved for him during his life by the politically conservative Neapolitan academy of those years.

But how did Italy, and Naples in particular, appear at that historical moment?

It was pointed out that at the beginning of the twentieth century Italian urban culture showed a considerable detachment from the European and American scenarios, pervaded by radical changes in technology and culture, and it had taken a position that the American historian Stephen Kern did not hesitate to define as expressing a nation 'mired in the past, obsessed with the relics and monuments of the glory of a dead civilization'.[5] Then, in the 1920s, when Gustavo Giovannoni inaugurated the new discipline, he substantiated the new identity by significantly drawing on European cultures characterized by a more advanced development. Trying to reconcile the reasons and the identity of the ancient city with the needs of the new building, he undertook to combine these traditions in a triple technical, artistic and humanistic value, referring to those whom, somewhat rhetorically, he defined the 'holy fathers' of urban planning: Camillo Sitte, Michel Dikanski, Eugène Hénard and Hans Ludwig Sierks.[6] A few years later, Luigi Piccinato assimilated Giovannoni's legacy, mediating it with modern elements and, as has often been pointed out, strengthening it with German specialist manuals and with a strong focus on the sociology of knowledge of Karl Mannheim.

After the war, when the general cultural orientation undertook the insistent search for a democratic horizon to escape from Fascism, two directions were crossed. On the one hand, the lesson of the modern was intertwined with the values of the new era, symbolized by the United States, the Anglo-Saxon world in general, and Marxism, taken as a synonym for democracy. On the other hand, an intransigent rejection of Modernity emerged, through a form of coercive planning, which found a long and controversial manifestation in the line drawn from Antonio Cederna to Salvatore Settis.[7]

An urban planner facing modernization

Domenico Andriello's work can certainly be placed along the first direction. Born in 1909, he graduated in civil engineering in Naples in

1936, having Cesare Valle as thesis supervisor, and proposed an idea for a plan for Addis Ababa. There, just that year, Valle had started working together with Ignazio Guidi. After collaborating with Valle on the construction of the Viceregal Palace in the Ethiopian capital, Andriello assisted him for three years, from 1938 to 1940, as a volunteer assistant in teaching *Tecnica Urbanistica*. He took on the job himself in 1940. However, the distrust of the Neapolitan academy, which was decidedly Christian Democrat at that time, prevented him from gaining the acknowledgement he aspired to.

The relationship with the Roman master appears as one of the fundamental formative moments of his path. Older by only seven years, Valle had graduated 12 years earlier in civil architecture at the Royal Higher Institute of Engineering in Rome, and he had immediately become a volunteer assistant to Gustavo Giovannoni. He had therefore engaged in a very wide range of disciplines, from historical to architectural subjects, combined with urban planning and technical issues, and he had immediately cultivated the habit of frequenting the key centres of architectural debate, including the editorial board of *Architettura e Arti Decorative*, where he consolidated his relationship with Luigi Piccinato, a person to whom Andriello, as we shall see, would also be particularly attached.

But in the years in which Andriello was trained, the concept of urban planning was also strongly influenced by the teaching of Cesare Chiodi in Italian engineering faculties. Chiodi was the holder of the first course in *Tecnica Urbanistica* from 1929, and author of the volume *La città moderna*, which appeared for the first time in 1935, published by Hoepli. He was also an urban planner who connected teaching with professional practice, with associations and with political activity, and he formed a collective awareness of urban planning after the Second World War, with a view to protecting the historic city, and taking the example of the European nations to which he attributed more significant advancement.[8] This question of urban planning awareness was cultivated in particular from 1949 by the well-known archaeologist-journalist Antonio Cederna in the pages of *Il Mondo*, the weekly directed by Mario Pannunzio.[9] The issue was combined with the necessity 'to finally make the citizens co-responsible for the development of their city, to convince them that the city can become what they want it to be, a place of civil life instead of segregation and punishment, and to enlighten them not to exchange some small action … for democratic politics'.[10] Moreover, from 1935, Chiodi extended the vision of the master plan from the city to the region, because he believed that the problem is no longer that of indefinitely increasing the capacity of the city to receive new crowds within it, but to keep those crowds in the surrounding territory.

In particular, then, after the Second World War, the Neapolitan environment – in which Andriello worked after graduating – being traditionally linked to the Roman one, was invested by the exegesis that Bruno Zevi made of the work of Frank Lloyd Wright and organic architecture. The latter was felt as a stylistic and ethical choice together: not only as a possible linguistic declination, but as an adhesion to values aimed at creating more 'human' spaces. Thus, two years after the foundation of the Roman nucleus of the APAO, in February 1947, the Campania section was also established: it included personalities such as Roberto Pane, Giulio de Luca, Luigi Cosenza, Carlo Cocchia, Michele Cretella, a young, just-graduated Roberto Mango, and importantly, Domenico Andriello (who was 38 years old at the time); all of whom would participate in the Association's First National Congress, organized in Rome from 6 to 8 December of the same year. In addition, from 1948 to 1952 Andriello was called to head the Campania section of the INU (which also included Luigi Cosenza and Carlo Cocchia), the Institute which, with the re-foundation initiated by Adriano Olivetti in 1948, became the constant point of reference for the most advanced forces of Italian architectural culture. In this context, the peripheral sections became decisive in the co-ordination of regional studies, as well as for the timely defence of the territory and local urban planning.

From October 1949, Andriello was also a member of the commission for the reform of the Urban Planning Law 1150 of 1942, among others, together with Giovanni Astengo, Francesco Cuccia, Amos Edallo, Eugenio Fuselli, Federico Gorio, Luigi Piccinato, Virgilio Testa and Cesare Valle.

But above all, as mentioned before, it must be considered that Luigi Piccinato was teaching in the Faculty of Architecture in Naples from 1930. Called by the then dean Alberto Calza Bini, Piccinato immediately held the course in *Edilizia cittadina e arte dei giardini*, called *Urbanistica* in all Italian architecture faculties from 1932. In the Neapolitan capital Piccinato taught until 1950, and was also in charge of the famous Plan of 1936–9. And he elaborated *Urbanistica: Compendio di tecnica urbanistica e di urbanistica generale*, based on the lessons held between 1942 and 1943: a volume that offered itself as a field of direct experimentation for the most famous *Urbanistica*, published by the Roman publisher Sandron in 1947. A lasting friendship was established immediately between the Neapolitan urban planner and the elder Venetian (of Roman adoption); it would continue even when Piccinato moved to Venice, after winning the professorship. This was testified, for example, by Piccinato's presence at the *Urbanistica e tecnica della pianificazione* seminars, organized in the early 1960s by Domenico Andriello. Convinced that urban planning could not coincide with urban art, but that it is a synthetic discipline, which combines economic and social considerations with renewed technical and artistic needs, Andriello was strongly influenced by the older master. [11] From Piccinato, in fact, Andriello borrowed, first of all, the idea of the city as an organism, in which 'the figure is one with the content', rather than a 'drawn crystal'; and thus he considered the problem of form fallacious and compromising of the real problems to which the urban planner is called to respond. Organism is the metaphor that alludes to the tendency of each city to adapt to the context and to change, expressed in socio-economic connotations; organism is the metaphor that defines the link that each civilization establishes between urban language and the structure of society.

In particular, Andriello argued that throughout the various ages our planet has been the scene of a great struggle between the autocratic (or, in the etymological meaning of the word, monarchical) principle and the democratic one. The dominance of one or the other idea has had direct repercussions on the organization of the social structure and consequently of its headquarters.[12]

Furthermore, referring to Frank Lloyd Wright's *When Democracy Builds*,[13] he wrote 'how the monarchy was the ideal of centralization – major axis and minor axis – men forced to rotate around an exalted common centre (exploitation of human unity); thus democracy is the ideal of reintegrated decentralizations – the reflection: many free units that develop strength in growth and function jointly in wide mutual freedom'.[14] Therefore, if the geometric city is an expression of autocratic society, the organic city – created by the free development of social forces, with due knowledge of the terrain, of the geographical characteristics, of the landscape – is the mirror of a democratic society, towards which the modern trends.

And it is always through Piccinato's mediation that Andriello came to frame these issues by taking them directly from some experiences from British urban culture, with respect to which, we could say that in turn he's a 'passatore'.[15] In fact, in the context of a scientific production that began in 1946 with an article in *La città nuova*[16] – the magazine of Giovanni Michelucci – and ended 20 years later, with the volume *Il pensiero utopistico e la Città dell'uomo*,[17] Andriello not only dealt with a variety of themes ranging from specifically disciplinary and terminological issues to tourism planning over a large area, but above all he was committed to studying and proposing Anglo-Saxon planning experiences and models, applicable to the Italian context. And he often did so, from the pages of *Urbanistica*, a magazine in whose editorial office he worked as a Neapolitan correspondent. The article 'Il precinct, unità urbanistica a funzione non residenziale' dates back to 1948.[18] And the arguments proposed therein would be resumed and developed in the subsequent intervention *Della preservazione precintuale dei nuclei storici*, which he illustrated at the National Urban Planning Congress, held in Naples in 1948.

The precinct, a term that in Italian can be translated as 'recinto' (but which Andriello reports always in English), represents a medium-sized protected area, in which vehicles do not enjoy free transit and the inhabitants can take advantage of spaces dedicated to them, of services and equipment typical of an urban centre, suitably located, as well as of vehicle or railway systems connecting one precinct to another. The precinct is 'an area with a simple or complex function, completely segregated from the crossing traffic, which flows around without invading it'.[19] According to Carlo Olmo, Andriello deduced this concept directly from the English urban planner Thomas Sharp, who had expounded it in the paper *Exeter Phoenix*, which appeared two years earlier.[20]

Furthermore, accepting the position of Patrick Abercrombie – the first, in his opinion, to have dealt with it concretely – as well as that of Gerhard Kallemann, Andriello specified that the size of the precinct must be studied in such a way that no part of it is segregated from the main traffic system, more than what appears compatible with the function, and its shape and size must be determined according to the 'innate vitality and character of the area'.[21] Furthermore, to allow the contraction and expansion of each unit, the limits should be identified independently of the network of secondary traffic routes. In this context, the precincts with a residential function (the so-called 'neighbourhoods'), developed around social institutions, must be considered separately, and also the historical-monumental nucleus constitutes a particular precinct, which urban planning must approach with 'loving and devoted care for the fear of destroying, with its daring modernism, even that imponderable "quid" that permeates every square, every street, every corner', and which cannot be treated according to a pre-established pattern.[22]

Therefore, since the organic city is made up of different parts, or organs, each with specific functions intended to carry out the tasks necessary for the life of the complex, precinctual planning became the founding basis of Andriello's conception. A concept that, in his opinion, is applicable to both newly formed agglomerations and existing cities, subject to an appropriate reorganization or reconstruction of parts. According to Andriello, in the Italian reality, this scheme can show great interest also and above all for 'the applications that it may have in the future restructuring of our old and historic cities'.[23]

Reflections on the precinct

The model, as is well known, was reworked in the US by Clarence Perry in preparatory investigations for the New York region plan in 1920, not only as a practical solution to the traffic problem in city neighbourhoods, but with the deliberate intent to help the inhabitants acquire a community sense of identity. Subsequently, it had been employed by Patrick Abercrombie and used extensively for the plans of the County of London (1943) and Greater London (1944), and applied in London's East End by Alker Tripp. Twenty years later, another Englishman, Colin Buchanan, would rejoin the idea in the well-known ministerial report on the traffic problem in Great Britain, published in 1963 under the title *Traffic in Towns*. However, it can be said that in fact it was Ebenezer Howard who imagined the garden city divided into 'precincts': wards of about 5,000 inhabitants, each of which containing shops, schools and services. The practical principle at its heart consisted in ensuring that some services, used daily by some groups of the population not inclined to long journeys, should have been placed in a central position relative to the small community they served and at a distance that could always be covered on foot.

Therefore, proposing to apply the precinct model to the Italian reality, Andriello took up the scheme of the garden city proposed by Howard, developing it on several occasions. The first of these was the report *L'idea della città giardino nella realtà urbanistica italiana* presented in 1963 at the Conférence du cinquantenaire de la Fédération Internationale pour l'Habitation, l'Urbanisme et l'Aménagement des Territoires in 1963; it was followed by the volume *Howard o dell'eutopia* in 1964 and *Il pensiero utopistico e la città dell'uomo* in 1966.

Even in this case the Neapolitan urban planner was linked to the ideas of Piccinato, who, in the well-known volume of 1947, had written:

> we are today on the threshold of a new urban planning era ... with new tasks, with new organization. From what fixed points must we move forward and what legacy handed down to us by our fathers? ... the last century, to those who know how to look at it precisely in its latest developments, which extend beyond the beginning of the

> twentieth century, has already said its word ... The battle found its champions in the men of the Ruskinian literary group: until the true cry of victory was launched by Howard in his now famous *Garden City of Tomorrow* (1898–1902). 'Return to the land' ... Ruralizing urban life; urbanizing the countryside ... These words contain the new basic position of modern urbanism, the verb that we must collect, the real conquest of last Century's urbanism.[24]

The problem of the modern city is then resolved in the dissolution of the city into an infinitely larger and more open organism, with a decentralization capable of bringing suitable conditions of social and urban life into the territory surrounding the city, and into the countryside. And it is precisely with this in mind that Andriello viewed Howard's theory from a different point of view from Carlo Doglio, for example.[25] Luigi Mazza remarked that according to Doglio, who considered urban planning a form of social action, the interest in Howard's utopia can only be modest; while, considering it a technique, it must be agreed that some essential characteristics of the strongest professional culture in the twentieth century can be traced back, directly or indirectly, to some of the themes developed by Howard's proposal.[26] Andriello, for his part, grasped in the theory of the garden city the interdependence between urban form and regional development, and the fact that the housing issue cannot be tackled in isolation, but must be considered an urban and urban design problem, within an overall reform programme of the city and the territory, capable of taking into account the interactions between home, work and leisure, between land use and mobility: just as there isn't a solution to the housing question outside of urban planning, so there isn't a solution to the urban question outside of regional planning. Moreover, Louis Mumford too, whose reflections Andriello never failed to praise, always had great sympathy for the garden city movement and for Howard's theories. In this perspective, in 1950 Andriello still expressed himself very positively on English planning culture, this time taking into consideration the study presented two years earlier by the West Midland Group on post-war reconstruction for the arrangement of Birmingham and the whole so-called conurbation of the area connected to this centre, known as the Black Country.[27] After having praised the role of Patrick Geddes (regarding the identification of a close connection between social sciences and human groupings, and the inclusion in the complex urban landscape of the geographical frame, climatic and meteorological factors, economic processes and historical traditions), attributing the primacy of the term conurbation, Andriello illustrated the plan. And he showed that he appreciated the principle of thinning applied to unhealthy central areas, the creation of specific commercial, social and cultural areas, the overall rethinking of the transport network based on the local administrative structure, the attention paid to the reclamation of more polluted areas and the parallel dislocation and segregation of harmful industries, as well as the demolition of unsanitary plants. In this case he also hoped that his indications could be understood and applied 'one day in the revision and arrangement of industrial, commercial or agricultural conurbations that are not lacking in the surroundings of some of our large cities'.[28]

Ultimately, for the Neapolitan scholar, the models and examples of planning offered by British countries were those that allowed him to 'anticipate the future and see far away', a term that summarizes what for him should be the goal of every urban planner.

In this regard, he wrote:

> and yet, we cannot prevent our generation from committing the future. We lay the foundations or not. We keep what the future will need or we waste it. We weave a texture; it may be extremely useful to our posterity or not serve them at all. The successes and failures of our fathers are before us to remind us that the results of urban planning last for centuries, for better and for worse. And what's worst of all, the process we initiate is practically irreversible. That's why we must strive to anticipate the future and see far.[29]

Notes

1 A. Belli 2015, 81.
2 Ward 2000, 40–60; Ward 2003, 83–106. Ward's reasoning is based on some particularly influential studies such as: Hall 1996; King 1990; Sutcliffe 1981.
3 A. Belli 2015, 81.
4 Ciccarelli 2019.
5 Kern 1983.
6 A. Belli 1996.
7 A. Belli 2015, 82.
8 Chiodi 1951.
9 A. Belli and G. Belli 2012.
10 Cederna 1965, 72.
11 Andriello 1958.
12 Andriello 1948, 5.
13 Wright 1945.
14 Wright 1945, cited in Andriello 1948, 5.
15 I refer to the expression used by: Todorov 2010. For Todorov, in fact, the 'passatore' is a subject who, after having personally crossed borders, tries to facilitate their passage for others: borders between countries, between languages, cultures; and then between fields of study and disciplines, but also between the banal and the essential, the everyday and the sublime.
16 Andriello 1946.

17 Andriello 1966.
18 Andriello 1948, 5–8.
19 Andriello 1948, 6.
20 See: Olmo 1992.
21 Andriello 1948, 7.
22 Andriello 1948, 7.
23 Andriello 1948, 8.
24 Piccinato 1988, 154–5.
25 Doglio 1953.
26 Mazza 2002.
27 Andriello 1950.
28 Andriello 1950, 59.
29 Andriello 1964, 114–15.

References

Andriello, Domenico. 'Intorno alla denominazione di una nuova scienza (urbanistica o geoproscopia?)', *La nuova città* 6–7 (1946), 7–10.

Andriello, Domenico. 'Il precinct, unità urbanistica a funzione non residenziale', *Metron* 28 (1948): 5–8.

Andriello, Domenico. 'Conurbation: Indagine su Birmingham e sulla Black Country', *Urbanistica* 5 (1950): 56–9.

Andriello, Domenico. *Urbanistica scienza dell'uomo*. Rome: Dapco, 1958.

Andriello, Domenico. 'L'idea della città giardino nella realtà urbanistica italiana'. Conference paper given at the Conférence du cinquantenaire de la Fédération Internationale pour l'Habitation, l'Urbanisme et l'Aménagement des Territoires (FIHUAT), Arnhem, 24–29 June 1963. Rome: Dapco, 1963.

Andriello, Domenico. *Howard o dell'eutopia*. Naples: Libreria Internazionale Minerva, 1964.

Andriello, Domenico. *Il pensiero utopistico e la città dell'uomo*. Naples: Libreria Internazionale Minerva, 1966.

Belli, Attilio. *Immagini e concetti nel piano: Inizi dell'urbanistica in Italia*. Milan: Etas, 1996.

Belli, Attilio. 'Il buon tradimento'. In *L'urbanistica italiana nel mondo: Contributi e debiti culturali*, edited by Alessandro Balducci and Luca Gaeta, 81–7. Rome: Donzelli, 2015.

Belli, Attilio and Gemma Belli. *Narrare l'urbanistica alle élite: 'Il Mondo' (1949–1966) di fronte alla modernizzazione del Bel Paese*. Milan: Franco Angeli, 2012.

Cederna, Antonio. *Mirabilia urbis: Cronache romane 1957–1965*. Turin: Einaudi, 1965.

Chiodi, Cesare. 'Comunicazione'. In *3. Congresso nazionale di Urbanistica, Roma 15–18 giugno 1950*. Rome: INU, 1951.

Ciccarelli, Lorenzo. *Il mito dell'equilibrio: Il dibattito anglo-italiano per il governo del territorio negli anni del dopoguerra*. Milan: Franco Angeli, 2019.

Doglio, Carlo. *L'equivoco della città giardino*. Naples: Edizioni RL, 1953.

Hall, Peter. *Cities of Tomorrow: An intellectual history of urban planning and design in the twentieth century*. Oxford: Blackwell, 1996.

Kern, Stephen. *The Culture of Time and Space 1880–1918*. Cambridge, MA: Harvard University Press, 1983.

King, Anthony D. *Urbanism, Colonialism and the World-Economy: Cultural and spatial foundations of the world economic system*. London: Routledge, 1990.

Mazza, Luigi. 'Ebenezer Howard, Garden Cities of Tomorrow (1902)'. In *I classici dell'urbanistica italiana*, edited by Paola Di Biagi, 19–31. Rome: Donzelli, 2002.

Olmo, Carlo. *Urbanistica e società civile*. Rome–Ivrea: Edizioni di Comunità, 1992.

Piccinato, Luigi. *Urbanistica: Compendio di tecnica urbanistica e di urbanistica generale*. Rome: Ferri, 1943.

Piccinato, Luigi. *Urbanistica*. Rome: Sandron, 1947. Subsequently published as: Piccinato, Luigi. *La progettazione urbanistica: La città come organismo*, edited by Giovanni Astengo. Venice: Marsilio, 1988.

Sharp, Thomas. 'Exeter Phoenix', *The Architectural Review* 99 (1946): 127.

Sharp, Thomas. *Exeter Phoenix: A plan for rebuilding*. London: Architectural Press, 1946.
Sutcliffe, Anthony. *Towards the Planned City: Germany, Britain, the United States and France, 1780–1914*. Oxford: Blackwell, 1981.
Todorov, Tzvetan. *Una vita da passatore: Conversazione con Catherine Portevin*. Palermo: Sellerio, 2010.
Ward, Stephen V. 'Re-examining the international diffusion of planning'. In *Urban Planning in a Changing World: The twentieth century experience*, edited by Robert Freestone, 40–60. London: Routledge, 2000.
Ward, Stephen. 'Learning from the US: The Americanization of Western urban planning'. In *Urbanism: Imported or exported?*, edited by Joe Nasr and Mercedes Volait, 83–106. Chichester: Wiley–Academy, 2003.
Wright, Frank Lloyd. *When Democracy Builds*. Chicago: University of Chicago Press, 1945.

11

From futurism to 'town-room': Hodgkinson, the Brunswick and the low-rise/high-density principle

Clare Melhuish

Prologue

Fifteen years on from the refurbishment of Patrick Hodgkinson's Brunswick Centre, now known simply as 'The Brunswick', it is hard to remember how bleak and uninhabited, yet memorable and in some ways poetic, the central public space between the imposing, linear housing blocks used to be.[1] For 30 years it fuelled security problems and anti-social behaviour, while falling into a progressive state of decay. But since 2006 (or at least until the COVID-19 pandemic struck) it has been a busy social hub, with a large high-end supermarket, refurbished cinema, numerous clothing shops, restaurants and cafés, and regular festival events, which offer a particular draw to the hundreds of students who frequent the area. But in the course of my observations and interviews with the residents who live in the flats above it between 2001 and 2006, I heard a range of views on this curious, concrete, traffic-free terrain, notably singled out for criticism by Richard Sennett as 'dead public space', typifying the decline of the public sphere,[2] and most commonly referred to as a 'precinct' in contrast to the verdant historic squares of the surrounding neighbourhood. The relationship between this space and the housing above it is acoustically very intimate; but to get a view of the precinct from the flats that look across it towards each other, and up to the sky, you need to stand up and look down with some deliberation. Once the shop fronts were extended into the space under the refurbishment scheme, with additional permanent canopies on each side

Figure 11.1 The Brunswick precinct, view to north, newly refurbished in 2006 by Levitt Bernstein, with the retail frontage extended by canopies: 'a high street for Bloomsbury'

further narrowing the central concourse, the visual boundary between the flats and the public zone below was further delineated, and so too was the social boundary for some residents who felt the formerly empty space, with its abandoned retail units, single café and affordable supermarket, had become out of reach.

Not all of course – Susan started to enjoy the buzz of the precinct, while on maternity leave, and would regularly meet up, outside the new Starbucks, with the other new mothers for whom it provided a convenient meeting-place. By contrast, Conal, working from home, had no need or reason to engage with the activities of the precinct during the day apart from shopping at Waitrose, and therefore found it disruptive and disturbing. Meanwhile Giulia, one of the oldest residents, had retreated into her private domain, a sad development for someone who used to enjoy sitting out in the precinct chatting with friends. Yet from an architectural and social perspective, the change in the character of the Brunswick's public space both highlights the failures of the original realization, and the idealism and potential of Hodgkinson's conception of a 'town room', which was key to his understanding of the need for a humanistic approach to the reconstruction of central city areas following the Second World War, rooted in a sense of historical continuity.

Introduction

The Brunswick Centre in central London was finally listed as a building of historical and architectural importance in 2000, on the cusp of redevelopment as 'The Brunswick: A High Street for Bloomsbury' by a commercial developer (completed 2006). It was described in the Department of Culture, Media and Sport's Listing Schedule as 'a pioneering example of a megastructure in England: of a scheme which combines several functions of equal importance within a single framework. It is also the pioneering example of low-rise, high-density housing, a field in which Britain was extremely influential on this scale ... Brunswick developed the concept of the stepped section on a large scale and for a range of facilities, whose formality was pioneering'.[3] This description echoed the appraisal of the building nearly 30 years earlier by critic Theo Crosby, in the *Architectural Review*'s special celebratory issue, published on its completion: '... perhaps the first built example of the idea of an urban "megastructure" – a building that is a city, rather than being merely a component in a city'.[4] Crosby's appraisal was mostly complimentary, and the megastructure tag was taken up enthusiastically by Reyner Banham in his eponymous volume a few years later. He immortalized the Brunswick as 'The most pondered, most learned, most acclaimed, most monumental, most bedevilled in its building history of all English megastructures – and seemingly the best-liked by its inhabitants'.[5] Hodgkinson, however, was not impressed. He was scathing about Banham's status as a critic, and always rejected the definition of the Brunswick as a 'megastructure', which bore no relation to what he had intended in the design he worked on from 1958 onwards, and had already, as a form, been condemned as a 'monumental folly' in an article condemning the authorities' clearance mentality by planner Peter Hall in 1968.[6]

This chapter will suggest that the historiographic emphasis on the Brunswick's 'megastructure' labelling, which was reiterated in the Italian press,[7] has obscured other influences on the conception of the building that were swirling around the Architectural Association (AA), where Hodgkinson studied from 1950–5, and the London-based architectural press during the 1950s and 60s. Among these, as other chapters in this volume reveal, the dialogue with Italian architects and writers was critical to debates about the right way to approach the post-war reconstruction of European cities, against the backdrop of the UK's short-lived embrace of the Welfare State, and the Italian reinstatement of democracy.

As principal of the AA from 1949–51, Robert Furneaux-Jordan (who taught ancient history and 'had a sense of humour', according to Hodgkinson[8]) hailed the Italian approach to architecture and planning as 'a third way' between vernacular Swedish empiricism and the International Style – 'between vernacular cosiness … and formalism',[9] in his introduction to the RIBA's exhibition Italian Contemporary Architecture of 1952. As Mingardi (this volume) recounts, the first CIAM summer school was held at the AA in 1949, following the CIAM 7 meeting at Bergamo that year, and paving the way for CIAM 8 at Hoddesdon (1951). Italian architects including Ernesto Rogers played a leading role in this meeting, which was dedicated to the theme of 'The Heart of the City', with a focus on Italian towns – particularly Venice and its Piazza San Marco. The following year, 1952, the first Italian CIAM summer school took place in Venice itself, attended by Giancarlo de Carlo and Joseph Rykwert among the younger generation of Italian and British architects, with Le Corbusier as distinguished guest. These meetings would pave the way for the codification of the Habitat Charter at Aix-en-Provence (CIAM 9, 1953) and the creation of Team X, in which de Carlo, Candilis and Woods, van Eyck, and the Smithsons would make a core contribution as members to the development of its critique of the Athens Charter. The group shared an interest in an anthropological or sociological approach to architecture, drawing on historical, cultural, and regional specificities.

In 1963, Joseph Rykwert's seminal text, *The Idea of a Town: The anthropology of urban form in Rome, Italy and the Ancient World,*[10] was published by Aldo van Eyck in the journal *Forum,* revealing the mythologies, morphology and sociology underlying the evolution of Rome and ancient city cultures, as a provocation to the prevailing ideology of functionalism and rationalization in urban planning that Team X also opposed. In London, the *Architectural Review* (*AR*), under the leadership of publisher Hubert de Cronin Hastings and his editorial team (J.M. Richards, Nikolaus Pevsner, Gordon Cullen and Kenneth Browne) had also started its 'Townscape' campaign, looking to Italian historic towns and cities as a source of inspiration for an approach to urban planning that celebrated a visual approach to design based on historical awareness and an ideal of public space. It was marked by the publication of Gordon Cullen's *Townscape* in 1961 (and *Concise Townscape*, now an urban planning classic, in 1971)[11] followed by *The Italian Townscape* by Ivor de Wolfe (de Cronin Hastings's pseudonym) with photographs of Italy by his wife Ivy (also a pseudonym).[12] The brief editorial to the 1972 issue of *AR* in which the Brunswick Centre was featured, referred to the development 'as the first fusion in one building of housing, commerce and townscape in a civilized way'[13] and headlined its introduction 'A good bit of city'.[14] Not coincidentally, the issue also featured Giancarlo de Carlo's project for the Law Faculty at the University of Urbino, entitled 'Urbino Renewal', and another feature on the competition for a new business centre in Perugia.[15]

Although Hodgkinson never explicitly referenced the influence of this intense UK–Italian exchange in architecture and planning, these concerns and principles, within a framework of resistance to Corbusian ideology and the Athens Charter, which Hodgkinson also strongly subscribed to, are fundamental to the design evolution of the Brunswick, as this chapter will show. It will focus on two key concerns – those of historical continuity, and ideals of public space, which are manifested in the Brunswick. Firstly, however, it will explore its ambivalent relationship with an earlier Italian artistic and architectural movement, futurism, which Banham had celebrated as the embodiment of 'the mechanical sensibility' defining modernism.[16] As Spina (this volume) explains, Banham positioned futurism in direct counterpoint to the post-war Italian historical and representational approach that he criticized in no uncertain terms, setting the Italian and Anglo-Saxon traditions at opposite ends of the spectrum in terms of their relationship to modernity. Banham also drew a direct line of connection between the work of the Italian futurist architect Sant'Elia and the Brunswick, highlighting the latter as a manifestation of an ultra-Modern outlook – one that Hodgkinson would strongly contest, insisting that the Brunswick was not intended to be modern at all.

Futurism and the Brunswick's rejection of modernism

Banham considered the Brunswick to be the high point of megastructure design in Britain, which he traced to two key sources: Sant'Elia's futurist city (1914), and Le Corbusier's Fort l'Empereur (1931) proposals, hypothetical though these were. He insisted that the Brunswick scheme owed much to the work of Sant'Elia[17] who, in his Manifesto of 1914, had famously rubbished traditional architecture, exalting 'the new beauty of cement and steel' in architecture, the construction of a futurist city modelled on 'an immense, bustling shipyard' with 'metallic catwalks and high-speed conveyor belts', and the futurist house as 'a kind of gigantic machine'.[18]

Banham described Sant'Elia as 'the virtual inventor of both the A-frame *Terrassenhauser* section and the vision of giant buildings spanning over traffic arteries'[19] and the Brunswick, therefore, with its

Figure 11.2 View looking due south of winter gardens to Foundling Court, prior to refurbishment

visually dramatic stepped 'winter gardens', as a tribute to him: 'one of the ultimate ancestors of megastructure ... Not only do the residential sections, with their *case a gradinate* over tall public access spaces within the A-frames proclaim his paternity; so also do the twinned towers flanking the entrances and stairs, the modelling and the battering of the surfaces around those entrances ... '.[20]

In reality, Sant'Elia's mechanical, inhumane vision of architecture and the city, which celebrated brutality and ugliness as the unavoidable counterpart of modernity, could not have been more opposed to the more traditional inclinations that Hodgkinson espoused, as this chapter will explain. He was infuriated by Banham's reference to the Brunswick's 'patent borrowings'[21] from Sant'Elia's work.

When English Heritage, in its 1992 listing appraisal of the Brunswick again emphasized a Sant'Elia connection, suggesting that the grand portico to Brunswick Square in particular was 'a direct crib' from Sant'Elia's Milan railway station project,[22] Hodgkinson was at pains to dissociate himself from it, insisting that he 'never knew' a Milan railway station project by Sant'Elia – indeed that it was 'a project he is not known to have done',[23] and that Banham had made a mistake. He distinguishes his own 'portico' at the Brunswick as a 'loggia',[24] pointing to its origins in an early scheme of his own for the site, which treated the entire east elevation to Brunswick Square as a long colonnade above the stepped profile. The portal as it stands today constitutes the remnant of this linear loggia, and was never conceived as a grand flourish or set-piece in the manner of the supposed Sant'Elia reference.

Hodgkinson admitted he was drawn to some aspects of futurism, in particular the idea of the sky as a transcendental plane of escape from mundane everyday life, particularly in the dreary streets of post-war London, as he saw it. But by his own account he was more interested in the work of the futurist artist and sculptor Boccioni than that of Sant'Elia. Boccioni published his own Manifesto in 1914, in which he also railed against the 'slavery' of architecture to the past, but emphasized the importance of expressing emotion through architectonic construction[25] – which struck a chord with Hodgkinson. It is hard to deny that the soaring A-frames framing the internal atria of the housing blocks give the place something of a futuristic, if not precisely futurist, feel that even

Figure 11.3 View through apex of concrete A-frame structure supporting housing block, with access level to atrium below

© C. Melhuish 2001

Hodgkinson did not deny: 'the A-frame is very modern – I slipped up with that! It's not traditional at all'.[26]

But the A-frame structure itself had not been part of the original design of the Brunswick, and emerged only as a by-product of changes in building legislation that meant the structure had to be engineered and executed in reinforced concrete instead of brick. The A-frame, developed with engineer Felix Samuely, who had taught at the AA, and whom Hodgkinson had worked with during his student days, provided a resolution of that issue.

Far more significant, in architectural and aesthetic terms, was the use of the stepped section. Hodgkinson believed this form eloquently expressed a direct connection with the sky while also retaining a firm link with terra firma:[27] an ideal 'liminal place' – between the homely and the transcendent – which perfectly embodied his aspirations. He stressed the importance of historical precedents and social continuity embodied in the Brunswick, as a considered piece of urban place-making rooted in the eighteenth/nineteenth-century central London neighbourhood of Bloomsbury, as the next section will show.

Historical continuity

Hodgkinson personally saw the Brunswick as the direct descendant of a much older, native model of urban form than the megastructure, and that was the Adelphi, designed and built in London as a grand speculative development of houses over vaulted warehouses, near the Thames, by the Adam brothers from 1768. The Brunswick was the first London development since the war to mix housing with other uses and, like the Adelphi, it represented a fusion of speculation on a grand scale with ambitious architectural vision and enormous risk. Banham's reference to the relentlessly rationalizing, aggrandizing Fort l'Empereur project designed by Le Corbusier for Algiers in 1931, as a key source for British megastructure design, further rankled with Hodgkinson, whose design approach was rooted in an explicit rejection of the Corbusian modernist values that dominated much of the teaching at the AA during his student days. Le Corbusier's technocratic rationalism and break with the past was fundamentally at odds with his own vision of architecture, which drew inspiration from a range of historical precedents.

In 1951 Hodgkinson had been to Marseilles to see for himself Le Corbusier's Unité d'Habitation, the first built example of his innovative prototype for mass housing designed as a concrete slab block raised on stilts. But his personal experience of the Unité convinced him that it was the wrong solution to future housing construction. As far as he was concerned, it was an 'impenetrable slab unacceptable for towns and society ... stranded, alien to its surroundings, severing the continuity of space or time'.[28] He noted that, while tall point blocks exert a radial force on their surroundings, producing 'residual and negative space'.[29] linear buildings, exemplified by the British Georgian terraces organized in streets, crescents and squares, characteristic of the Bloomsbury area of London in which the Brunswick is located, have the potential to contain space positively.

While studying at the AA school, Hodgkinson also worked at the firm of Ward and Austin on the design of the Riverside Restaurant beneath Waterloo Bridge for the 1951 Festival of Britain on the South Bank. Hodgkinson loved the Festival, unlike peers of his such as Jim Stirling, who considered it much 'too Swedish', and other critics who disliked its populist character and derided what was called 'People's Detailing'. That agenda actually fitted in with Hodgkinson's own idea of architecture as a 'humanist' profession, as well as an interest in Scandinavian modernism that was to develop through his experience of working for Alvar Aalto in Finland in 1953.[30]

He found further inspiration in a range of other sources, especially the architectural traditions of his own country – notably the English Gothic and other medieval building traditions. He loved the English hall tradition represented by 'magical great houses like Penshurst, Haddon and Lacock and their smaller, manorial sisters'.[31] By the end of his student years he had also become interested in the nineteenth-century revival of these traditions, in the work of the 'good' English Arts and Crafts architects, notably Lethaby and Voysey, which was regarded with some scorn by his contemporaries. While they continued to focus on the built and published manifestos of Le Corbusier and the Bauhaus, Hodgkinson made the decision at the end of his third year to leave London and work with Alvar Aalto in Finland for nine months.

Although Hodgkinson always stressed his non-academic approach to architecture, he had also been reading Lewis Mumford's books, particularly the *Culture of Cities* (1940), in which he introduces the concept of the superblock.[32] Hodgkinson explained that, 'In this he describes some New York planners' ideas of rebuilding areas of the city as "superblocks" for whole communities with traffic kept to the perimeters, with the social advantages this would bring. The Brunswick was a smaller area – even for its intended length – but then Bloomsbury was smaller scale than New York.'[33] Mumford seemed to point the way towards a brighter future after the dreadful war years, while his later book

The Highway and the City (1963) offered an overt criticism of the Unité concept, or 'the Marseille "Folly"', as he put it.[34] Hodgkinson was happy for the Brunswick to be defined as 'superblock' rather than 'megastructure',[35] affirming 'that Mumford was my largest inspiration … As for directly architectural influences, I was not drawn by Corbu, Gropius or Mies, more by futurism than Cubism. I much admired Mendelsohn's German buildings – I thought of him as a futurist, not an Expressionist, but I was not too impressed by Sant'Elia because he built nothing … '.[36]

At that time, in an architectural and planning climate dominated by the ruthless thinking and practice of Le Corbusier and the European school of functionalist modernism, Hodgkinson's rich mix of influences and referents – English Gothic, Arts and Crafts and the Festival of Britain, from Scandinavian and modernism to futurism, and from Sartrian existentialism to Lewis Mumford – was unusual. While working during the late 1950s in the office of Leslie Martin, the former head of the London County Council's architecture department, and architect of the point towers of the Alton Estate, Hodgkinson began translating this eclectic mixture directly to his design work. His guiding principle was, he wrote later, 'not to play with an English translation of Le Corbusier's urbanism, as the LCC had done over the summer of that same decade, but to advance a way of building which instead started with the found, and sound, fabric of city'. At the Brunswick, it was 'about making a new village for central London, rich with the panoply of life of the West End's villages of old yet possessing a new, life-giving spirit'.[37]

Hodgkinson was deeply opposed to the *tabula rasa* approach that had underpinned the slum clearance policies of the 1950s, writing of the County of London plan's authors: 'Sir Patrick Abercrombie with his henchman Forshaw – but without much foresight – was to improve away the life a pre-war London had known … The Foundling Estate presented an opportunity to again bring together living, work and recreation to stimulate each other, against normal practice of the time … it would have been a rich village … I have never believed in a modern architecture as "art", but rather as the craft of making liveable towns and cities.'[38] He looked to the native eighteenth- and nineteenth-century traditions of English 'town making', and viewed housing, 'ordinary stock', as a crucial component of this equation: 'housing, after all, is the stuff of which towns are made, rather than public palazzos which only serve to decorate'.[39] He stressed that his design for the Brunswick was about engagement with the local context of Georgian terraces, while looking to Mumford's superblock proposition as a way of potentially dissolving and reshaping the rigid social hierarchy they historically embodied, into a more egalitarian and socially acceptable model fit for the future.

Notably, among this range of references, the influence of Italian historical town-making traditions, and the ongoing dialogue between British and Italian architects and writers of the time, contributing to the development of the Habitat Charter and a more humanistic approach to architecture, is never mentioned. Indeed, as a Suffolk farmer's son, Hodgkinson consciously adopted a role of championing English artistic and cultural traditions, the English landscape and its vernacular building forms, in opposition to the European interests of his metropolitan contemporaries, and later wrote that 'I have never really forgiven Elizabeth David for trying to teach us to cook Mediterranean food, simply because it does not suit our raw materials or our climate'.[40] By contrast, he praised the English Georgian model of housing design as eminently suitable to the temperate British climate, supporting high densities of occupation in conjunction with open spaces. He believed he could re-present at the Brunswick a romantic evocation of a unique, native tradition of construction and settlement patterns, fused with the English landscape and climate, in the form of 'a village ... overlooking nature ... [a] green valley'.[41]

Hodgkinson maintained that he fundamentally disagreed with the Team X approach launched in Aix-en-Provence in 1959, and had deliberately avoided being taught by Peter Smithson in his last year at the Architectural Association, stating that the Smithsons' acclaimed school building at Hunstanton 'appeared to me to be the very opposite of what a school should be, and something like Team X, which was political, was the last way I wanted to make my architecture'.[42] On the other hand, he also had close connections with Joseph Rykwert, with whom he studied both at school and as fellow architecture students at the AA in the early 1950s, and would subsequently fraternize with during the 1960s and 1970s when they both held visiting teaching posts in the United States. He could not have failed to be influenced by his thinking and writing on place and culture, immersed in the long Italian tradition of town-making, and the humanistic approach to architecture that he promoted specifically in opposition to 'those urban planners who consider the city exclusively through the perspective of the economy, hygiene, traffic problems or services' during the 1950s, as Rykwert put it in his preface to *The Idea of a Town*.[43] Later, as director of the Architecture Diploma course at Bath University from 1981, and Professor of Architecture from 1990–5, Hodgkinson would draw explicitly on this book as a starting-point for student design projects with teaching colleagues Pierre d'Avoine and Richard Padovan, while in 1998–9 Rykwert would join the School of Architecture at Bath as British Academy Visiting Professor.

The next section will therefore explore the correlations between these ideas, the 'Heart of the City' theme launched at Hoddesdon in 1951, the position of Team X, and the design of the Brunswick from 1958 onwards, focusing particularly on the centrality of the concept of public space to the project, as a focus for human interaction across both the everyday and sacred dimensions, and as a critique of the prevailing urban planning practices of the time.

Ideals of public space

> The squares of Italy, cozy areas, like a large vase, are a wonderful example of "Hearts" ... The heart of the city should be a place suitable for the most relaxed of human connections: conversation, discussion, shopping, "piropeo", "flâneur", and the priceless "dolce far niente" which, in its best meaning, is the most natural expression of contemplation (leisure, in quiet enjoyment of body and soul). Ernesto Rogers, Hoddesdon 1951[44] (see also chapter 8).

As previously referenced, Hodgkinson always maintained that the Brunswick was not modern at all, despite its oft-cited futuristic visual appearance as a 'megastructure'. He preferred to describe it in simple, traditional terms as '*a glass-covered market hall*' (not subsequently built), and 'a long quiet square with gravel and trees'.[45] Indeed, his low-rise, high-density approach to the housing development, explicitly conceived in opposition to the radial, point block typology of the Ville Radieuse, placed a fundamental emphasis on the sheltered space between the blocks, and the public gardens on the terrace above it, rather than the form of the blocks themselves. It chimed with the idea of bringing back a central core, or 'heart', for human life and interaction, as debated at CIAM 8, in a central London, bomb-damaged neighbourhood that was widely felt to have become institutionalized by over-scaled university, hospital and hotel buildings. The newly created London Borough of Camden (1962; the local municipal and housing authority) would identify it as ripe for a return of 'ordinary family life', in the form of the Brunswick housing scheme.[46] As such it can further be understood, notwithstanding Hodgkinson's denial, as strongly connected to the anthropologically conceived principles of Habitat and human settlement put forward in 1959 at Aix-en-Provence, contextualized by climatic and cultural context, human scale, and the language of local materials.

In 1972, Hodgkinson crystallized this idea in the ‘Notes’ he published on the conception of the scheme in *AR*’s special issue, as that of a ‘town room’: ‘Although linear in plan the completed building will present an entity of urban scale which should not be extended in length. It is a town room; an interval on a possible future pedestrian route linking the stations of Euston Road with the offices of Holborn’.[47] Fifteen years later, however, this terminology had evolved to describe his vision of the Brunswick development restrospectively, in an almost identical quote, as ‘a *major public place* on a proposed pedestrian route linking the rail termini of Euston Road with the offices of Holborn’[48] (my italics). I will consider the implications of this conceptual and scalar shift in emphasis over a period of two decades.

The term ‘town room’ is clearly linked to the London planning context of the 1950s and early 1960s, specifically the slum clearance programme enshrined in the principle of radical development (published in Abercrombie and Forshaw’s Statutory Development Plan of 1951); and the Ministry of Transport’s *Traffic in Towns* report (1963), which set out recommendations to create traffic-free ‘environmental areas’ in cities, surrounded by new highways for fast-moving traffic.[49] Professor Colin Buchanan, the author of the report, compared these areas to the corridor-and-room system of a house, also referring to them as ‘urban rooms’.[50] In 1972, Leslie Martin cited the concept in the following words, in a chapter illustrated by Hodgkinson’s Brunswick scheme among others: ‘“environmental areas” ... are recognizable working units. They are areas in which a pattern of related uses holds together: local housing, shopping, schools etc. would be one obvious example. They form, in Professor Buchanan’s terms, “the rooms of a town”... ’.[51]

By the early 1960s, planned road widening and enhanced traffic circulation seemed to be inevitable in the environs of the Brunswick site, and the long Brunswick shopping arcade, with housing stacked above it, was regarded as an appropriate replacement for the neighbouring shopping street. Facing inwards, away from the traffic, it would bound a sheltered public space, elevated above ground level, across which linear blocks of housing would face each other creating a neighbourly context for social interaction – what Hodgkinson himself would describe as a ‘town room’. He prided himself on the fact that it contributed to a return of 70 per cent of the site to public and private open space.

The idea of ‘linear terraces enclosing garden courts’, as he described them, had already been present in Hodgkinson’s student project for housing at the Loughborough Estate in south London of 1953, in which he ‘had taken the Unité 3-floor pack and developed it to suit our climate and habits in a way that produced the social mix of any traditional street'.[52] This project attracted Martin's attention, leading to him employing Hodgkinson in his office, where he initially worked on designs for Oxford and Cambridge university colleges, and then on the Brunswick scheme for the developer Alec Coleman of Marchmont Properties. Hodgkinson's work on the college projects, particularly Harvey Court in Cambridge (1957–62), further developed his ideas on enclosed public spaces in town settings: 'The collegiate plan ... breaks down the town population in appreciable stages with which we identify at different scales and levels of privacy', he wrote.[53] The first version of the Brunswick that Hodgkinson produced owed much to this model, comprising a 'blanket' of brick courtyard buildings, internally subdivided into small vertical blocks arranged around staircases (1958–60).

But Hodgkinson's espousal of the collegiate model was also influenced by Mumford's 'precinctual' approach, promoting the importance of the discrete, traffic-free neighbourhood unit in town planning.[54] Predating Buchanan's *Traffic in Towns*, Mumford had emphasized the social advantages that the creation of similar 'environmental areas' would bring in cities dominated by motor traffic, and in 1966 he would also identify the significance of Oxford and Cambridge universities' contribution to town planning, as 'the superblock and the urban precinct divorced from the ancient alleys and streets'.[55] Hodgkinson saw Mumford's proposition as a straightforward enlargement and expansion of Georgian principles of town-building based on the construction of households integrated with community facilities and shops in squares and crescents: a celebration of everyday life and interaction, which chimes with Rogers's evocation of the characteristics of the 'heart of the city' at Hoddesdon, but implies an expansion of scale and loss of 'cosiness'.

The concept of the 'superblock' is reflected in the subsequent modification of the early Brunswick Centre proposals,[56] and the re-imagining in retrospect of traffic-free 'town room' as 'major public space'. This was prompted by the developer's desire to minimize the cost of redeveloping the site, which led to the redesign of the collegiate-inspired proposal as a single large floorplate slightly elevated above street level, bordered by continuous linear blocks with relatively few points of vertical access and long horizontal internal access galleries instead – the Outline Planning Scheme of 1960–3, and the basis of the structure we see today. The blocks were higher on the internal elevation, to give a more 'civic' presence onto the precinct, and lower on the external elevation, to achieve a more domestic scale in relation to the street. The elevated plinth allowed for underground servicing and car parking, but the precinct itself would materialize as an awkwardly over-scaled and windswept space between concrete blocks that never succeeded in hosting the buzz of human interaction and exchange in the way Hodgkinson hoped. It was much criticized for its alienating qualities, most memorably by Sennett, until its refurbishment in 2006.

The stepped section of these blocks had been in place from an early stage, to provide midday sun into all the living rooms, east or west facing, and glass-enclosed 'winter-gardens' for every flat, with a view of the sky. However, in contrast to the exposed concrete facades and the monumental and 'futuristic' reinforced concrete A-frame structure, introduced after 1963 due to changes in building regulations, and compared by Banham with Sant'Elia, the early Brunswick project, like Harvey Court, was conceived in a very different palette of materials – defined by its use of brick. Hodgkinson attributed this to the influence of the still little-known Louis Kahn while he was a student.[57] Kahn's use of brickwork was inseparable from his interest in the spatial ideas embedded in the architectures of the past, particularly the monumental and spiritual qualities of ancient buildings that he visited in Greece, Rome and Egypt, and sought to recreate in a new architecture for the present. The pervasive influence of Kahn and these sources on Hodgkinson was indirectly highlighted by Colin Rowe in his 1971 essay, where he wrote of the Brunswick, and its central public space, not as a 'town room', but, evoking a grander scale, as a modern-day Classical forum or arena. Rowe suggested that '[in] Hodgkinson's central space, it is sometimes difficult to avoid the impression that we are in an arena for the celebration of some archaic and not wholly known religious ritual. Are we in the Palace of Knossos or the Ball Court at Monte Alban?'[58]

Later, the archaic grandeur of the structure and spatial organization of the Brunswick was again evoked by David Hamilton Eddy, referencing Rowe: 'we are in a pagan world ... The walkways that give access to the flats on the upper floors and the broad decks of the first floor bear no relation to the Christian cloister of Gothic and Palladian architecture ... one is reminded of the great causeways and monuments of ancient civilisations, the Egyptian, the Mayan and Aztec with their ziggurats and intimations of entombment and human sacrifice'.[59] Rowe's and Hamilton Eddy's romantic-classical interpretation of the Brunswick as a descendant of the ancient tradition of monumental architecture imbued with spiritual quality further chimes with Rykwert's work on the sacred and profane ritual spaces of ancient Italian towns that was so influential in changing the course of architecture and urban planning during the post-war reconstruction years in the UK and beyond. Indeed, Hodgkinson concurred that 'I was always interested in the ancient ... there was something there that I couldn't grapple with and nonetheless it interested me tremendously'.[60] This shared interest informed the character of the Brunswick, and would further manifest itself in his engagement with Rykwert's work while Professor of Architecture at Bath University in the early 1990s.

The continuing shift towards a more monumental conceptualization of the Brunswick project, away from the more human scale of the 'town room' on different levels, and towards the creation of a 'major public place', on a monumental axis, with a quasi-ritualistic dimension, followed on from the granting of Outline Planning consent in 1963.

At this point, Hodgkinson was asked to revise the scheme again to a more speculative and commercial brief, which included both

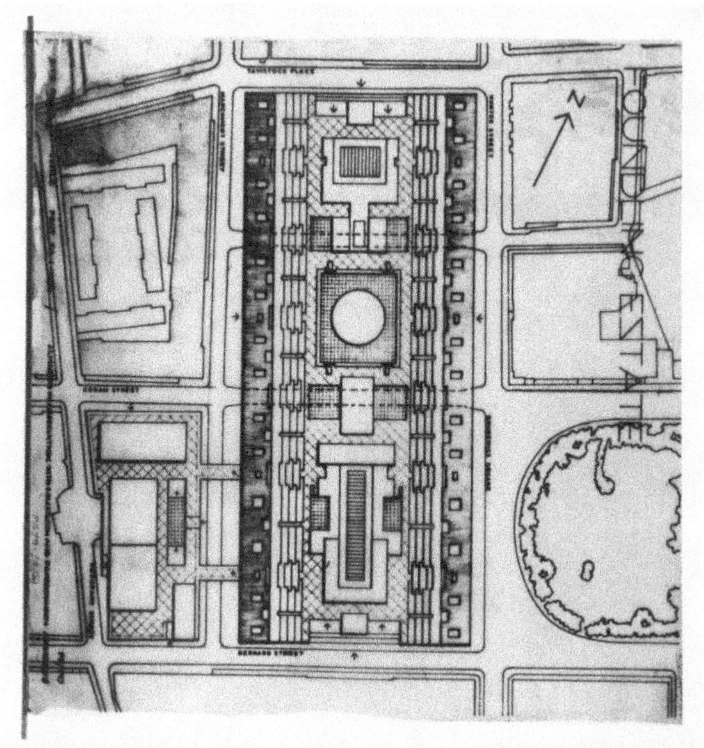

Figure 11.4 Outline Planning Scheme 1963, showing a more formalized axial emphasis to the public space, with circular recital hall at centre between two linear blocks

the introduction of the A-frame structure, and the replacement of the proposed circular recital hall in the centre of the internal space by a covered shopping hall as the focus of the arcade. Hodgkinson wrote, 'It will give a meeting place to the area and allow the terrace above to become one large space: a piece of quiet tree-lined ground (not just a raised deck) separating the housing from street bustle'.[61] The extended central axis through the scheme, intended to be twice the length of what was eventually built, was said by Hodgkinson to have been influenced by an unexecuted eighteenth-century plan by a forgotten architect named Merryweather, for a long wide street stretching from Queen Square to Tavistock Place. However, it also displays superficial similarities to the Charles Holden schemes for the University of London in the early 1930s, comprising a long 'spine' of university accommodation stretching from Montague Place in the south to Byng Place in the north.

A grand staircase rising from the raised ground plane of the Brunswick's public precinct was also introduced, to provide access to the wide public terrace above, further emphasizing the ambitious urban scale of the project by this stage, and its increasingly existential qualities (it would provide a significant backdrop for a scene in Antonioni's 1975 film *The Passenger*, before later being demolished for security reasons). But between 1965 and 1970, the evolving character of the scheme came increasingly into conflict with the new programme introduced by the handover of the housing element to the local council, resulting from the developer's financial difficulties. The reduction to the housing specification and overall detailing demanded by the council, plus the eventual loss of the glass-covered shopping galleria, eventually led to Hodgkinson's resignation in 1970 and a truncation of the intended extent of the project marked by the end of construction two years later.

Conclusion: Contradictions and compromise

As discussed in the first section of this chapter, Hodgkinson always distanced himself from the early critiques of the Brunswick as a megastructure, with futuristic ambitions, declaring the social concept and tight-knit human scale of the *village*, or *town room*, to be far more apt. He expressed a strong commitment to the native forms and materials of the UK, and the need to reject internationalist and universalizing typologies, evoking the concept of the 'town room' and low-rise housing as key to the reconstruction and revitalization of this central London neighbourhood after the war, in direct opposition to the prevailing ideology of the London County Council (LCC). Yet he also publicly rejected the 'political' values of Team X as he saw them, and the discourse around habitat, never explicitly referencing the strong influence of historic Italian urban landscapes and architectural approaches to reconstruction on British architects and thinkers associated with the Architectural Association, and *Architectural Review*. And indeed, the Brunswick project, for many decades dubbed a 'concrete monstrosity' by everyday critics, or 'a spaceship landed from outer space', exhibited a peculiar tension between the localized, human scale and values that he propounded, and the pull towards a more monumental and aggrandizing form of architectural and tectonic expression better represented by the Brunswick's listing definition as one of the most important exemplars of the megastructure typology in the UK.

It is perhaps not surprising then to know that Hodgkinson felt there was only one critic who, at a later stage, really grasped the contradictory essence of the Brunswick. David Hamilton Eddy, cited in the previous section, described the building in architectural-anthropological terms as a composition of 'two related but ultimately separate dimensions, each of which is facing in opposite directions, both practically and symbolically … these can be seen as traditional-communal and futurist-autonomous'.[62] He defined the former as the public area, the 'thriving bazaar of shops … open to the surrounding neighbourhood', and the latter as the housing – 'a different world … rows of glazed apartments … like the serried ranks of two alien armies … a dream world, familiar and entrancing and disturbing at once … '. Hamilton Eddy celebrated what he saw as the futurist spirit of the housing design, a liberating force within the 'conventional restraining order of Georgian and Victorian London, with its closely arranged social system where everyone is "placed" and knows their place'. He understood the idealism of the architect's social ambitions, and the source of his inspiration as a heady fusion of traditional forms with a very modern notion of social identity and individuality in a world that had been turned upside down by two world wars.

Far from being a statement of purist aesthetic and ideological conviction, the Brunswick embodies the ambiguities, conflicts and compromises that determine the outcome of most real-life large architecture projects, and the mix of influences that typifies any architect's output. Hodgkinson did not, as the Smithsons did, embrace the techniques of industrialized mass production as an authentic expression of a modern vernacular, and actively distanced himself from an ethical or ideological approach to materials, especially concrete. However he did share their, and Rykwert's, interest in ancient Mediterranean sites. His commitment to a form of spatially and visually led town-making that was being promoted by the townscape movement in the early 1960s, with reference to historic Italian urban landscapes, is exemplified in the early conceptualization and development of the Brunswick. Although it became veiled by the increase in scale, ambition and radical changes in materials and construction methods that lent the Brunswick a more futurist identity, the legacy of the development as a 'heart' for the city, represented in a typology of bounded public space designed to host everyday communal interaction, thrives today.

Notes

1 Melhuish 2007.
2 Sennett 1977. It is, he says, 'dead public space', which typified the reshaping of contemporary Western cities to reflect the decline of the public sphere. The concourse that lies between the two 'enormous apartment complexes' consists of 'a few shops and vast areas of empty space ... an area to pass through, not to use ... isolated ...' The glazed terraces of the two blocks themselves, generate a 'permeation of the house and the outside' which is 'curiously abstract': 'one has a nice view of the sky but the buildings are so angled that they have no relationship to, or view out on, the surrounding buildings of Bloomsbury ... The building is sited as though it could be anywhere.'
3 DCMS 2000.
4 Crosby 1972, 212.
5 Banham 1976, 185.
6 Hall 1968.
7 De Angelis 1974, in *Casabella* 38, no. 4, 2–3: 'Is this megastructure repressive? A lesson from the Brunswick Centre in London.'
8 Hodgkinson 2005b.
9 Mingardi, this volume.
10 Rykwert 1963.
11 Cullen 1961, 1971.
12 De Wolfe 1963.
13 Editorial, AR 1972, 193.
14 Editorial, AR 1972, 195.
15 Unauthored, AR 1972, 242 and 250.
16 Banham 1960.
17 Banham 1976.
18 Sant'Elia 1981.
19 Banham 1976, 19.
20 Banham 1976, 188.
21 Banham 1976, 185.
22 English Heritage 1993.
23 Hodgkinson 2000.
24 Hodgkinson 2007, 42.
25 Boccioni 1981 [1914].
26 Hodgkinson 2004.
27 Hodgkinson 2001b.
28 Hodgkinson 1987, 19.
29 Hodgkinson 1972, 216.
30 Hodgkinson 2005b.
31 Hodgkinson 1987, 19.
32 Mumford 1940.

33 Hodgkinson 2000.
34 Mumford 1963, 53–66.
35 Hodgkinson 2001b.
36 Hodgkinson 2000.
37 Hodgkinson 1992a.
38 Hodgkinson 1992a.
39 Hodgkinson 1987.
40 Hodgkinson 2001a.
41 Hodgkinson 1992b.
42 Hodgkinson 2001a.
43 Rykwert 1963.
44 Tyrwhitt, Sert and Rogers 1952.
45 Hodgkinson 1987, 20.
46 Barsley 1967.
47 Hodkginson 1972, 218.
48 Hodgkinson 1987.
49 Ministry of Transport 1963.
50 Buchanan 1963, para 101, cited in Headicar 2015.
51 Martin 1972, 22–3.
52 Hodgkinson 1987, 19.
53 Hodgkinson 1987, 20.
54 Mumford 1940; 1954.
55 Mumford 1966, 319.
56 Hodgkinson 1972, 217.
57 Hodgkinson 2004.
58 Rowe 1971.
59 Hamilton Eddy 1989, 31.
60 Hodgkinson 2006a.
61 Hodgkinson 1972, 218.
62 Hamilton Eddy 1989, 31.

References

Banham, Reyner. *Megastructure: Urban futures of the recent past*. London: Thames and Hudson, (1976): 185–9.

Banham, Reyner. *Theory and Design in the First Machine Age*. Cambridge, MA: MIT Press, 1980 [1960].

Barsley, M. 'The changing face of Bloomsbury', *Evening Standard* 3 May 1967, 8.

Boccioni, Umberto. 'Umberto Boccioni: Manifesto 1914'. In *AD Profile* 32, 'From Futurism to Rationalism: The origins of modern Italian architecture', 17–19 (supplement issued with *Architectural Design* 51 1/2) (1981).

Crosby, Theo. 'Brunswick Centre, Bloomsbury, London', *The Architectural Review* 908 (1972): 212.

Cullen, Gordon. *Townscape*. London: Architectural Press, 1961.

Cullen, Gordon. *The Concise Townscape*. London: Routledge (Architectural Press), 1971.

De Angelis, Almerico. 'Is this megastructure repressive? A lesson from the Brunswick Centre in London', *Casabella* 384 (1974): 2–3.

Department for Culture Media and Sport, 'Listing Schedule 798–1/95/10155: Brunswick Square (west side)', London: DCMS 2000.

De Wolfe, Ivor, with photos by Ivy de Wolfe. *The Italian Townscape*. London: Architectural Press, 1963.

English Heritage, London Advisory Committee, 5 November, item 6 g. The Brunswick Centre, planning application at consultation stage, London: EH 1993.

Hall, Peter. 'Monumental folly', *New Society* 317 (1968): 602–3.

Hamilton Eddy, David. 'Castle mythology in British housing', *RIBA Journal* 100/12 (December 1989): 28–33.

Headicar, Peter. *Traffic and Towns: The next 50 years* (ITC Occasional Paper 6). London: Independent Transport Commission, 2015.

Hodgkinson, Patrick. 'Foundling conception', *The Architectural Review* 908 (1972): 216–17.
Hodgkinson, Patrick. 'A handful of homes: British post-war housing'. *A3 Times No 9, Modern Urban Living*. London: Polytechnic of North London (1987): 19–21.
Hodgkinson, Patrick. 'Speculation with Humanity?'. Architect's objection to Tranmac's planning application, 10 July 1992a.
Hodgkinson, Patrick. 'How green, this Bloomsbury valley?'. Architect's statement, 31 July 1992b.
Hodgkinson, Patrick, letter to author, 3 Sept 2000.
Hodgkinson, Patrick, letter to author, 22 May 2001a.
Hodgkinson, Patrick, in conversation with author 7 Jun 2001b.
Hodgkinson, Patrick, in conversation with author, Nov 2004.
Hodgkinson, Patrick, interview with author and Pierre d'Avoine, October Gallery, 3 November 2005.
Hodgkinson, Patrick, interview with author and Pierre d'Avoine, 8 February 2006.
Martin, Leslie. 'The Grid as Generator', in Lionel March and Leslie Martin (eds.), *Urban Space and Structures*, Cambridge: Cambridge University Press, 1972, 6–27 (Foundling Estate 23–7).
Melhuish, Clare. 'Visiblity regained', *The Architectural Review* 1321 (2007): 42–8.
Mumford, Lewis. *Culture of Cities*. London: Secker and Warburg, 1940.
Mumford, Lewis. 'The neighbourhood and the neighbourhood unit', *The Town Planning Review* 24, no. 4 (1954): 256–70.
Mumford, Lewis. *The Highway and the City*. New York: Harcourt, Brace and World, 1963.
Mumford, Lewis. *The City in History*. London: Secker and Warburg 1966.
Rowe, Colin. 'A palais royale for London?'. Unpublished essay, 1971.
Rykwert, Joseph. *The Idea of a Town: The anthropology of urban form in Rome, Italy and the Ancient World*. Cambridge, MA: MIT Press 1988 [1963].
Sant'Elia, Antonio. 'Antonio Sant'Elia: Manifesto 1914'. In *AD Profile* 32, 'From Futurism to Rationalism: The origins of modern Italian architecture', 20–23 (supplement issued with *Architectural Design* 51 1/2) (1981).
Sennett, Richard. *The Fall of Public Man*. London: Faber and Faber, 1977.
Tyrwhitt, Jaqueline, José Luis Sert and Ernesto Rogers. *The Heart of the City: Towards the humanisation of urban life*. London: Lund Humphries, 1952 (Italian edition: *Il cuore della città: per una vita più umana della comunità*. Milan: Hoepli, 1954).

Part III
Building the Welfare State

12

A Janus-faced approach to the new universities of the 1960s: monumentality and pedagogy at Sussex and Essex

Jack O'Connor

This chapter will examine the traditional, classical and humanist references present in modernist campus architecture of the English New Universities of the 1960s, and in relation to Italian influences. The New Universities were conceived as part of a renewal of the public sphere in Britain following the Second World War. In response to the horrors of war and the demands of a modern economy, the nation reconstructed physically and renewed politically the institutions of democracy as part of a new welfare state. This vision was materialized spatially in the New Universities, through the deployment of classical themes, the emergent New Monumentality and elements of avant-garde New Brutalism. Basil Spence's visits to Rome and his work on the British Embassy in the city were major influences, as well as the ideal model of the Greek agora, deployed as a democratic meeting space at the centre of the Sussex campus. Meanwhile Kenneth Capon's designs for the interlocking piazzas at Essex displayed the influence of Italian hill towns (namely San Gimignano, Tuscany) another ideal space for people to circulate and for impromptu meetings to occur.

The campus architecture of Spence and Capon embodies a new vision for modern democratic education based on traditional ideas of institutional life. But why did the architects turn to Ancient Greece and Rome, and Medieval Italian towns, to provide the spaces for the new modern universities? How did university reformers imagine the dialogue between built environment and modern pedagogies? How should we assess this part utopian, part regressive, and part futurist vision of higher education? This chapter draws on the spatial-philosophy of Hannah Arendt, who also turned to classical humanist references, in order to answer these questions and theorize the construction of an edifice for human political action to reside in.

In 1957 the *Architectural Review* published a feature on university architecture and the history of its form. Nikolaus Pevsner established how the idea of the university was a vital component of western civilization that formed a community of learned scholars, which in turn was bonded to and valued by the wider public sphere of society. Pevsner traced the origins of the institution's architectural form back to twelfth-century Italy where a monastic cloistered form was established, which then developed and evolved, taking on other architectural styles through the centuries in various national settings.[1] In the same issue Lionel Brett critiqued contemporary university architecture, arguing that its problems should be redressed by turning to tradition, and by establishing that the university is a special architectural site and not just another educational institution.[2] These conversations reveal the growing importance of universities in the British post-war public sphere and architectural culture, but also show how the architectural profession began to debate more intensely the form university buildings should take, in order to explore their representational status. Moreover, they establish how, through the centuries, university architecture had been linked to Italianate and classical styles.

A year earlier the University Grants Committee (UGC), whose role was to advise and deliver on national needs in higher education and manage university funding, decided that the post-war growth in student numbers could no longer be absorbed through the expansion of existing universities. Therefore the UGC advised the Treasury that they should support the creation of new university institutions, beginning with the existing proposal for a University of Sussex at Brighton. In February 1957, the government authorized this recommendation, which in turn led to the creation of six more institutions – York, East Anglia, Essex, Kent, Warwick and Lancaster – which came to be known as the New Universities of the 1960s.[3]

Each institution appointed an architect to devise a masterplan for the architecture of the new university. At Sussex this was to be Basil Spence, at Essex, Kenneth Capon of Architects Co-Partnership (ACP). This chapter will explore how the modern architectural designs they produced came to feature a series of classical and humanist references. In seeking to understand this Janus-faced approach, I shall explore how, in tackling questions of education and citizenship in a post-war mass society, architectural and pedagogical allusions to supposed humanist continuities produced meaning in the modernist campus architecture at Sussex and Essex. To do this one must understand the factors behind their creation, the status attributed to them and how the individual architects assimilated these factors with their own architectural ideals, to conceive a masterplan. In this analysis I shall use elements of Hannah Arendt's philosophy of the public sphere, to understand the concepts present in the New Universities, as Arendt enables one to conceive the university as a space of appearance; a site for renewing the common world through human agency.[4] Like the New Universities, Arendt's theories were consciously situated between the past and the future; Arendt used classicism as a resource from which to excavate 'thought fragments' to inform the present.[5] Therefore by examining the New Universities through this lens, they are seen as sites for renewing the common world, by educating generations of young people for a modern Britain, while also giving a sense of permanence by establishing communities of learning and providing a physical space for this sphere of experience. Especially as they were to be social, cultural and political spaces of national importance; meaning those architects appointed to design them had to respond to these factors, by synthesizing tradition and modernity, monumentality and community.

New universities and the post-war context

The UGC concluded that the New Universities would be established as national institutions, and, as they would have no existing traditions, they were given a licence to create innovative pedagogies to meet changing demands and developments in scientific knowledge. The UGC decreed that they would be situated on a large campus of 200 acres and cater for a minimum of 3,000 students. To meet these requirements the New Universities would receive capital grants and recurring quinquennial grants, which the UGC had secured from the Treasury.[6]

To meet the criteria set out by the UGC both Sussex and Essex created a school system in order to foster interdisciplinarity both within and between the arts and sciences. They aimed to break from the Oxbridge college models and insular departments of the Redbrick Universities (like Manchester, Liverpool, Leeds – built at the turn of the twentieth century), but also to meet the demands of contemporary British society and industry.[7] Further to the academic plans was the ambition to create communities of learning. At Sussex the aim was mostly described as creating an 'academic community', whereas at Essex, it was more often described as a 'democratic community' or a 'self-governing academic community'.[8] The architects were also reacting to various contemporary and historical contexts. Despite this most of the historiography on New University architecture places them as socio-educational welfare state creations. They were certainly a result of or a reaction to post-war welfare state reforms, notably the Education Act of 1944, which was a key factor leading to the expansion of higher education in Britain during the post-war period.[9] However, they were products of further contextual factors that can be broadly defined as technocratic modernization and the historic idea of the university, which therefore placed them between the past and the future; an emblem of a university system beginning to move from elite to mass higher education. All of these factors contributed to elevating the status of the New Universities, from mere educational institutions to representational buildings.

The combination of neoclassical and modernist styles at the universities of Sussex and Essex is something that has been established in articles by Maurice Howard and Jules Lubbock respectively.[10] Both highlight the modern influences – Le Corbusier, the Townscape movement and second wave New Towns – and more classical influences – the Colosseum, the Greek agora as a site of social intercourse, the medieval Oxford quad, and the piazzas of Italian hill towns. Meanwhile others have focused on the lineage of university architecture that influenced the New Universities designs from the Oxbridge collegiate model to the US academic village and campus. Most notably Stefan Muthesius's study focuses upon the mutations and combinations of the American campus and English college design models to forge an 'understanding of', what he terms, 'the utopianist mood which shaped the institutions and their architecture' during the post-war years; a period when, according to Muthesius, 'educational reformism united with a new social and architectural impetus'.[11] These histories identify the stylistic and typological influences present in the architectural design of the New Universities, and the presence of a social-educational ethos. Much like Muthesius, McKean states that the social purpose of post-war modern architecture found its epitome in the New Universities. Despite this McKean argues that their architectural conservatism served to create separate elite communities, an argument that prompts the question as to whether these architectural spaces failed.[12]

The socio-educational welfare state thesis places the creation of the New Universities, educationally and architecturally, as one pillar of the welfare state in Britain. However, their creation and architectural form is also the result of other contextual and historical factors, which contributed to elevating their status. Reports published during the immediate post-war period projected an increase in student numbers, but also indicated that an expansion in higher education was about increasing national scientific and technological capability, and producing managers for the welfare state as part of a modernizing nation state, and therefore not simply about social-democratic idealism.[13] These factors placed the New Universities as one element in the expansion of higher education that was linked to a technocratic and meritocratic moment in the post-war years, during which a university system was formed to meet national demands, driven by the expanding state and less by democratic ideals, particularly in the fields of science and technology.[14] International concerns were also driving the expansion of higher education in Britain, as the nation was seeking a role globally following the impact of war and decolonization in its empire during the post-war years, while Cold War geopolitics would influence the international outlook of the curriculums at the New Universities.[15]

Higher education was therefore becoming one sphere of experience within an expanding post-war public sphere dominated by experts and professionals, as the problems, crises and future of higher education became more hotly debated during and after the war.[16] The pages of the journal *University Quarterly*, founded in 1946, covered the key topics affecting universities in the post-war period; expansion, the purpose of the university, modernization, specialization versus general education, science and technology, increased government involvement, 'the student', and accommodation. The expansion of the universities and the foundation of the New Universities thrust higher education firmly into the public sphere, which saw national newspapers begin to widely report on universities, and the new Vice Chancellor of Essex, Albert Sloman, presented his vision for the new university as a BBC Reith Lecture in 1963.[17] The combination of these factors – the educational reform of the welfare state, expansion of science and technology graduates for increased national output, education of experts and managers for the welfare state, and the expanded higher education sphere – meant that the New Universities had an elevated status when they came to be constructed.

Upon these contemporary factors weighed heavily the history of the idea of the university and its many divergences. From the liberal tradition in England, specifically at Oxbridge, which was rooted in literary, philosophical and moral humanist trends; to the nineteenth-century German idea, with philosophy as the unifying discipline; and to the American idea where, as Sheldon Rothblatt states, the 'notion of education for a national citizenry received a special American emphasis', therefore displaying a somewhat Arendtian notion of education for citizenship.[18] These ideals resonated for the two New Universities at Sussex and Essex, where the founders of both institutions laid out the blueprint of their idea, in reference to the past idea of the university and how it was to be reformed in the new institutions. Meanwhile Halsey has argued that the post-war university system was stuck between trying to serve an advanced industrial society while also maintaining the elite character of the liberal establishment – a problem that he feels lies within the 'British conception' – the *idea* – 'of a university and its relation to wider society.'[19] This is an analysis that demonstrates how the idea of the university held particular ideological force in British society. Furthermore, the diverse idea of the university had an architectural heritage rooted in Italian and classical typologies, as demonstrated in Pevsner's article from 1957.

Both Spence and Capon were architects interrogating the boundaries of modern architecture, mixing traditional references with functionalism, and thus were well placed to design the New Universities as symbols of modernity. Modernity in this case may be understood as the condition of living imposed upon individuals by the socio-economic process of modernization, experiences that are reflected in modernism, 'the body of artistic and intellectual ideas and movements that deal with the process of modernization and with the experience of modernity.'[20] However, as Heynen registers, modernity is complex and multifarious, it can mean present or current; 'new' as opposed to old, describing time experienced as a period; or something that is momentary, of the transient; furthermore modernity can be seen to be in constant conflict with tradition, even a rupture with tradition.[21] However, following Harvey's assessment that 'high-modernism' became hegemonic after 1945 – the establishment arts and culture practice of choice in a corporate capitalist version of the Enlightenment project – the architects called upon to produce monumental and representational buildings would need to reconcile tradition with modernity.[22] The post-war debate concerning 'new monumentality' and its relationship to creating representational buildings, would therefore be significant for university design.

New monumentality and the new universities

In 1944 the architectural historian and critic Sigfried Giedion called for a 'new monumentality' within modern architecture, describing how, historically, monumentality was represented in buildings of perennial power, from the Acropolis to Gothic cathedrals, from renaissance churches to eighteenth-century squares. However, Giedion stressed how this had descended into a 'pseudo-monumentality' during the nineteenth century, which had become 'veiled and even poisonous', particularly due to its use by Fascist regimes.[23] He postulated that modern architecture must begin anew to reach a new monumental expression for buildings such as museums, theatres, churches, concert halls and, crucially, universities. If they failed to meet this demand, he warned that architecture may fall into mere academicism. Giedeon's writings on modern architecture have been described by Heynen as 'pastoral', as they attempted to smooth out differences and conflicts in modernity, but ultimately reveal the ambiguity of a position that at once challenges modernity by aligning with the avant-garde, yet clings to the traditional architectural values of harmony and permanence.[24]

Monumentality, wrote Giedion, was linked to the eternal need of humanity to reveal their inner life, actions and social conceptions, an analysis that, to an extent, intersects with Arendt's political theory, where the monument builder provides a stable world, a space of appearance for humanity's actions to take place.[25] Giedion also cited the Latin meaning of monuments as 'things that remind, things to be transmitted to later generations' and, despite calling for something new, he still reflected on past 'periods of real cultural life' that had the 'capacity to project creatively their own image of society' through community centres such as the agora, the forum and the medieval square.[26] However, the Arendtian concept of *natality*, the idea of a common world that is created by humans and has permanence, which is then transmitted to and renewed by later generations, diverges from this.[27] Here renewal offers the potential for something new and different, breaking the repetition of old harmonies and values. The tensions in these positions reveal those present in New University architecture, which on one hand were new spaces of appearance for education, youth and renewal, but on the other were monuments repeating existing institutional traditions.

The debate on monumentality was brought into the milieu of British architecture when Giedion delivered a lecture on the subject at the Royal Institute of British Architecture (RIBA) in 1946, and via the subsequent symposium convened by the *Architectural Review* in 1948.[28] The concept of a 'new monumentality' was held back in Britain due to the lack of resources in the immediate post-war years, with priority given to utilitarian buildings. However, as constraints loosened, attentions turned to redevelopment and public projects, thus again raising the question of what architectural form they should take. Forming part of these public buildings would be the New Universities of the 1960s.[29]

With the growing importance of universities in the public sphere and the expansion of existing universities throughout the 1950s, the architectural profession began to debate more intensely the form that these representational buildings should take, as seen in Pevsner and Brett's analysis from 1957. The fervour around universities and their architecture increased as the New Universities began to be designed and built in the 1960s, with one commentator comparing the building programme to the cathedral building movement of the twelfth century.[30] By the end of the decade the architectural theorist and Professor of Art at Essex, Joseph Rykwert, described the university as the archetypal building of the age.[31]

Meanwhile the search for a 'new monumentality' would be a key factor in two major architectural competitions of the post-war period, both of which were relevant to the design approaches for the New Universities. Firstly, the competition to rebuild Coventry Cathedral, which was won in 1951 by Basil Spence, whose design for the cathedral has been described by Louise Campbell as 'the greatest single monument of Britain's reconstruction'.[32] Secondly, the competition to design Churchill College, Cambridge, in 1958, where Basil Spence sat on the judging panel, and an entry was submitted by Capon's practice ACP. One of the architects who worked on the project stated that 'Churchill College was to be a memorial', they were 'to design a "monument".'[33] This instance was representative of a new post-war public sphere dominated by experts and professionals. In designing these new spheres of experience, architects had the opportunity to work with intellectual clients, who were part of this same new post-war public sphere, and who were understanding and sympathetic to their design concepts.

The themes of monument and memorial are present in the literature surrounding the New Universities. Muthesius labels the Sussex design as 'monumentalism on a parkland campus', meanwhile Lubbock posits that the residential towers at Essex were imbued with a sense of memorial to the war, due to towers being a traditional symbol of memorial, arguing that the New Universities were a 'manifestation of the final stage of post-war reconstruction'.[34] Underlying this remains the question of how modern architecture was to represent a 'new monumentality', those questions that were debated in the immediate post-war years. How was it to represent the ideology of liberal democracy in its public buildings, its spheres of experience? How was it to reconcile this with an architecture that was to have a social and human orientation? Would architects devise an expressly 'new monumentality', or would there be an element of historicism, a turn to tradition and classicism to realize it?

In January 1959 Basil Spence was appointed architect at Sussex, then the most well-known architect in the country, following his success in the competition to design Coventry Cathedral. Spence was already on his way to establishing himself as a key proponent of public sphere architecture and, as master planner of the campus at the first New University, he had the responsibility of conceiving the abstract production of space for this new sphere of experience. Henri Lefebvre, who theorized the production of space in the technocratic moment of the post-war years, writes that conceived space is the space of architects, scientists, urbanists and technocratic subdividers, who 'identify what is lived and what is perceived with what is conceived', which finds expression in monuments as well as town planning, and therefore universities.[35] Spence was supported by the first Vice Chancellor John Fulton, who explained that Sussex would not be organized in colleges but in schools, with new approaches to learning; Fulton stated that it would be an 'institution with its own identity' and 'strong esprit'.[36] Despite these guiding words from Vice Chancellor Fulton, it was clear that Spence was to be given considerable scope to conceive of the vision for Sussex's physical realm and it would be his background, architectural training and influences and experiences on previous projects that would guide his design, which sought to unite the modern of the New University with the traditional and the classical.

As a modernist architect, Spence remained nonetheless attached to his arts and crafts training in Edinburgh, which gave him an understanding of classical orders, a deep reverence for the relationship between context and landscape, and the traditions of modern architecture; establishing a humanist lineage in the history of art and design – all of which would have a bearing on his design at Sussex.[37] An interplay between tradition and modernism, between the past and the present, would become a hallmark of Spence's work. This was particularly evident in his design for Coventry Cathedral, which occupied a middle ground between the other traditional and avant-garde entries, displaying deference to the heritage of cathedral and church architecture and 'to the way in which buildings could provide a powerful bridge between past and present for their users'.[38] This theme of modernization and tradition continued as a feature of Spence's university work. A particular sensitivity to tradition was required in the design of halls of residence at Queens College, Cambridge in 1958. Meanwhile his design for a science complex at Nottingham University has been labelled a 'technopolis', and the series of buildings for

Southampton University, enclosing a quadrangle, pools and a bronze sculpture, was described as a 'science piazza'.[39]

With this background and influences, his awareness of the pedagogical vision for the new university at Sussex and its licence to innovate, Spence appeared to agree with the architectural press of the period that the university was more than another educational institution. In Spence's own assessment the university and its buildings were to take on a sense of agency, they were to be mother and father to the undergraduate, stating that the 'bricks and mortar should help sixth-formers over the fence into manhood and womanhood.' The task was also to be political, as Spence felt the students would also 'learn to be good citizens' within this space.[40] Underlying this was the representational value of such a new institution, and the cultural and political position it was to hold in British society. With his approach to Sussex and previous university work, Spence displayed an understanding of the historic liberal concept of the idea of the university and placed the university as part of a democratic tradition.

This understanding led Spence to develop 'a robust and sculptural vocabulary' to represent these ideals, turning to the perceived cradle of Western civilization's knowledge and democracy, Ancient Greece, as well as established British university design traditions.[41] Spence described the Acropolis, which he visited in 1958, as 'that great monument to the first democracy', a site that represented the vitality of a young civilization coming to life.[42] The arrangement of space in the Acropolis and medieval towns was influential to Spence because it spoke to his humanist view of modern architecture: they were 'attune to the individual and people' – the human condition – therefore he felt that a collection of buildings for Sussex, in this lineage, could stimulate 'thinking and feeling and living … a fuller existence'.[43] Here Spence establishes, in an Arendtian sense, the university as a monument to the democratic tradition, a permanent space of appearance in the public sphere, while also displaying a deep concern for the human condition and how it cares for the world. Importantly the architecture was also to signify youth and vitality, and foster thinking and feeling, therefore having the potential to become a site between past and future where the common world may be renewed by the young students.

The early site plans revealed the fusion of classical and traditional themes that was informing his modernist vision. A plan from 1960 echoes the Greek polis, from its central agora and monumental structures, right down to the amphitheatre.[44] Meanwhile later plans reveal the evolution of the design and the use of the quadrangle shape for most of the major buildings, a form synonymous with Oxbridge, which had also been deployed in a modernist guise for the recent designs at Churchill College. The Agora and Ancient Athens represented to Spence the idea of incompleteness, a Greek philosophy and wisdom, 'in which they try to get as much perfection as possible in each part of a development and yet constantly allow for growth.'[45] This idea was used by Spence to meet the design brief for a university that was to be continuously growing over the coming decades, while also cloaking the environment in a specific democratic ideal to elevate these buildings to a representational level. This notion was carried by Spence into the design of the first major building on the site, Falmer House, but it also extended to the Great Court complex, which was to be a forum of completeness for the university to expand from.

Falmer House, the first building on campus and the university's social centre, perhaps best demonstrates Spence's approach to monumentality. For inspiration Spence turned to the great monument of Imperial Rome, the Colosseum. However, it was not the glory of ancient

Figure 12.1 Falmer House, North Entrance. The classical arched entrance to the Falmer House courtyard and great court beyond, echoing the arches of the Colosseum

© University of Sussex

empires that Spence intended to revive here. In fact, Spence claimed to be interested in the ancient arena only in its ruined form; its casual appearance interested him because the exposed arches framed and cosseted the individual.[46] Falmer House was also described as a 'gateway to the university', which therefore can symbolically demarcate and restrict access to the main 'democratic' space of the agora beyond.[47] The classical arched entrance of Falmer House resembles the main axial entrance to the Colosseum, and lies on its own axis leading up to the sculptural monument of incompleteness at the entrance to the Arts building, which in early designs was to contain its own arched entrance way.

Spence himself felt Falmer House was 'a rather noble expression of the university idea', however, when seen in this way the landscaped parkland space takes on a tougher, more deterministic appearance.[48]

At the University of Essex Kenneth Capon, of ACP, was also given considerable freedom to design the masterplan of the new university, and he established a close client–architect relationship with Vice Chancellor Albert Sloman in order to understand the academic vision for the university. Capon's importance was emphasized by the fact that the architect was the second appointment to the university, following the vice chancellor.[49] While they registered the picturesque quality of the development, both were concerned about the isolation of the site and the problems it presented for creating a university town that integrated with the existing town of Colchester, with Capon explaining that students did not want a sense of segregation while learning; 'however attractive the parkland site might be the student still wants his every day … facilities.'[50] Despite the physical distance Vice Chancellor Sloman explained that they had wished to orientate the university to the town and foster strong links with the community.[51]

Following the discussions between architect and vice chancellor, Capon presented a development plan that would represent 'a physical realization of the educational ideas that underlie the academic planning of the University of Essex – emphasis on the relationship between fields of knowledge which have all too often been treated in isolation, a strong sense of democratic community, and the capacity to respond to changing and expanding needs of society and industry in the twentieth and succeeding centuries. The University is conceived as an efficient modern community for learning and living.'[52]

Key to Capon's conceived plan for this new sphere of experience was the concept of creating a democratic 'university town', an idea initially based upon contemporary notions of town planning and concepts from the Townscape movement, but which extended to the traditional influences of Italian townscapes.[53] The intention of this vision was to break from the collegiate traditions of Oxbridge, as well as the nine-to-five character and lack of architectural harmony at the Redbrick universities, to achieve a compact, 'organic' space of appearance. Capon attempted to meet the interdisciplinary challenges of the academic brief with a continuous teaching block, and the design would also incorporate monumentality through its sheer projected scale, but also with the inclusion of residential towers, which gave visual representation to a complex of buildings that had a higher public standing. To reconcile size and concentration Capon arrived at the principle that every element should be within five minutes' walk of the centre, which meant a '10-minute walk from one edge to another.'[54] This concentrated design began with Capon's decision to build in and over the valley, where a constructed offset pedestrian platform would cover an access road below in the valley floor, giving access to the basements of buildings.

'Townscape': A humanist planning model

Integral to these town planning ideas was a particular subset of the Townscape movement, a study titled *The Italian Townscape* by 'Ivor De Wolfe', a pseudonym of the *Architectural Review* editor Hubert de Cronin Hastings, first published as a special issue of the *Architectural Review* in June 1962 and then as a book in 1963, both contemporaneous to the design of Essex.[55] In this publication, Italian townscapes, and particularly medieval hill towns that had survived into the modern age, were displayed to show the many possibilities of street life, and offer British architects a way to 'rediscover some humanist core to its urbanism' and a paragon of how to 'bind together community and architecture.'[56] 'De Wolfe' stated that 'the object of the exercise' was 'to compile a case-book of the past in the interest of the present' – again an Arendtian and Benjaminian notion of excavating thought fragments or pearls from the past to inform the present.[57] The study depicted the Italian town as a whole, as well as identifying specific typological elements, such as squares, convex streets, arcades, cloisters and vistas, and also the function of water, natural light and neon, to exemplify a quintessentially Italian street life. Hill towns were espoused for their site conditions and their economical use of land, but also their aesthetic profile on the skyline. It was to be these very characteristics that Capon's 'university town' design aimed to emulate in modern form. A university press release captures almost all of the elements in the study:

> Platforms each the size of a small Italian town square linked by shallow flights of steps. These platforms will form the university "high street" busy squares surrounded by buildings. A student walking up the university's high street will pass from one square to another, each with its own style and vistas ... the still water of the lake contrasting with the bustling activity of the central street.[58]

The piazzas, designed by Capon with cloistered arcades, were to provide the 'street life' of shops, coffee bars and bookshop that would fulfil the ideal of the university town, both day and night, with lights at 'midnight streaming across the squares'.[59]

Indeed *The Italian Townscape* spoke of neon lights from cafes illuminating arcades, just as Capon spoke of neon lights and a 'controlled vulgarity' in the central 'street' at Essex.[60] The ideas of Townscape theory were adopted at Essex to achieve compactness, and because the spaces described in *The Italian Townscape* could aid the academic interchange and casual social contacts desired; as Capon's deputy explained 'a

Figure 12.2 Drawing of square at University of Essex by Conrad Schevenels, Architects Co-Partnership c. 1963. The architect's conceived vision for the Essex squares as a social space

University of Essex Collection. Used courtesy of the Albert Sloman Library, University of Essex

concentrated urban environment was the intention ... the intention to get a hot sort of matrix of education and life, where things will grow.'[61] Here again, like with Spence at Sussex, there is a turn to historic and traditional architectural spaces for inspiration in fulfilling the physical ideal of a New University. The squares of Essex, like those at Sussex, are reminiscent of those at Oxbridge, but in the Essex case there is also the influence of medieval and renaissance Italian towns for their humanizing scale and density.

The 'romantic' conception of Italian hill town architecture was referenced by Capon as part of his rationale for the use of residential towers, 'there was' explained Capon 'still a certain romance about the San Gimignano towers around'.[62] They provided a visually varied and strong skyline from a distance, but the town also represented the 'desirable picturesque characteristics, of enclosure, surprise and juxtaposition.'[63] The influence of Italian hill towns was present in other New University designs, namely Denys Lasdun's design for the University of East Anglia.[64] It also surfaced in the avant-garde; the Smithsons, as part of their 'Cluster City' project, published comparisons of Italian and Greek hill

Figure 12.3 The monumental residential towers at Essex, on the skyline and contrasting with the trees in the parkland

University of Essex Collection. Used courtesy of the Albert Sloman Library, University of Essex

towns along with Louis Kahn's drawings of Siena.[65] The towers at Essex were to house the student accommodation flats, consisting of study bedrooms, study rooms, a shared kitchen and living space. It was envisaged that the students would live in these towers of flats just like Londoners and New Yorkers, and they would be managed by committees of residents, marking them out as a key component in the conceived ideal of a democratic community.[66] The towers also had monumental qualities. The development plan stated that towers 'like monoliths across the skyline' would 'contrast with the trees in the foreground'.[67]

The towers of San Gimignano and the profile of the town provided the 'romantic' influence for this project. Reflecting on the towers, Albert Sloman remarked that Capon also used them to make a statement about the status and importance of the university: the scale of the library building and towers embodied the 'strength and confidence of the university' stated Sloman, thus displaying that it was to be more than a local teaching institution.[68]

This analysis demonstrates how Sussex and Essex, as examples of the English New Universities, were significant spaces of appearance in post-war Britain, conceived as communities to represent certain ideals, which in turn reveals the complexities of modernity within post-war Britain. To represent these ideals the architects excavated themes from architectural history, shared European 'sites of cultural memory', spaces of democracy and conceptions of communality.[69] Turning to classical and traditional architecture from Europe, and more specifically Italy, as embodiments of humanist ideals, was not unprecedented in English architectural culture, nor indeed within the tradition of university architecture. In the post-war period this interaction with Italian culture was revived, as humanist ideals that had been degraded in war were considered anew. Introducing *The Italian Townscape* Erten and Powers explain how this coincided with the revival in the arts of design and film in Italy, and with Wittkower giving scholarly respectability to baroque and humanist architecture.[70] Italian architectural debates of the period offered English modern architects ideas to consider the contextual and historical conditions of their designs, something that was particularly resonant for those designing representational buildings.[71] More specifically Muthesius argues that in the early 1960s 'Italian' became a 'euphemism for a dense development with perhaps some towering structures', ideas that were present in New University designs, as well as in housing and town planning.[72]

In light of this analysis we see that like Arendt, Capon and Spence were seeking a route to rethink social life, between the past and future.

Their references to classical architecture and medieval townscapes in post-war campus architecture in Britain manifested an interest for democratic and communal ends, while it created stimulating sites for human action to take place. However, the interaction with ancient sites and Italian townscapes is often conducted at a distance, at a purely visual level. Indeed, the touristic gaze of the architect reveals a particularly romantic conception of Italy during its post-war return to democracy. This uncritical excavation of the past remains therefore potentially problematic. Spence and Capon cast themselves as 'monument-builders', to provide a stable world, communities of learning, spaces of appearance for humanity's actions to take place.[73] Both architects, along with the vice chancellors, certainly displayed an understanding that these spaces were for the young. However, by embedding certain notions of tradition and classicism in their buildings, the spaces took deterministic forms and remained wedded to an elite liberal idea of the university. Capon and Spence inadvertently negated the new in the New Universities, the potentiality of natality, represented by the ability to renew a common world. Something that was expected by those staff and students attracted to these New Universities, who would bring their own concepts of community, and question the traditions supposedly built into these spaces, as well as the traditional structures of governance.

Notes

1 Pevsner 1957.
2 Brett 1957.
3 University Grants Committee 1964, 91–3.
4 Arendt 1998.
5 Arendt 2015.
6 University Grants Committee 1964, 69–101.
7 Briggs 1964; Sloman 1964.
8 Daiches 1964; Sloman 1964.
9 'Education Act 1944'.
10 Howard 2015; Lubbock 2002.
11 Muthesius 2000; Darley 1991.
12 McKean 2007.
13 Tight 2009, 58–61.
14 Ortolano 2009, 105; Edgerton 2006, 2.
15 Cragoe 2014, 226.
16 Silver 2003.
17 Sloman 1964.
18 Rothblatt 1997, 29; Arendt 2006a; Arendt 2006b.
19 Halsey 1992, 8.
20 Heynen 1999, 3; Berman 1988.
21 Heynen 1999, 9.
22 Harvey 1989, 35; Hughes 2000, 84.
23 Giedion 1944, 550.
24 Heynen 1999, 4–5 and Chapter 2.

25 Giedion 1944, 552–3; Arendt 1998, 173.
26 Giedion 1944, 553–6.
27 Arendt 2006a; Arendt 2006b.
28 'In Search of a New Monumentality', 1948.
29 Bullock 2002, 50.
30 'The University in the City', 1964.
31 Rykwert 1968, 61–3.
32 Campbell 2012.
33 Harwood 2000, 40.
34 Muthesius 2000, 107; Lubbock 2002, 116.
35 Lefebvre 1991, 39; Merrifield 2006, 109.
36 Spence 1964.
37 Long and Thomas 2007, 9; Fenton 2007.
38 Campbell 2012, 72.
39 Campbell 2007, 51.
40 Spence 1964; 'University of Sussex Archive Film', Interview with Basil Spence c.1961.
41 Basil Spence and Partners, 1961.
42 The Pacemakers 1965.
43 The Pacemakers 1965.
44 'Influences of Greek and Roman Architecture in the Proposed Sussex University', 1960.
45 Basil Spence and Partners 1961.
46 Spence 1964, 210.
47 Spence 1964, 206.
48 Campbell 2012, 159.
49 Sloman 1964, 73.
50 Tucker 1964.
51 Sloman 1967, 48.
52 'Guide to the Exhibition of the Development Plan for the University of Essex', 1963.
53 Cullen 1961; London County Council 1961.
54 Capon 1967, 49.
55 Wolfe and Browne 2013.
56 Hughes 2000, 64.
57 Wolfe and Browne 2013, 14.
58 McKean 1972, 644.
59 Tucker 1964.
60 Capon 1967, 49.
61 McKean 1972, 648.
62 McKean 1972, 648.
63 Hughes 2000, 64.
64 Muthesius 2000, 142.
65 Hughes 2000, 64.
66 Sloman 1964, 55–60.
67 'Guide to the Exhibition of the Development Plan for the University of Essex', 1963.
68 'Transcript of Interview of Albert Sloman, Re: Designing the Campus', 1996, 18–19.
69 Kedward 2013, 94.
70 Wolfe and Browne 2013, 15.
71 Rogers 1955.
72 Muthesius 2000, 142.
73 Arendt 1998, 173.

References

Arendt, Hannah. *The Human Condition*. 2nd edition. Chicago: University of Chicago Press, 1998.

Arendt, Hannah. 'The crisis in culture: Its social and its political significance'. In *Between Past and Future: Eight exercises in political thought*, 194–222. New York: Penguin Books, 2006a.

Arendt, Hannah. 'The crisis in education'. In *Between Past and Future: Eight exercises in political thought*, 170–93. New York: Penguin Books, 2006b.

Arendt, Hannah. 'Introduction: Walther Benjamin: 1892–1940'. In *Illuminations*, by Walter Benjamin, 7–55. London: Bodley Head, 2015.

Basil Spence and Partners. 'University College of Sussex, College House – Building summary', 2 February 1961. SxUOS1/1/5/3/1/5/7. University of Sussex Collection.

Berman, Marshall. *All that is Solid Melts into Air: The experience of modernity*. New York: Viking Penguin, 1988.

Briggs, Asa. 'Drawing a new map of learning'. In *The Idea of a New University: An experiment in Sussex*, ed. David Daiches, 60–80. London: André Deutsch, 1964.

Bullock, Nicholas. *Building the Post-War World: Modern architecture and reconstruction in Britain*. London: Routledge, 2002.

Campbell, Louise. '"Drawing a new map of learning": Spence and the University of Sussex'. In *Basil Spence: Architect*, edited by Philip Long and Jane Thomas, 97–103. Edinburgh: National Galleries of Scotland in association with RCAHMS, 2007.

Campbell, Louise. 'Coventry Cathedral'. In *Basil Spence: Buildings and projects*, by Louise Campbell, Miles Glendinning and Jane Thomas, 72–103. London: RIBA, 2012.

Capon, Kenneth. 'University of Essex: Part 2'. In *University Planning and Design: A symposium*, by Michael Brawne, 48–53. London: Published for the Architectural Association by Lund Humphries, 1967.

Cragoe, Matthew. 'Asa Briggs and the University of Sussex, 1961–1976'. In *The Age of Asa: Lord Briggs, public life and history in Britain since 1945*, edited by Miles Taylor, 225–47. New York: Palgrave Macmillan, 2014.

Cullen, Gordon. *Townscape*. London: Architectural Press, 1961.

Daiches, David. *The Idea of a New University: An experiment in Sussex*. London: André Deutsch, 1964.

Darley, Gillian. 'Visions, prospects and compromises', *Higher Education Quarterly* 45, no. 4 (1 October 1991): 354–66. https://doi.org/10.1111/j.1468-2273.1991.tb01578.x.

Edgerton, David. *Warfare State: Britain, 1920–1970*. Cambridge: Cambridge University Press, 2006.

'Education Act 1944'. Queen's Printer of Acts of Parliament. Accessed 5 May 2020. http://www.legislation.gov.uk/ukpga/Geo6/7-8/31/contents/enacted.

Fenton, Clive B. 'First buildings 1932–9: Arts and crafts to modernism'. In *Basil Spence: Architect*, edited by Philip Long and Jane Thomas, 35–47. Edinburgh: National Galleries of Scotland in association with RCAHMS, 2007.

Giedion, Sigfried. 'The need for a new monumentality'. In *New Architecture and City Planning: A symposium*, by Paul Zucker, 549–68. New York: Philosophical Library, 1944.

'Guide to the exhibition of the Development Plan for the University of Essex', October 1963. Foundation Papers Box 3b. University of Essex Collection.

Halsey, A. H. *Decline of Donnish Dominion: The British academic professions in the twentieth century*. Oxford: Clarendon Press, 1992.

Harvey, David. *The Condition of Postmodernity: An enquiry into the origins of cultural change*. Oxford: Basil Blackwell, 1989.

Harwood, Elain. 'The Churchill College competition and the Smithson generation'. In *Twentieth-century architecture and its histories*, by Louise Campbell, 35–56. London: Society of Architectural Historians of Great Britain, 2000.

Heynen, Hilde. *Architecture and Modernity: A critique*. Cambridge, MA: MIT Press, 1999.

Howard, Maurice. 'Ancient spaces in modern dress: Basil Spence at the University of Sussex'. In *British Design: Tradition and modernity after 1948*, edited by Christopher Breward, Fiona Fisher and Ghislaine Wood, 101–11. London: Bloomsbury Academic, 2015.

Hughes, Jonathan. '1961'. In *Twentieth-Century Architecture and Its Histories*, by Louise Campbell, 57–84. London: Society of Architectural Historians of Great Britain, 2000.

'Influences of Greek and Roman architecture in the proposed Sussex University'. *The Architect and Building News*, 13 April 1960. SxUOS1/1/5/1/3/6. University of Sussex Collection.

Kedward, Rod. 'The University of Sussex and the modern European mind'. In *The Transformation of an English University from the 1960s: Fifty years of societal and religious developments at the University of Sussex*, by Geoffrey Victor Whitfield, 93–102. Lexington, KY: Emeth Press, 2013.

Lefebvre, Henri. *The Production of Space*. Translated by Donald Nicholson-Smith. Oxford: Blackwell, 1991.

London County Council. *The Planning of a New Town: Data and design based on a study for a new town of 100,000 at Hook, Hampshire*. London: London County Council, 1961.

Long, Philip and Jane Thomas. 'Introduction'. In *Basil Spence: Architect*, edited by Philip Long and Jane Thomas, 9–10. Edinburgh: National Galleries of Scotland in association with RCAHMS, 2007.

Lubbock, Jules. 'The counter-modernist sublime: The campus of the University of Essex', *Twentieth Century Architecture* 6 (2002): 106–18.

McKean, John. 'University of Essex: Case study', *The Architects' Journal* 156/38 (20 September 1972), 637–78.

McKean, John. 'The English university of the 1960s: Built community, model universe'. In *Man-made Future: Planning, education, and design in mid-twentieth century Britain*, edited by Iain Boyd White, 205–22. London: Routledge, 2007.

Merrifield, Andy. *Henri Lefebvre: A critical introduction*. New York: Routledge, 2006.

Muthesius, Stefan. *The Postwar University: Utopianist campus and college*. New Haven, CT: Yale University Press, 2000.

Ortolano, Guy. *The Two Cultures Controversy: Science, literature and cultural politics in postwar Britain*. Cambridge: Cambridge University Press, 2009.

Pevsner, Nikolaus. 'Universities: Yesterday', *The Architectural Review* 122/729 (1 October 1957): 234–9.

Rogers, Ernesto. '"Preexisting conditions and issues of contemporary building practice" from *Casabella-Continuità*, Feb 1955'. In *Italy Builds: Its modern architecture and native inheritance*, by George Everard Kidder Smith, 200–4. London: Architectural Press, 1955.

Rothblatt, Sheldon. *The Modern University and Its Discontents: The fate of Newman's Legacies in Britain and America*. Cambridge: Cambridge University Press, 1997.

Rykwert, Joseph. 'Universities as institutional archetypes of our age', *Zodiac* 18 (1968): 61–3.

Silver, Harold. *Higher Education and Opinion Making in Twentieth-Century England*. London: Woburn Press, 2003.

Sloman, Albert. *A University in the Making*. London: British Broadcasting Corporation, 1964.

Sloman, Albert. 'University of Essex: Part 1'. In *University Planning and Design: A symposium*, edited by Michael Brawne, 46–8. London: Published for the Architectural Association by Lund Humphries, 1967.

Spence, Basil. 'Building a new university: The first phase'. In *The Idea of a New University: An experiment in Sussex*, ed. David Daiches, 201–15. London: André Deutsch, 1964.

The Pacemakers: Basil Spence (film). Central Office of Information, 1965. Online. https://www.bfi.org.uk/films-tv-people/4de83927ef787.

'The university in the city', *The Architectural Review* 136/809 (1 July 1964): a8–12.

Tight, Malcolm. *The Development of Higher Education in the United Kingdom since 1945*. Maidenhead: Open University Press, 2009.

'Transcript of Interview of Albert Sloman, Re: Designing the Campus', 27 February 1996. Foundation Papers Box 1b. University of Essex Collection.

Tucker, W.E. 'Bright Lights at Midnight'. *Essex County Standard – University Supplement*, October 1964. Box 5 – Newspaper Articles and special supplements 1964–7. University of Essex Collection.

University Grants Committee. *University Development, 1957–1962* (Cmnd. 2267). London: House of Commons Sessional Papers, 1964.

'University of Sussex Archive Film', Undated. Item Ref: SxUOS1/1/5/1/20. University of Sussex Collection.

Wolfe, Ivor de and Kenneth Browne. *The Italian Townscape*. New ed. London: Artifice, 2013.

13

Italy assessing the UK assessing Italy: a battle of perspectives on cities and learning

Francesco Zuddas

'The sooner the university is back in town and making its unique contribution to the quality of life of the town the better for all concerned'.[1]

There is more than a polemic about university planning in these words by the editors of the *Architectural Review* (*AR*). Published in February 1972 with the unequivocal title 'A Florentine Fiasco', the text was a commentary on the results of the design competition for the expansion of the University of Florence. At a time when new academic buildings and settlements were often being located on virgin land or in the outskirts of towns, speaking of universities inevitably meant discussing an idea of urbanism for cities in expansion. But in the article and the related diatribe between the UK and Italy that was fired by the Florence competition also stood the mirror image of a deep divide of urbanistic philosophies between the two countries – a divide that had deepened during the post-war years.

The UK assessing Italy: A fiasco?

The Florence competition brief asked for the combination of a new academic axis in the outskirts and the reorganization of the university presence in the historic city.[2] As such, it was a call for ideas on how to conceive of the city beyond its historic boundaries, or what the post-war Italian architects throughout the 1960s had been calling a *Città territorio*. The new academic axis was to be located along the westward corridor for

A FLORENTINE FIASCO

One of the lessons learnt from this country's post-war university building programme is that a campus of culture, learning and athleticism, sitting in 200 acres of playing fields and parkland two miles from town, is not a final, ideal solution. It is administratively tidy, and it is also much cheaper and easier to build on virgin land. But a university needs more than isolation from the bubbub of town. It is a romantic dream that research and academic study is best undertaken in rural bliss, and growing ideas of continuing education, adult education and re-education suggests that the sooner the university is back in town and making its unique contribution to the quality of life of the town the better for all concerned.

To judge from an architectural competition recently held by Florence University, Italy would seem to be following this regrettable British practice, despite strong protests made by James Gowan, the one British architect among the 17 assessors.

Florence University issued the vague, generalised conditions for what they called an international competition in 1970 but without having asked the assessors to help prepare them, and issuing them only in Italian which formed a considerable handicap to foreigners. The conditions contained quite inadequate information about the existing university organisation and the location of departments—another factor prejudicial to any non-natives competing. In the event the International Union of Architects ruled that the competition did not fulfil the necessary conditions to merit the title 'international' and member nations of the IUA were so warned, but not, it seems, James Gowan.

Florence University with a prewar nominal capacity of about 5000 students has now, apparently, 20 000 and is still growing. So is the town. What more logical therefore for the promoters than to devise a plan to accommodate the growth of both. Unfortunately the site chosen was farming land north-west of Florence through which runs, with attendant ribbon development, a motorway to Prato.

The paucity of information and the size of the project seems to have effectively limited

The winning design in an international competition for a new university and satellite town for Florence. 1 (opposite page), the overall development plan, spreading from Florence, bottom right, to Prato, centre, and Pistoia, top left. West of the road junctions shown on the outskirts of Florence is the site for the proposed university and town centre shown in the birds-eye perspective, 4, with Florence in the distance, and also in the model, 2, 3, the university buildings seen from the administration and research centre. In the foreground is the trellis structure of the elevated railway. 5, internal piazza. On the left is the overhead railway and regional offices. In the background, the chemistry, physics and maths buildings.

Figure 13.1 'A Florentine Fiasco'. *The Architectural Review* 900 (1972): 79–82. Endorsing the critique by juror James Gowan, the editors of the *Architectural Review* polemicize with the premises and results of the international competition for the expansion of the University of Florence. The illustrations in the article are from the winning project by Vittorio Gregotti, Edoardo Detti *et al.*

Courtesy of the *Architectural Review*

urban expansion envisaged in the most recent City Plan authored in 1962 by urbanist Edoardo Detti. Eventually, Detti was also pronounced the winner of the competition in a team of architects that included Vittorio Gregotti and Franco Purini among others.[3] Their proposal, named *Amalassunta*, combined the objectives of the City Plan with Gregotti's own research on the 'anthropogeographic project', which he defined as architecture's role of providing formal and figurative meaning to existing landscapes, especially at a large scale.[4] *Amalassunta* did so by devising an archipelago of formally finite interventions around the core of Florence and along the westward development corridor. The new university was meant to be a major anchor for such city-territory.

The large transport hubs located as a ring around the city centre, and more generally the complex infrastructural network set out by the project to mix private and public transportation, placed the proposal within the 1960s international scene of architect-authored large-scale master plans, finding references in cases such as Kenzo Tange's Tokyo Bay Plan or, even more evidently, Louis Kahn's proposals for the centre of Philadelphia.[5] Like those examples, *Amalassunta* impressed for its heroic size ('five Whitehalls, or 20 Pitti Palaces, to put it in Florentine terms', in the words of the *AR* editors)[6] but also raised in the British observers as many doubtful feelings as to its practicality. While praising the addition of a civic centre with shops and offices to complement the academic spaces, the absence of student residences was considered a crucial mistake that would turn the new academic/civic settlement into a commuter's destination 'virtually dead for two-thirds of the day'.[7]

The *AR*'s polemic was an endorsement to the decision of James Gowan to quit his role in the competition jury. Gowan himself clarified his reasons in a short piece published in *Casabella* two months later, where he listed the competition's main problems: the deceitful international character of a contest that was really Italo-centric; the inadequate level of the entries, none of which deserved a prize; and the generally ill-conceived brief that relocated the university outside of the city.[8] On this last point the *AR* editors insisted particularly, backing their condemnation for the alleged exile of the university out of town with a comparison to recent British university planning:

> One of the lessons learnt from this country's post-war university building programme is that a campus of culture, learning and athleticism, sitting in 200 acres of playing fields and parkland two miles from town, is not a final, ideal solution.[9]

Italy assessing the UK: Beyond nostalgia

The UK was a pioneer in the international university building programme of the 1960s, founding and building several new academic institutions. Seven of these, alternatively referred to as Plateglass Universities or just New Universities, had been rapidly instituted, built and opened by the mid-1960s in a showcase of a remarkable capacity at implementing complex plans in the country's interest. All were located on virgin land sites outside small and medium-sized towns.[10]

Italy started observing what was happening in British university planning and design in the early 1960s, at a time when indigenous discussions on how to reform the country's higher education were still far from reaching the architects' drawing boards – something that would only happen nearer the turn of the 1970s, with the competition for the University of Florence marking an important moment.[11]

In 1962, an article in *Casabella* penned by Matilde Rivolta Biffa discussed projects from an early period of post-war British university design that was mostly marked by somewhat small expansions of existing universities. Biffa did not yet comment on the controversial decision of building brand new developments in outlying sites, which in 1962 had not been much publicized yet, despite most of the seven Plateglass being already on the drawing boards if not starting construction. Focusing on mostly inner-town cases, she particularly praised those projects that managed to confirm the embedded nature of British town and gown. Among these were some new colleges and buildings for Oxford and Cambridge, and the expansion of the University of Edinburgh planned by Sir Basil Spence. The latter was presented as an example of integration between academic and city functions that confirmed the 'structuring role of university areas inside the urban fabric' considered typical of the best British tradition.[12]

Biffa's article appeared right in the middle of a series of issues that *Casabella* devoted to a discussion of cities beyond their historic limits under the alternative labels of *Città regione* and *Città territorio*. We will come back to this discussion later, but it is here important to note that by 1962 the Italian architectural discourse was comfortable in praising a somewhat traditional understanding of universities inside towns as it was emerging from an early stage of post-war British academic planning.

Six years later, in 1968, the Italian reception of the next phase of UK higher education expansion showed a much more critical attitude. A few publications came out in and around that year that reviewed the by then mostly accomplished experience of the Plateglass Universities, all of which were up and running. Giancarlo De Carlo and Paola Coppola Pignatelli, respectively from their academic posts in Venice (IUAV) and Rome (La Sapienza), published the findings of two research projects on university planning and design, and included the British experience among the case studies.[13]

Concomitantly, some Italian architectural periodicals investigated the reasons and counter-reasons of such experience. The Adriano Olivetti-founded magazine, *Zodiac*, was one of these with its eighteenth issue being monographic on twentieth-century British architectural discourse. Besides including Henry-Russell Hitchcock's review of English architecture in the earlier part of the century, the issue focused on some major preoccupations and concepts of the post-war era, such as Brutalism, infrastructural design, and regional and metropolitan planning.

Inserted within such table of contents were a few articles that contributed a reading of what could be rightly considered as two stages of the same urbanistic discourse: the New Towns and the New Universities. Starting from the latter, two articles critically assessed the newly built academic complexes. Joseph Rykwert's 'Universities as Institutional Archetypes of Our Age' claimed that if anything was to be learnt out of the construction of a new university settlement, it had not to do with a demonstration of how to build a miniature self-contained city. Instead, the strong demand for building new academic institutions had to be taken as an opportunity to provide more spaces for practising social dissent – a conclusion clearly imbued in 1968 ethos.[14]

A second article, penned by Bianca Raboni, echoed Rykwert's position claiming that 'the problem [of higher education], is anything but resolvable in terms of a nostalgic image of café life and bohemianism.'[15] She duly acknowledged some noticeable innovative aspects of the Plateglass, such as their construction technology, the widening of teaching and learning methods, and the indubitable proof of strong top-down decision-making orchestrated jointly by the central government and the universities. Yet, her conclusions argued for the need of 'an actual qualitative leap forward.'[16] On this point, she found the company of two British names that had been voicing criticism of the architectural response to higher education reform from within their country's discourse.

Intermission: The UK assessing itself

Reyner Banham was one of these critical voices. He polemicized with the architects' response to the epochal calls for change coming from post-war society and condemned the architects for their 'offering to paralyse change by fixing the first concept in expensive and monumental structures'.[17] Next to him was Cedric Price, who added to the critique with a practical counter-example. His project, Potteries Thinkbelt, clearly set against the small, nostalgic, backward-looking and isolated Plateglass, about which Price polemically wrote in 1966, ridiculing them as variations on a 'medieval college with power points'.[18]

Elaborating on this critique, Raboni noted that all the British new universities 'present themselves as autonomous units … and the frequent comparison with the convent of medieval society or the post-war new towns expressively underlines this aspect.'[19] She thus applauded the alternative response offered by Price for its ability to go beyond the 'codified image of the university as a place which is physically defined within precise boundaries, the expression of an alternative, privileged function.'[20]

Anticipating a future reality to which we have become accustomed in the twenty-first century where students are equalled to the status of labourers deprived of certainties and fixed points, Potteries Thinkbelt merged mobility, learning and production to reinvent what was meant by higher education.[21] In so doing, it also reframed the scale of reasoning, going much beyond any possible academic building or citadel to encompass a vast territory crossed by multiple transport infrastructures and activated by production/learning plants complemented with more or less temporary forms of residential accommodation.

Interest in Price's project was also shown by Giancarlo De Carlo who included it in his mentioned research on projects and plans for new universities published in 1968.[22] Potteries Thinkbelt lent itself as one possible representation of a freer society enabled by architectural thinking and, for this reason, it appealed to the Italian architect who had been pursuing a similar line of research with his own work. In fact, a few years later, in 1971–6, De Carlo's Plan for the University of Pavia re-proposed some of Price's ideas, such as mobile research poles moving across a regional territory. Matched with the adaptive reuse of inner-city buildings, De Carlo's plan would implement an idea of the university understood as something more than a specialist location, and as a fundamentally urban space open to a broad, anonymous audience.[23]

Price and De Carlo shared a similar attitude towards questioning the status quo and breaking through the barriers of top-down decision-making. The space of the university lent itself perfectly to such end, and it is not surprising that these two architects remain particularly remembered for their projects and writings about universities. At the same time, the Price/De Carlo pairing testifies to wider Italian interest on some British counter-proposals for higher education, cities and their territories, which contrasts with the discredit of the New Universities.

A review of counter-proposals was offered by Piero Sartogo and Carlo Pelliccia's fifth instalment in their article series titled 'Campus Design'. The series was published in *Casabella* in 1968–9 and followed on a visiting professorship by the two authors at the University of Virginia. Interspersing analysis of built cases, proposals and the projects of their own architecture students in Virginia, Sartogo and Pelliccia insisted that the problems posed by the mass university were not merely quantitative but 'qualitative in nature and such as to transform radically the preceding university.'[24] Their fifth article discussed the 'individual roads to education as alternatives to educational institutions', and spotted a gap between the new learning technologies and media available at the time, and the obsolete traditional formats of learning, thus arguing that:

> The truly new meaning of education lies not so much in the multiplication and spread of new educational organisms whose processes are under institutional control, as in apparatus whose educational processes are under the individual's control. The objective is the generalization of education throughout all levels of society.[25]

Cedric Price's arguments clearly resound in these words, and in fact the article was illustrated with examples coming from the most experimental parts of British architectural culture of the time, including Price's own project Atom and Archigram's Ideas Circus. Variations on the argument that learning needed to break from the fixity of a four-wall classroom, the two projects proposed mobile systems of education that were in line with the ideas of plug-in cities and looser uses of spaces and institutions advocated by the British avant-garde as ways towards individual freedom and self-empowerment. These projects appealed to Sartogo and Pelliccia also because they showed that education could claim back a 'level of anonymity' by retrieving the educational capacity of existing or projected new urban structures.

In particular, Price's Atom project was produced during the design charrette 'New Schools for New Towns' (Rice University, 1967) that asked participants to reflect on 'the opportunity that the new towns present as laboratories for approaching educational and school building problems in better ways.'[26] Making the link between new-town planning and planning for new educational spaces, Atom and other projects from the charrette offered a radical counter-voice to the type of link between those two planning objectives that had been implemented in the real world, and especially in the UK.

Reprise: Italy assessing the UK: The road backwards from universities to new towns to garden cities

Biffa's 1962 *Casabella* article on the British universities already made the connection with the experience of the New Towns, in turn bringing both back to their common originating point: Ebenezer Howard's Garden City. Six years later, Lina Marsoni thoroughly reviewed for *Zodiac* the story of the New Towns. Marsoni retraced the main steps from the Barlow Report of 1940, through the first stage of development, all the way to the most recent general rethinking of the very idea of the new towns, which aimed at loosening the closed and rigid character of the urbanistic idea lying behind them.[27]

On this last aspect Marsoni's article built its own criticism. The New Towns suffered, she claimed, from an original sin located in Howard's anti-urban sentiments. Howard conceived of planning as a limiting force to urban growth, and this relied on the possibility of thinking in terms of an ideal size – of a community and, therefore, of a physical settlement. The notion of an ideal size grounded the concept of neighbourhood communities or units, which Marsoni discounted for not leaving any 'place for confusion, ambiguity, uncertainty', namely the key attributes of urbanity.[28] Contrary to the proven fact, as she argued, that 'no town may be prevented from growing indefinitely', the New Towns prescribed 'only one correct way of living, and this one only was made possible.'[29]

Rethinking the New Towns 20 years after their first formulation, and 70 since the Garden City idea came into planning currency, meant breaking with the rigid 'new town-monad'[30] and seeking instead 'a dynamic town the functions of which should be integrated at any level of implementation'.[31] These words remind of those used in 1962 by Giancarlo De Carlo to conclude a seminar on the 'City Region'. On that occasion, which is often signalled as a key moment in the evolution of the post-war Italian architectural/urbanistic discourse, De Carlo talked of the city as a 'dynamic set of relations that contrasts with the static condition of the traditional city'.[32] Part of an intense debate on cities understood beyond their traditional boundaries, the *Città regione* and *Città territorio* discussed in Italy in the early 1960s presented scenarios opposed to an urban planning culture that had, instead, preached about possible escapes from the city by means of self-regulating entities.[33] This was the culture prescribed by the Garden City and New Towns of British origins, which was widely criticized in some of the most influential Italian texts published at the turn of the 1950s and 1960s.

Among these texts, Giuseppe Samonà's *L'urbanistica e l'avvenire della città* (1959) argued that the main problem that the British still had to resolve was how to overcome Howard's ideas. A 'cult of personality'[34] towards Howard was so pervasive in the UK to prevent his de-sanctification, so that Samonà saw a fundamental problem persisting in the post-war period: understanding the new town/garden city solely in terms of a decongesting agent to cure large metropolises, instead of thinking of 'activating the productive forces of territories by putting the new town as their fulcrum'.[35]

Samonà admitted that the Garden City was one of the greatest technical achievements of modern urbanism, but its technicality was all that there was to it. On this aspect, he was surely indebted to the criticism of Howard's idea that Carlo Doglio had elaborated a few years earlier. In an essay published in 1953, Doglio had discussed the Garden City as a mere technocratic act that was devoid of the socialist spirit animating other utopian thinkers of the late nineteenth century, from William Morris to Charles Fourier. His analysis pointed to unveil the false consciousness of an idea and its creator that, while proclaiming willingness to change society, actually aimed at strengthening the existing one with its current class structures.[36] Or, to put it in the words used in *Zodiac* in 1968, it prescribed one way of living, and that one only.

What Doglio first formulated in a most explicit way was that the Garden City merely 'worked', and perfectly, so that it would easily be accepted as an example of pragmatic planning capable of *actually* achieving results. Invariably, therefore, the Italian criticism of the Garden City/New Towns nexus could not avoid highlighting its ultimate merit: their mere being a fact, existing in reality and not only on paper. This was enough reason for it to be worthy of study and consideration, and the 1968 *Zodiac* article on the New Towns concluded precisely in this way, praising them as the demonstration that only through realizations can ideas be tested and discussed.

Such praise extended also to the appreciation of the British new universities, which in fact were widely looked at by the Italian architects who in the early 1970s started to *actually* design universities. But the way they looked at them was always with a technical eye, searching for standards and technological details, but invariably retaining the same critical position towards their underlying ideas as nothing but the vitiated continuation of the Garden City/New Town tradition – a tradition inappropriate to solve the problems, desires and anxieties of post-war urban society.

At the same time, the type of Italian praise of the main moments in recent British planning and architecture anticipated an intimate sense of frustration related to their own country, where the debate on city-territories was coupled with heroic visions and projects that mostly remained on paper. Scenarios for new business districts (*Centri direzionali*), development corridors (*Assi attrezzati*) and, ultimately, new universities were destined to a very different fate from the British perfection of translating from drawing to building, eventually promoting an image of 1960s Italy as a place of prodigious theoretical thinking and great practical inconsequentiality.

Assess or pillory: Keep it in the city

Back to the Florentine diatribe of 1972. It is now possible to understand the defence brought forward by the winning architects against the accusations moved by Gowan and the *Architectural Review*. The latter had indicated the abandonment of the old city and the absence of student residences integrated with the new academic pole as major reasons why the very premises of the competition needed to be disregarded altogether. In response, Gregotti, Detti and their team noted how:

> The intention was to give meaning to the university, to consider it principally as a place of public exchange (a 'social condenser', as the Soviet avant-garde called the factory) that directly affects the region. To do this, it was necessary to break the ideology of the campus.[37]

The word campus was here used as the academic-related alternative to Garden City or New Town: namely, another self-regulating monad promising to solve contradictions from within its clearly defined boundaries. And even if the detractors could go further to argue that also *Amalassunta*'s university was based precisely on its finiteness as a figure (indeed an important aspect of Gregotti's own theorizations about the nexus of architecture and landscape), the aim of the project was in line with the type of urbanistic discourse that had developed in post-war Italy: to devise a *Città territorio* (even if this term was not explicitly used by Gregotti) by means of:

> a chain of interventions (the university represents one of the central ones) [to ultimately provide] a clearly complementary and geographically well-defined system. To speak in these circumstances of the university as either in or outside the city is completely meaningless.[38]

A city with no outside is what *Amalassunta* proposed by taking advantage of the urgency of rethinking an institution, the university, that was understood as playing a key role in the years to come for shaping what we have since then come to call knowledge-based societies. Of course, the divide between the idea indicated by *Amalassunta* (and other similar Italian projects of the early 1970s) and its respective British counterparts would not be washed away. And in the light of the Florentine fiasco diatribe it is not a surprise to read, two years later in 1974, another *Architectural Review* article praising the stubbornness of the University of Leeds to resist 'the classic advice of the architect to his large-scale client ... to "Go Out"'.[39]

The title of the article could not be more explicit: 'Keep it in the city'. Seventeen years had passed since the British magazine offered the first thorough consideration of university design. In 1957, Lionel Brett had warned about some universities having 'surrendered and moved out'.[40] What was most alarming, for Brett, was that the move did not bring the student accommodation along, thus starting a commuter-culture that put unnecessary and dangerous pressure on transport infrastructure. The caricature could not be fuller in irony:

> [The students] were likely to be scattered over acres or square miles of urban or suburban streets. And so, like other workers, they caught the 8.30, heavily loaded with books and notes, distinguished from other commuters only by tired look and hideous muffler.[41]

That these words work perfectly (still today) as a description of the typical day of an Italian university student would give enough reason to the advocates of the Florentine fiasco. But read within the context of an architectural community such as the Italian one of the 1960s attempting to break with a planning ideology of British origins, it helps understanding a bit better how, after all, what Gregotti and others were proposing was a far more daring future that accepted as a fact, albeit reluctantly, the impossibility of controlling urban growth. Declaring the futility of reasoning in terms of inside or outside cities, they showed that there could only be one single reality created out of the blurring of what were traditionally known as city and countryside. Ironically, this had exactly been the declared aim of Ebenezer Howard – a crucial figure of twentieth-century urbanism that the post-war Italian architects somehow pilloried in order to try to *actually* achieve his vision.

Notes

1 'A Florentine Fiasco' 1972, 79.

2 The competition was reviewed in *Casabella* 361 (1972): 19–29; *Controspazio* 1–2 (1972): 5–31; *Domus* 509 (1972): 1–12; *Urbanistica* 62 (1974): 45–63.

3 Besides Detti and Gregotti the team consisted of: Emilio Battisti, Gian Franco Di Pietro, Giovanni Fanelli, Teresa Cobbò, Raimondo Innocenti, Marco Massa, Hiromichi Matsui, Mario Mocchi, Paolo Sica, Bruno Viganò Bruno, Marica Zoppi; Collaborators: Francesco Barbagli, Peo Calza, Gian Franco Dallerba, Franco Luis Neves, Franco Purini.

4 Gregotti 1966.

5 Gregotti's interest in Kahn's project had been evidenced in his writings, examples being the book *Il territorio dell'architettura* (1966) and one of the issues of *Edilizia Moderna* (no. 80, 1963) curated by Gregotti during his tenure as the magazine's editor.

6 'A Florentine Fiasco' 1972, 80.

7 'A Florentine Fiasco' 1972, 80.

8 Gowan 1972. Gowan lamented the poor English text of the competition brief, which he related as evidence of the very fact that only Italian architects took part. Among the latter, he singled out four that 'by implication ridiculed the competition'. While not naming names, it is likely that Archizoom were among those four. The Florentine collective entered a polemical project that went against the brief and was used as a test bed of their project No-Stop City, which was published in a *Casabella* article in 1971 almost concomitantly with the competition's deadline.

9 'A Florentine Fiasco' 1972, 79.

10 The seven universities were: Sussex (established in 1958, first buildings started in 1960), York (1960, 1963), East Anglia (1960, 1964), Essex (1961, 1964), Kent (1961, 1964), Warwick (1961, 1964), and Lancaster (1962, 1964). In 1961, the British government appointed a committee chaired by Lord Lionel Charles Robbins to study the state of the country's higher education and advise on its development. The committee published its report – known as the Robbins Report – in 1963, advising for an expansion of higher education. The report helped push forward the plans for the seven universities as well as for other ones to be established in the following years. For a discussion on the British New Universities from the time of their creation see Brawne 1967. For a more recent account see Muthesius 2000.

11 In 1966–7, a national competition for the University of Chieti pre-dated the one for Florence. Despite being won by the important office BBPR, the competition was little advertised or commented on in the architectural press. The University of Florence competition was comparatively much more debated, thus signalling itself as the real starting point of an Italian higher education design season that would include other similar competitions for the universities of Cagliari (1971–2), Calabria (1972–4) and Salerno (1973–5). For a discussion of these cases see Zuddas 2020.

12 Biffa 1962, 22.

13 De Carlo 1968; Coppola Pignatelli 1969. Other research projects conducted by architect/academics of the Italian faculties of architecture and planning in the late 1960s included Clemente 1969; Canella and D'Angiolini 1975. In October 1970, a conference on university planning and design was organized by ISES (an institute for the management of public housing) in Rome. The conference saw the participation of most of the architects and academics that had been dealing with the topic, including among others Ludovico Quaroni, Guido Canella, Paola Coppola Pignatelli and Piero and Francesca Sartogo. The conference was covered in *Casabella* ('The Ises meeting ...' 1971). The proceedings are held at Archivio Bottoni, Milan: VVAA 1970.

14 Rykwert 1968.
15 Raboni 1968, 280.
16 Raboni 1968, 280.
17 Reyner Banham, 'The Outhouses of Academy', *New Society*, 1966, cited in Raboni 1968, 279.
18 Price 1966, 483.
19 Raboni 1968, 279.
20 Raboni 1968, 281.
21 Aureli 2011.
22 De Carlo 1968.
23 On De Carlo's plan for Pavia see Zuddas 2015.
24 Sartogo and Pelliccia 1969, 12.
25 Sartogo and Pelliccia 1969, 12.
26 Cannady 1967, 4.
27 Marsoni 1968.
28 Marsoni 1968, 268.
29 Marsoni 1968, 268.
30 Marsoni 1968, 194. My translation from the Italian. The English translation reads 'the self-regulating new town' (Marsoni 1968, 268).
31 Marsoni 1968, 269.
32 De Carlo 1962.
33 For a review of the post-war Italian urbanistic and architectural discourse see Conforto *et al.* 1977; Ferrari 2005.
34 Samonà 1959, 121.
35 Samonà 1959, 122.
36 Doglio 1985, 34.
37 Gregotti *et al.* 1972, 63.
38 Gregotti *et al.* 1972, 63.
39 'Keep it in the City' 1974, 3.
40 Brett 1957.
41 Brett 1957, 241.

References

'A Florentine Fiasco', *The Architectural Review* 900 (1972): 79–82.

Atti del convegno di studio sull'edilizia universitaria. Rome: ISES Istituto per lo Sviluppo dell'Edilizia Sociale, 1970.

Aureli, Pier Vittorio. 'Labor and architecture: Revisiting Cedric Price's Potteries Thinkbelt', *Log* 23 (2011): 97–118.

Brawne, Michael (ed.). *University Planning and Design: A symposium* (Architectural Association Paper 3). London: Lund Humphries for the Architectural Association, 1967.

Brett, Lionel. 'Universities: Today', *The Architectural Review* 729 (1957): 240–51.

Canella, Guido and Lucio D'Angiolini (eds) *Università: Ragione, contesto, tipo*. Bari: Dedalo, 1975.

Cannady, William (ed.). *New Schools for New Towns*. Houston: Rice University School of Architecture, 1967.

Clemente, Ferdinando (ed.). *Università e territorio*. Bologna: S.T.E.B., 1969.

Conforto, Cina, Gabriele De Giorgi, Alessandra Muntoni and Marcello Pazzaglini. *Il dibattito architettonico in Italia, 1945–1975*. Rome: Bulzoni, 1977.

Coppola Pignatelli, Paola. *L'università in espansione: Orientamenti dell'edilizia universitaria*. Milan: Etas Kompass, 1969.

De Carlo, Giancarlo. 'Relazione conclusiva al seminario dell'ILSES sulla nuova dimensione e la citta-regione.' Stresa: Istituto Lombardo di Studi Economici e Sociali, 1962: 19–21.

De Carlo, Giancarlo (ed.). *Pianificazione e disegno delle università*. Rome: Edizioni universitarie italiane, 1968.

Doglio, Carlo. *La città giardino*. Rome: Gangemi, 1985. First published as an essay in Carlo Doglio. *L'equivoco della città-giardino*. Naples: RL Edizioni, 1953.

Ferrari, Mario. *Il progetto urbano in Italia: 1940–1990*. Florence: Alinea, 2005.

Gowan, James. 'Firenze Università: Appunti di un membro fuggiasco', *Casabella* 364 (1972): 10.
Gregotti, Vittorio. *Il territorio dell'architettura*. Milan: Feltrinelli, 1966.
Gregotti, Vittorio and 17 others. 'Florentine Fiasco: To the editors', *The Architectural Review* 905 (1972): 63.
'Keep it in the City', *The Architectural Review* 923 (1974): 2–18.
Marsoni, Lina. '20 anni di New Towns: Rilettura di un intervento parametrico', *Zodiac* 18 (1968): 188–200. English translation pp. 266–72.
Muthesius, Stefan. *The Postwar University: Utopianist campus and college*. London: Yale University Press, 2000.
Price, Cedric. 'Life conditioning', *Architectural Design* 36/10 (1966): 483.
Raboni, Bianca. 'Le università in Inghilterra: Un problema aperto', *Zodiac* 18 (1968): 212–19. English translation pp. 278–82.
Rivolta Biffa, Matilde. 'Aspetti e prospettive dei complessi universitari in Gran Bretagna', *Casabella* 268 (1962): 17–24.
Rykwert, Joseph. 'Universities as institutional archetypes of our age', *Zodiac* 18 (1968): 61–3.
Samonà, Giuseppe. *L'urbanistica e l'avvenire della città*. Bari: Laterza, 1959.
Sartogo, Piero and Carlo Pelliccia. 'Campus Design 5: Le vie individuali all'istruzione come alternativa alle istituzioni educazionali', *Casabella* 332 (1969): 12–17.
'The Ises meeting on university building', *Casabella* 357 (1971): 19–30.
Zuddas, Francesco. 'Pretentious equivalence: De Carlo, Woods and Mat-Building', *FAmagazine* 34 (2015): 45–65.
Zuddas, Francesco. *The University as a Settlement Principle: Territorialising knowledge in late 1960s Italy*. London: Routledge, 2020.

14
The jewel of the Triennale: dialogues between Italy and the UK around a school

Gabriele Neri

Set in the Palazzo dell'Arte, the magnificent venue built by Giovanni Muzio in 1932–3 at the edge of Sempione Park, the post-war Milanese Triennali provided an outstanding stage where Italian design culture would establish a connection with the international scene.[1] From Alvar Aalto to Max Bill, from Josep Antoni Coderch to Aldo Van Eyck, the most famous – or emerging – architects and designers attended these recurring events, intertwining a dense web of relations, contacts and exchanges.

Among the many episodes that constitute the history of the Triennali, one of them in particular marked the post-war cultural exchanges between Italy and the UK. As this chapter will show, British participation in the twelfth Milan Triennale of 1960 – consisting of the construction of a prefab model school in front of the Palazzo – would foster a wide range of dialogues, thoughts and opportunities for interaction between the two countries, creating a network that wouldn't run out at the end of the show.

A school in the park

Organized at the peak of the Italian economic boom, the twelfth Triennale was dedicated to 'Home and School', two of the most crucial themes of the time, on which a great debate was taking place, linking architecture, construction industry and politics.

Figure 14.1 CLASP British School at the XII Triennale, Milan, 1960
Courtesy of Triennale Milano – Archivio Fotografico

In 1960, in Italy, a major educational reform was just about to be set. Two years earlier, the government headed by Amintore Fanfani had worked on a 10-year School Development Plan, which was unfortunately stopped, but whose ideas would return in the early 1960s, with the development of a special programme of the Department for School Building, part of the Ministry of Education, for the construction of new schools. Among its main aims, there was the will to systematically introduce the concepts of prefabrication, standardization, industrialization, flexibility and openness in school building, as a counterpart to the new educational models that were introduced at school, as well as an answer to productive changes for the Italian economy.[2]

With regards to the construction industry, the effects of the Italian miracle had been profound, 'stretching to its limits the productive capacity of the building industry on the one hand offering numbers of opportunities for profit but on the other drying up the traditional sources of site labour'.[3] In particular, factors like the lack of qualified manpower (due to the expansion of the building industry and the better working conditions offered by other sectors) and new commercial agreements (such as the CECA for steel), these factors were changing dramatically the ratio between the cost of material and the cost of labour, provoking the need for a revolution in the field.

For many authorities, prefabrication seemed the perfect solution for these new conditions, giving a renewed incentive to the work of many Italian architects and engineers, whose impetus in that direction had been softened by certain Italian post-war politics. The measures taken by the Fanfani Government at the end of the 1940s, in particular, had favoured the continued use of traditional construction procedures, in order to employ a large-scale unskilled labour.[4]

The twelfth Triennale, instead, showed a precise effort towards a modernization of the building industry. Its Committee organized – together with the Ministry of Education and the newly established Italian Prefabrication Association (AIP) – an international conference upon the theme, as well as a competition for the study of industrial elements for primary schools building.[5]

Even without producing any immediate concrete results (some outcomes would be built and put on show at the Triennale in 1962, within the First Exhibition on Prefabrication), these initiatives offered a large overview upon the situation of the Italian construction industry, setting the ground for real applications that would start in later years, when the ministry of Education promoted the construction of over 300 industrialized schools and the extension of mandatory education demanded more classrooms.[6]

Within this frame, Britain's contribution was perfectly fitting. It consisted of a primary model school, composed of three classrooms and assembly hall, in the park around the *Palazzo dell'Arte*. It was a total prefab and furnished one, according to the principles set up by the Consortium of Local Authorities Special Programme (CLASP).[7]

The CLASP system was thought to give an answer to the great lack of school buildings in the country, which had been the topic for a great deal of research in the early 1940s. In 1943, the government had published new ideas for the post-war reconstruction of the education service, and, the following year, Parliament made these proposals the basis of the 1944 Education Act.[8] A process of updating schools had started, not only in terms of construction, but also as educational reform, which included the variety of teaching groups and the wider scope of school life.[9]

As the small catalogue released for the twelfth Triennale stated: 'A Victorian school building may look comfortingly familiar to the grandparents of the children attending it, but the activities going on inside the neo-Gothic exterior are as refreshingly up to date as next year's new car. They need only the environment of a new building, soon to be provided, to complete a revolution in the British approach to education'.[10]

Riding this wave, in 1955 Nottinghamshire started to carry out research on the prefab system for its school building programmes, and decided to develop a new one. Realizing that if the production had been left to the manufacturing industries, these would end up imposing their own standards, penalizing the expected quality and costs, the county – with the support of the Ministry of Education – decided to establish a consortium of local authorities that could have direct control over the programme, chaired by Donald Gibson, who in 1954 had become county architect to Nottinghamshire. Thus, CLASP was established in 1957, promoting the production of modular elements to be assembled in a variable way, rather than the idea of designing a model-building to replicate wherever. This research was based on the system developed by F.W. Heathcote, an engineer of Brockhouse Steel Structures, a Midlands engineering firm previously specializing in military vehicles, which would become involved in CLASP.[11]

CLASP represented an interesting experiment from both an administrative and technical point of view. In terms of organization, it was initially based on an agreement between nine local authorities, six counties and three towns. In some cases, the Ministry of Defence and the Ministry of Education also joined in. The aim of the agreement was the study and the improvement of the system, sharing the technical knowledge with all the participants. The consortium co-ordinated all the building process, organizing tenders and choosing each supplier, that would be officially nominated by the specific county. The more the programme developed, the more the costs fell and the quality increased.[12]

Architectural issues, often undervalued in other prefab systems, were in the foreground, since the consortium was at the same time the architect and the client of the building, and also thanks to the flexibility of its technical concept. It was an open system, based on a modular grid, which allowed maximum flexibility in planning, the only constraint being a module of 1m in plan and 60cm in vertical. Apart from the main steel structure, all constructive elements were interchangeable; therefore, prefabrication didn't mean the repetition of the same architectural outcome. Usually, a main company managed the production and assembly of the bearing steel structure (such as Brockhouse). Smaller local factories provided the other elements. Often, the frame was covered with cladding tiles, following a traditional method used in Kent and Sussex to cover timber-framed buildings so that, superficially, they appeared to be built of brick.[13]

As it was noted:

> CLASP cannot be considered as just a kit of components to be assembled into buildings; it is in its original form a highly complex 'unicum' in which technical details and building programmes, contract procedures and functional standards are inextricably interlocked. In this situation, the client, the architects of the building and the designer of the components are never very far from one another ... What is more they are closely associated in their interests in the ultimate result ...[14]

The British Model School at the twelfth Triennale summarized all these statements and was intended to explain them to the Italian public, also through a small exhibition within the building.

A great success

The Milanese CLASP school obtained an excellent outcome. It won the Grand Prix Special Mention of the Jury of the Triennale, and it also received good feedback from architectural critics and journalists, in both countries.

In Italy, it is worth mentioning the enthusiastic comment of Gio Ponti, the well-known architect and director of the review *Domus*, in which in 1950 he had already published a generous report on the new British schools. In his own words:

> This school is the jewel of the Triennale, and considering the harsh criticism that the XII Triennale has aroused, this school, if need be, would be enough to redeem it. And when we will talk about this Triennale, we'll say, "that of the English School".[15]

Gio Ponti particularly appreciated the way its architecture was 'form of a substance', since it reflected the 'active' pedagogical approach applied in the UK:

> Its plan is the form of his didactic system in action. It is a *true* form. But, the value of this school is not merely in the architectural solution of the design and economical problem of repetition, approached on a national scale. Its value lies in the context of reproducible prefab elements, conceived for a program of reproductions and distribution, with a result of outstanding reliability and worth.[16]

THE OBSERVER, SUNDAY, AUGUST 14, 1960

A Lesson in English

From PATIENCE GRAY

Portrait of an Italian designer (neo-Liberty).

Inside the Nottingham primary school.

The school in its leafy setting.

Neo-Liberty

The Challenge

Figure 14.2 Patience Gray. 'A Lesson in English', *The Observer*, 14 August 1960

Courtesy of CASVA – Archivio Francesco Gnecchi Ruscone

On the other side of the English Channel, the construction of the British model school was reported with attention and pride.[17] According to *The Observer*, the modernity of CLASP school was 'A Lesson in English' for the Italians, since it was considered as a sort of antidote to the *Neo Liberty* fever that affected the Peninsula.[18] 'Finally while the North Italians have been involved in the last few years in stylistic altercations and architectural pyrotechnics, Britain has been quietly solving her social problem on a tremendous scale. Serious-minded Italians feel the challenge of this achievement.'[19]

Of course, those words referred to the famous debate that had occurred the previous year, between Reyner Banham and Ernesto Rogers. In a sharp article published in *The Architectural Review* in April 1959, the English critic had denounced 'the Italian retreat from modern architecture', identified in a dangerous wave of historicist eclecticism – the Neoliberty – which called the whole status of the Modern Movement in Italy in question.[20] Soon after, Rogers wrote a 'Response to the keeper of the Frigidaire' in the pages of his *Casabella-Continuità*, defending the role of history and its conscious contribution to architectural practice:

> Our modernity resides in continuing the tradition of the Masters (including Wright's one) ... the critical and meditated retracing of the historical tradition is useful for an artist, when he refuses to accept in a mechanical way a certain matter. For Mr Banham, instead, the determinism of the forms through an abstract development line, it seems to take the place of the concept of history. Hence his aptitude for absolutions and excommunications that can only mummify reality.[21]

Not by chance, then, it was Reyner Banham who wrote the most articulated comments on CLASP school at the twelfth Triennale, defining it '"une architecture autre", something different from the architecture to which we have been accustomed since the Renaissance'.[22] He also commented in *The Listener*:

> No one, not even its designers, would want to pretend that the school was a great masterpiece of architecture. With its snug plan, white wall frames, big windows, and panels of red-brown tile-hanging, it looked perfectly at home in the *Parco Inglese*, and exactly what it was: a summation of all we have learned since the war about mass-production schools for a reformed pedagogy ...[23]

Not by chance, CLASP's designers stated that 'they "don't want aesthetics—you look after the children and the components, and the aesthetics will look after themselves" ... They were delighted when the *Architects' Journal* quoted the claim of a private architect writing on CLASP that "it is not Architecture"'.[24]

Behind the scenes

The CLASP school at the twelfth Triennale was built only at the end of a long series of negotiations, contacts and intercession. The path was not easy: the idea of building a real model building in front of the Palazzo dell'Arte developed slowly, with many stops and doubts, due to the lack of funds, the need for permission from the municipality, the scepticism of the British authorities, and so on.

Contacts between the Milanese institution and the Ministry of Education in London started in early 1959. They followed the refusal of the British Government to take part in the previous edition of the Triennale (1957) – due, it was said, to a lack of money.[25]

One of the first contacts regarding an English participation in the twelfth Triennale was laid by Lisa Ponti, Gio Ponti's daughter, in March 1959.[26] She had just received a letter from Paul Reilly, member of the Council of Industrial Design in London, who wanted to promote an official participation by England, with a specific section to be organized by its institution. These preliminary contacts triggered long correspondence between the Council and the Triennale, in order to set up this participation, as well as several personal communications between Italian and British actors of the two architecture and design scenes.

The first official contacts between the Triennale and the Council of Industrial Design in London, concerning an English participation in the twelfth Triennale, were managed by Marco Zanuso, one of the most talented Italian architects and industrial designers of the time.[27]

On 20 May 1959, Philip Fellows, head of the exhibitions division of the Council of Industrial Design of London, wrote to the Secretary of the Triennale, Mr Tommaso Ferraris, proposing the construction of a special building made out of a British prefab system, in the park around the *Palazzo dell'Arte*.[28] An exploratory committee – composed of Sir Gordon Russell, Paul Reilly, Misha Black and J.M. Richards – was appointed to evaluate the participation proposal.

Besides the logistical and bureaucratic difficulties, the main obstacle to Britain's participation was the lack of funds. Still in September 1959, Philip Fellows was pessimistic.[29]

It is worth mentioning the involvement of Nikolaus Pevsner, contacted by Tommaso Ferraris in April 1959. Pevsner, who had been member of the Curatorial Committee of the eleventh Triennale of 1957, informed Ferraris about the progress made by the exploratory committee, and contributed to convince its members about the participation.[30]

After exerting a lot of pressure and building up support, positive feedback emerged. And finally, on 30 November 1959, Sir David Eccles – the Minister of Education – announced Britain's official participation:

> The Government has been much impressed by the volume of informed opinion which has called for a British exhibit at the Milan Triennale. It is impossible to estimate, in terms of material advantage, the benefits to be derived from a British participation in international events of this kind. But when, in this occasion, the exhibition is

devoted to "The House and the School", it is right to tell the story of Britain's outstanding post-war record in school building. Schools are the best example of what Britain has done over the whole range of building; our lead in school building is recognized throughout the world. This is, therefore, an opportunity not to be missed.[31]

After the confirmation, the Italian architect Vico Magistretti, member of the Technical Executive Committee of the twelfth Triennale, and engineer Cesare Fera, member of the Commission of the School, went to England. During their trip they aimed to visit a CLASP school, meet W.D. Lacey (County Architect for Nottinghamshire and designer of the Milanese structure, together with Trevor Prosser), and also to discuss 'any articles that you would like them to submit for consideration in the main Italian exhibition, particularly on the home'[32] with the Council of Industrial Design.

The latter aim was of great importance for both the Triennale and the Council, which was keen on spreading British products internationally. Therefore, in the following months the Triennale would receive many requests by national companies to participate in the British section. With this purpose, Magistretti got in touch with the Council of Industrial Design, which proposed the display of those projects to be awarded with the Design Centre Awards in 1960 at the Triennale.[33]

The presence of Vico Magistretti in this story is also worth highlighting. One of the most gifted Milanese architects of the 1950s, he developed a profound relationship with the UK during his entire career, of which the short experience linked to the British Model School constitutes an important – and so far, unmentioned – episode.[34] It is particularly true if we consider that the same year, one of his works – the Arosio House in Arenzano, in which the lessons of the Modern movement opened up to regional influences and the echo of Charles Rennie Mackintosh and Josef Hoffmann – was presented by his master Ernesto Rogers at the Otterlo's CIAM, making him one of the involuntary protagonists of the already mentioned 'Italian retreat' denounced by Banham, and its consequent debate.[35] In contrast with such a label, the involvement in the process of realizing the British Model School at the twelfth Triennale shows Magistretti's interest in prefabrication and standardization, which, however, was evident in other contemporary works, such as the office block he realized in Milan in 1957, also published in the UK.[36]

Magistretti's relationship with the UK would get tighter in the following years: his 'Carimate' Chair, which was exhibited for the first time at the 12th Triennale in 1960, would be exported – thanks to Terence Conran and his Habitat Store in South Kensington – in Great Britain, becoming one of the icons of 'Swinging London'. Later on, from the end of the 1970s, he was appointed visiting professor at the Royal College of Arts, for many years, influencing an entire generation of young designers, such as Jasper Morrison and Konstantin Grcic.[37]

A bridge between Italy and the UK: Francesco Gnecchi Ruscone

Once the project had officially started, the British Minister of Education invited Nottinghamshire County Council to design the Milanese CLASP school according to their experience. Their architectural and educational services were given without charge; some of the manufacturers and appliers of the components used by the CLASP generously offered their products free of charge.

Mr L.W. Norwood, the administrative officer in the Architects and Building Branch of the Ministry of Education, was charged with particular responsibility for the organization and administration of the UK participation in the Triennale. The contract for erecting the school in Milan was given to the British firm of CD Productions, which intended to use the Italian firm of IPI as sub-contractor.

The CLASP school at the twelfth Triennale was built in nine weeks (within the normal Ministry cost limits). It included furniture and fabrics by the Ministry and CLASP, as well as creative toys by the exhibition designer James Gardner, as samples of new creative learning techniques.[38]

Finally, it was inaugurated on 16 July 1960, attended by Sir David Eccles and Cardinal Montini (Archbishop of Milan) among others. A further question was, nevertheless, still unsolved. What to do with that structure, once the exhibition was over?

Some months previously, in February 1960, the Minister of Education Sir David Eccles offered the donation of CLASP school to the Italian Government after the end of the exhibition. It was a very kind act, which also saved Great Britain a lot of money, avoiding the dismantling and repatriation of the construction.[39] The gift was accepted, and the City Council started to think about a new location.

It was eventually found in another Milanese Park – the *Parco Trotter* – where, after the Great War, a series of school buildings had been erected as innovative pavilions in a small oasis of nature.[40] In other words, the British Model School would be added to other model schools.

Due to the complexity of such an operation – dismantling and reassembling a prefab school made according to British methods in Italy – in Spring 1961 the City Council asked a 36-year-old Milanese architect to analyse the matter and give an estimate of the operation's cost. His verdict was not positive for different reasons, like the impossibility – due to the different metric system – of an easy replacement of the prefab elements, if broken, with others produced in the country. In addition, the architect affirmed that building a totally new CLASP school, using Italian CLASP elements, would have almost the same price as dismantling and moving the Triennale's school.[41] Furthermore, in this preliminary phase, no company accepted to provide an estimate of the operation's cost. Waiting for a solution, the school remained abandoned for more than a year.

Who was this architect? Why was he talking about 'Italian' CLASP elements?

He was Francesco Gnecchi Ruscone, who will be the main character of the rest of this story. His biography, in fact, traces a noteworthy connection between Italy and Great Britain in the post-war period.[42] He was born in 1924 in Milan with an international background: his grandfather graduated at the University of Leipzig, while his mother had studied in France at Sacré Coeur. He learnt English pretty soon thanks to his nanny, Miss Jessie Mason. In 1942, he began studying architecture at the Politecnico di Milano, where he met professors such as Piero Portaluppi, Antonio Cassi Ramelli and Gio Ponti.

In March 1944, he joined the *Resistenza* (the Italian resistance movement), during which he was captured and tortured. In the same period, he also collaborated with the British Army, giving information about the enemy lines. For all these activities, he was awarded with a Bronze Medal of Honour.[43]

Back to civilian life, he continued his studies and graduated in 1949 in architecture. Thanks to his language skills, Gnecchi Ruscone was invited by Ernesto Rogers – with whom he collaborated as assistant from November 1962 – to participate in the CIAM 7 congress in Bergamo, as Secretary of the session on Architectural Industrialization. The same year, 1949, he joined the CIAM summer school in London, organized by the MARS Group at Bedford Square, where he also met two other Italian colleagues: Franco Berlanda and Giovanni Pericoli.

The CIAM 1949 summer school was the first episode of a long-lasting relationship with Great Britain. Some weeks later, Gnecchi Ruscone was appointed full member of the teaching staff at the Architectural Association in London. He was re-appointed to this position in the following years, remaining a member of the AA until 1985.

Thanks to his contacts on both side of the English Channel, Gnecchi Ruscone became a reference figure in both countries, for instance collaborating with *The Architectural Review* and *Domus*. As Gio Ponti stated in an ironical letter to Gnecchi Ruscone on 16 September 1949, written in English: 'Dear Sir, I have the pleasure to confirm you that you have been appointed as correspondent from London for *Domus*'.[44] Actually, he limited these collaborations to some information on events, exhibitions, debates, and the like, but in this way, he got in touch with many key figures such as Reyner Banham, with whom he had various exchanges about modern architecture in Italy.[45]

In 1950 Gnecchi Ruscone worked together with the Architects' Co-operative to design the entrance structure of the Festival of Britain, whose drawings are still kept in his archive.[46] In the same year, he was also actively involved in the organization of a significant exhibition on Italian Contemporary Architecture, prepared by the Italian CIAM Group and held at RIBA in 1952, with the support of the Italian Institute.[47]

During the 1950s, the focus of his activity changed back to Italy. However, his relationship with London deepened again at the end of the decade, just before the twelfth Triennale. In 1959, he would be appointed temporary assistant to the Fourth Year Master at the Architectural Association, and some months later, in September 1960, he organized a guided tour of Milan for AA members. On that occasion, he toured his colleagues and students through the brand-new icons of Milanese Modernity[48] (such as the Pirelli Tower, the Galfa Tower, the Velasca) and – of course – to the ongoing Triennale.

It is also worth mentioning that Gnecchi Ruscone participated in the twelfth Triennale presenting a scheme for the re-planning of part of Milan's old city centre. The project – which included the creation of a nursery school, proposed the exclusion of all motor traffic – was well received by the British press: his friend Banham, for instance, praised its qualities in *The Listener.*[49]

Meanwhile, contacts between Milan and London continued. In November 1960, the British Ministry invited the Study Commission of the Triennale, including some members of the Ministry of Public Works, to visit England to evaluate the use of prefabricated systems of school buildings first-hand, while an important debate on the new reform was ongoing.[50] Being the right man at the right place, Gnecchi Ruscone was asked to organize the trip, which took place at the beginning of December. The Italian Commission included some members of the Ministry of Public Works, some of the Ministry of the Education and members from the AAI and UNRRA CASAS. The Commission had a series of interesting meetings,

Figure 14.3 The Italian Ministry of Public Education representatives, visiting a CLASP building in the UK in September 1960, puzzled by British bureaucratic recklessness

Courtesy of CASVA – Archivio Francesco Gnecchi Ruscone

with such figures as D.H. Merrell, administrative director of the building department of the Ministry of Education; and Dan W. Lacey, county architect of Nottinghamshire, one of the main experts of the CLASP system and later chief architect of the Ministry of Education. The Commission also visited a series of prefab schools in Nottinghamshire and in the city of Coventry.

In his memoirs, Gnecchi Ruscone remembers that experience as a peculiar one. 'I felt like a tour guide on Mars',[51] he wrote, underlining the huge gap between the Italian and British approach to public building management: the Italians were puzzled by British bureaucratic recklessness.

Nevertheless, some results were to come.

The CLASP translation

The great success of the British Model School at the twelfth Triennale, the expected need of prefab schools in Italy, the visit of the Italian Commission in December 1960, all these elements convinced Brockhouse to create an Italian branch, while the system was going to be exported also to West Germany, France, Switzerland and Israel. Within the Italian building context, characterized by fragmentation and small-scale production, it represented one of the few cases of importation of foreign construction systems for school building.

With this purpose, in 1961 Gnecchi Ruscone was asked to find an Italian company, specialized in metal carpentry, which would be able to produce the metal bearing structures of CLASP system. After some epic meetings in Glasgow – where the respective managers spoke in Oxford English and Milanese dialect[52] – the Brockhouse Company chose the Fratelli Biraghi (Biraghi Brothers) company, with whom Gnecchi Ruscone had already collaborated.

Surprisingly, the Fratelli Biraghi factory in Milan was much more modern and productive than those of the Brockhouse. As Gnecchi Ruscone remembers, the cutting and drilling of steel sections was already automated; productivity was at least double.[53]

The Italian *Costruzioni Modulari* (modular constructions) company was born. It defined itself as a technical and logistical consultant, its duty being to assist both the architect and the building company for the right application of the project, supplying all the technical details and checking the production line of all the prefab elements. Thanks to his Italian contacts and British background, Gnecchi Ruscone was appointed consultant architect for Brockhouse and managing director of the Costruzioni Modulari.

From that moment on, he focused his work on the translation of British CLASP system into a new Italian version, one that could fit the Italian situation.

In the autumn of 1960, Gnecchi Ruscone became the chief designer for a school in Biella, a small town in Piedmont, sponsored by the Cerruti wool mill and then donated to the city. The client had just visited the British Model School at the twelfth Triennale: therefore, he wanted to have a building realized according to CLASP system, for the first time in Italy.

The process of 'translation' of the CLASP system was not simple, since the project started before it was totally converted into something feasible for the Italian context. Building works were delayed, due to the slowness of the negotiations regarding the building site; in addition, it was difficult to find a contractor that accepted this particular method of managing the tender:

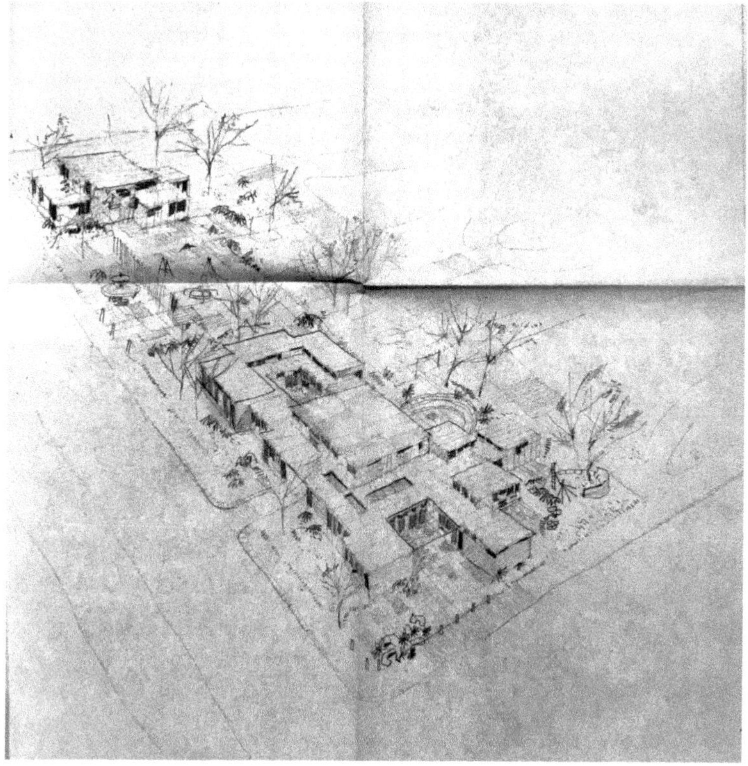

Figure 14.4a Francesco Gnecchi Ruscone, CLASP school in Biella, Italy. Aerial view, 1960

Courtesy of CASVA – Archivio Francesco Gnecchi Ruscone

> No company has agreed to make a global construction contract in a system unknown to them … This of course led to the burden on the construction manager of an infinite number of practical and managing details that normally are under the responsibility of the construction company. The main suppliers (metal structures, roofing and wooden frames) had their work blocked by strikes in the Spring / Summer period for many days, with effects on material deliveries and assembly, that you can imagine. Construction workers in Biella repeatedly went on strike in July and August.[54]

For these reasons, works were delayed for three months, but finally the school was built. At the CASVA's archive in Milan, there are some sketches by the artist Broggini for an artwork for the Biella school.

Figure 14.4b Francesco Gnecchi Ruscone, CLASP school in Buccinasco, Italy, 1962
Courtesy of CASVA – Archivio Francesco Gnecchi Ruscone

In October 1961, Gnecchi Ruscone participated in a competition for a primary school in Monza, but without success.

Another school was built by him in Buccinasco (on the outskirts of Milan) in 1962, according to CLASP system, now entirely translated for the Italian context.

Such a translation was not neutral, since it implied not only a technical system but also a managing one. For instance:

> the use of timber had to be cut down to a minimum because of its cost, because contractors do not normally have carpenters on their teams and joiners would be too expensive if employed ... It has caused the practical impossibility of using cladding tiles, a major component of CLASP language as we know it. On the other hand – continues Gnecchi Ruscone – it has determined a new range of partition panels that need no site cutting or adapting. It will certainly produce other changes from the present form of the CLASP.[55]

The 'translation' of CLASP also implied the use of metal sheet for slabs and plaster panels as internal partitions. The original module, originally set on 3'4" (101.6 cm), was adapted to 1m.

The work of Costruzioni Modulari – and, above all, the economic outlook offered by Italian politics about school building, after the Law no. 17 of 1962 – attracted some bigger companies. In March 1962, Gnecchi Ruscone was contacted by Comansider, part of FINSIDER Group (which

Figure 14.5 Francesco Gnecchi Ruscone, IRCOM School in Rome, early 1960s

Courtesy of CASVA – Archivio Francesco Gnecchi Ruscone

would later become the ILVA), which initially wanted to acquire the rights to use the CLASP system for Italy. As this was not allowed, they found an agreement that led to the creation of IRCOM (Industrie Riunite Costruzioni Modulari), based in Milan, Rome and Naples. The aim of IRCOM was to build by using existing prefabrication systems and to set up new ones, as well as building elements, to be sold to others.[56] At the same time IRCOM also wanted to make use of the CLASP system for some buildings, in view of the tenders to be announced by the Ministry of Education.

Gnecchi Ruscone became consultant for IRCOM, managing projects and the dialogue with Costruzioni Modulari. At the same time, he was asked to supervise the design and realization of a new system for residential buildings. Therefore, in the following months Gnecchi-Ruscone tried to optimize the CLASP system for IRCOM's purposes.

This phase of his career did not last long: on 13 August 1962, Gnecchi Ruscone resigned from Costruzioni Modulari. As he wrote in a letter to a friend: 'I have had a lot of difficulties with the Brockhouse organization and have eventually resigned. They were in practice asking me to give up my practice to be a full-time employee of the firm. Apart from a number of very good reasons for wanting to remain independent, their manners were not such to encourage anyone to become their employee'.[57]

The main reason for this divorce consisted in the kind of work that he was supposed to do: more administrative and economic tasks, rather than design challenges. This also had a profound impact on architectural results. In fact, Italian companies such as IRCOM intended to use CLASP system mainly as a catalogue of standardized solutions, losing the real concept of the system, which was – at its origin – the potentiality of doing everything.

Gnecchi Ruscone insisted on this point on several occasions. Freedom, in his view, was one of the main aims of CLASP translation, because the degree of validity of such a system was directly proportional to the amount of possible variations. Therefore, he stated, 'if "national ways to CLASP" can be developed, the system will have passed a major test. Naturally these differences, to be of positive value, must amount to an enrichment of possibilities and not just reflect limitations imposed by different circumstances such as building regulations or cost of materials'.[58]

Such an enrichment involved deeper meanings and procedures. On the one hand, a coherent translation of the system would have required an original administrative set-up, since when CLASP as a technical system was divorced from its consortium, several major conditions were altered: 'the building programme is no longer a known datum in the problem but at most a working assumption; the architect may well be very unfamiliar with the system; on the other hand there is no longer any need to operate through local contractors competing with one another: the competition takes place at an earlier stage, against other systems of prefabrication and points to the advantage of one or a few contractors specializing in the erection of CLASP buildings. All these new conditions tend necessarily to tighten up discipline in the system, to reduce the number of alternative components and possible combinations, in short to make it more rigid'.[59]

These considerations led to a fundamental starting point:

> the original design of CLASP and the choice of materials were influenced at the root by a decision to produce architecture and not "prefabs", obviously not in a snobbish and dubious distinction, but in a conscious attempt to avoid that just-landed-flying-saucer-look to which quite a few prefabricators seem to be romantically attached, and this to the point of using a very traditional (and traditional looking) material, such as cladding tiles.[60]

Gnecchi Ruscone believed that such a methodological approach could be extremely fitting in Italy, where the presence of landscapes and townscapes imposes respect towards what is already existing, but also where, at the same time, there is the need for modern and functional buildings:[61] 'San Gimignano needs schools too'.[62]

He even saw a sort of analogy between CLASP and the 'expressive consistency that was offered to those who built the vernacular, spontaneous architecture of the past', in which predetermined parts and techniques were used in a free composition. But, with an important warning: 'a vernacular, even a new one, is by definition popularly understood'.[63]

Somehow, these statements close the circle, showing – at least in theory – how to mend the intellectual rift that had opposed Rogers's and Banham's perspectives on history, technology and modernity. On the one hand, Gnecchi Ruscone was – thanks to his Anglo-Saxon experiences – totally aware and confident with the British know-how which had triggered the birth of CLASP, but on the other, in his mind the cultural influence of the Milanese school gathered around Rogers was sound and entrenched.

A few years before, for instance, the Italian philosopher Enzo Paci,[64] close to Rogers, had expressed his ideas upon the application of the industrial method in buildings and its aesthetical consequences. This is a point of view that we can also track down in Gnecchi Ruscone's words and works, as well as in those of other young Milanese architects who tried to blend prefabrication and tradition.[65]

Talking about building techniques, Paci noticed that they could reach 'a degree of abstraction such that it could be difficult to find their relationship with the real situation'[66], leading to an alarming contrast between a formal methodology and concrete human situations. On the one hand, the methodology of the industrial design could not be in harmony with the historical and psychological character of those for which dwellings and other constructions are built; on the other, an industrialization methodologically perfect in terms of design could not find workers able to realize what is abstractly planned, with all the consequent political, social and psychological related problems. These warnings would lead to an industrial design able to consider contents, natural conditions, social and cultural situations, in relation both to the inhabitants and the workers. If not, the aesthetical dimension would also fail.

'As an artist, if the architect has to find harmony with industrial technique, with the socio-historical conditions and with all his collaborators, at the same time he must go beyond the facts with the invention of new forms suggested by the application of a project as well as by the participation of the architect in the execution of the work, the behaviour of the workers and the behaviour of the inhabitants of the constructed buildings. This participation may suggest new possible forms and suggest new types of standardized elements'.[67]

In his fleeting but determined attempt to translate CLASP system into the Italian context, Gnecchi Ruscone tried to blend British empirical realism into the Italian awareness of (and sometimes obsession with) human and architectural traditions. Many factors impeded him from fully achieving this task (such as the fragmentation of the national building industry and the short-sightedness of local authorities), but his efforts marked one of the most interesting attempts in the process of importation of foreign building methods into the Italian context of the 1960s.

His involvement in this field, however, did not stop after his resignation. Gnecchi Ruscone continued to collaborate with IRCOM on a number of jobs as an independent architect, on projects such as some model schools with 12, 18 or 24 classrooms on different floors. Even dealing with a simplification of the approach, due to a larger application of the system, the buildings he designed for IRCOM in Caserta, Naples and Rome in 1962–5 show original interpretations each time.[68] Thanks to the experience he gained in the field, in the following years he was also appointed consultant for the Organisation for Economic Co-operation and Development (OECD) on the prefabrication of school buildings. After Italy and the UK, new international perspectives had opened up.

Notes

1 Pansera 1978.
2 Semeraro 1999; De Giorgi, Gaudio and Pruneri 2019; Leschiutta 1975.
3 Gnecchi Ruscone 1963, 319–20.
4 Talanti 1970.
5 Triennale Milano Historical Archive (TMHA), Proceedings of the International Conference on School Building, 13–16 October 1960 (transcription of the speeches).
6 Giannetti 2016.
7 Gnecchi Ruscone 1962; Zaffagnini 1967; Harwood 2020.
8 *Britain's New Schools* 1960.
9 Maclure 1984; Fera 1964.
10 *Britain's New Schools* 1960, 6.
11 Harwood 2020.
12 Gnecchi Ruscone 1963, 319–20.
13 Harwood 2020.
14 Gnecchi Ruscone 1963, 319.
15 Ponti 1960.
16 Ponti 1960.

17 *Laurels at Milan* 1960.
18 Gray 1960.
19 Gray 1960.
20 Banham 1959.
21 Rogers 1959.
22 Banham 1961; 1962; Whiteley 2002, 151.
23 Banham 1960.
24 Harwood 2020.
25 TMHA, letter from T. Ferraris (Triennale di Milano) to the Italian Institute of Culture in London, 4 September 1959.
26 TMHA, letter from L. Ponti to T. Ferraris (Triennale di Milano), 6 March 1959.
27 TMHA, letter from M. Zanuso to P. Reilly (Council of Industrial Design), 28 April 1959.
28 TMHA, letter from P. Fellows to T. Ferraris (Triennale di Milano), 20 May 1959.
29 TMHA, letter from P. Fellows to T. Ferraris (Triennale di Milano), 4 September 1959.
30 TMHA, letter from N. Pevsner to T. Ferraris (Triennale di Milano), 29 April 1959.
31 TMHA, Ministry of Education, *Background Notes. The Milan Triennial*, 30 November 1959.
32 TMHA, letter from W.D. Pile (Joint Head of Architects and Building Branch – Ministry of Education, London) to T. Ferraris (Triennale di Milano), 30 November 1959.
33 TMHA, letter from Tommaso Ferraris (Triennale di Milano) to W.D. Pile (Ministry of Education), 4 January 1960.
34 Neri 2021.
35 Newman 1961.
36 *Walls and partitions* 1958.
37 Neri 2021.
38 Harwood 2020.
39 TMHA, letter from I.M. Lombardo (President of the Triennale) to the Italian Ambassador in London, 4 November 1960.
40 Costa and Dentis 2005.
41 Gnecchi Ruscone 1961.
42 Cimoli 2004.
43 Gnecchi Ruscone 1999; 2011.
44 CASVA, letter from G. Ponti to F. Gnecchi Ruscone, 16 September 1949.
45 CASVA, letter from R. Banham to F. Gnecchi Ruscone, s.d.
46 CASVA, Architects' Co-operative Partnership, Festival of Britain, drawing 73/290.
47 CASVA, letter from F. Gnecchi Ruscone to E. N. Rogers, 10 October 1950.
48 Irace 1996.
49 Banham 1960, 254.
50 CASVA, letter from David Eccles to Guido Amorosi (Chief Engineer, Milan City Council), 1 November 1960.
51 Gnecchi Ruscone 2014, 136.
52 Gnecchi Ruscone 2014, 165–8.
53 Gnecchi Ruscone 2014, 167–8.
54 Gnecchi Ruscone 1964.
55 Gnecchi Ruscone 1963, 319.
56 CASVA, letters, March 1962.
57 CASVA, letter from F. Gnecchi Ruscone to J. Morton, 11 August 1962.
58 Gnecchi Ruscone 1963, 319.
59 Gnecchi Ruscone 1963, 319–20.
60 Gnecchi Ruscone 1963, 320.
61 Gnecchi Ruscone 1963, 320.
62 Gnecchi Ruscone 1963, 320.
63 Gnecchi Ruscone 1963, 320.
64 Paci 1957.
65 Neri 2020.
66 Paci 1957, 76.
67 Paci 1957, 80.
68 Morganti, Tosone, Di Donato and Franchi 2013.

References

Banham, Reyner. 'Neo Liberty: The Italian retreat from modern architecture', *The Architectural Review* 747 (April 1959): 231–5.

Banham, Reyner. 'School of today – Homes of yesterday', *The Listener*, 18 August 1960, 253–4.

Banham, Reyner. 'A gong for the Welfare State', *New Statesman*, 6 January 1961: 26–7.

Banham, Reyner. 'On Trial 4: CLASP-Ill-Met by Clip-joint?', *The Architectural Review* 131 (May 1962): 349–52.

Britain's New Schools: A Record of Achievement 1945–1960, booklet published in occasion of the XII Triennale di Milano, 1960, Chapter 3.

CIAM Group. *Italian Contemporary Architecture: An exhibition*, catalogue of the exhibition at the RIBA (London, 24 March–30 April 1952). London: RIBA, 1952.

Cimoli, Anna Chiara (ed.). *L'archivio dell'architetto Francesco Gnecchi Ruscone presso il C.A.S.V.A.* Milan: Comune di Milano, 2004.

'CLASP', *Architects' Journal* 129/3348 (April 1959): 645–50.

Costa, Emilia and Emanuela Dentis (eds). *La città del sole al parco Trotter: Un progetto per le bambine e i bambini*. Milan: CLUP, 2005.

De Giorgi, Fulvio, Angelo Gaudio and Fabio Pruneri. *Manuale di storia della scuola italiana: Dal Risorgimento al XXI secolo*. Brescia: Schole, 2019.

Fera, Cesare. *Scuole in Inghilterra*. Milan: Görlich, 1964.

Giannetti, Ilaria. 'Prototypes of industrialized construction systems at the XII Triennale of Milan', *Annali delle Arti e degli Archivi: Pittura, scultura, architettura* 1 (2015), 217–26.

Giannetti, Ilaria. 'The design of a system: Industrialized schools in Italy (1960–1975)', *Tema* 2, no. 1 (2016): 134–44.

Gnecchi Ruscone, Francesco. *Report on the Dismantling and Reassembling of the Prefab School Offered by the British Government to the City Council of Milan*, 22 December 1961. Milan: CASVA Archive.

Gnecchi Ruscone, Francesco. 'Un'esperienza inglese: Il C.L.A.S.P. come consorzio, come programma, come sistema', *Abitare* 11 (November 1962): 14–17.

Gnecchi Ruscone, Francesco. 'CLASP in Italy', *The Architectural Review* 83 (May 1963): 319–20.

Gnecchi Ruscone, Francesco. *Report on the Construction of the School in Biella*, 16 September 1964. Milan: CASVA Archive.

Gnecchi Ruscone, Francesco. *When Being Italian Was Difficult*. Milan: Isabel, 1999.

Gnecchi Ruscone, Francesco. *Missione Nemo: Un'operazione segreta della Resistenza militare italiana 1944–1945*. Milan: Mursia, 2011.

Gnecchi Ruscone, Francesco. *Storie di architettura*. Milan: Lark, 2014.

Gray, Patience. 'A lesson in English', *The Observer*, 14 August 1960.

Harwood, Elain. 'System Building', in https://www.e-flux.com/architecture/education/322668/system-building/ (accessed 2 July 2020).

Irace, Fulvio. *Milano moderna*. Milan: Motta, 1996.

'Laurels at Milan', *The Times Educational Supplement*, 22 July 1960, 124.

Leschiutta, Fausto E. *Linee evolutive dell'edilizia scolastica: Vicende–norme–tipi 1949–1975*. Rome: Bulzoni, 1975.

Maclure, Stuart. *Educational Development and School Building: Aspects of public policy 1945–73*. Harlow: Longman, 1984.

Morganti, R., Alessandra Tosone, Danilo Di Donato and Daniela Franchi. 'Il CLASP: Un sistema costruttivo d'importazione in acciaio per le nuove scuole d'Italia'. In *Giornate italiane della costruzione in acciaio: L'Acciaio e la sfida delle prestazioni,* 940–7. Naples: Doppiavoce, 2013.

Neri, Gabriele. 'Hundred (and one) years of Vico Magistretti: A blend of architecture and design, Milan and the world'. In *Vico Magistretti: Architetto milanese*, edited by Gabriele Neri, 31–56. Milan: Electa, 2021.

Newman, Oscar. *CIAM '59 in Otterlo*, edited by J. Joedicke. Stuttgart: Karl Krämer Verlag, 1961.

Paci, Enzo. 'L'applicazione del metodo industriale all'edilizia e il problema estetico', *La Casa: Quaderni di architettura e di critica* 4 (1957): 73–80.

Pansera, Anty. *Storia e cronaca della Triennale*. Milan: Longanesi and Co., 1978.

Ponti, Gio. 'I padiglioni stranieri alla XII Triennale di Milano', *Domus* 372 (November 1960), 23–4.

Rogers, Ernesto. 'L'evoluzione dell'architettura: Risposta al custode dei frigidaires', *Casabella-Continuità* 228 (June 1959): 2–4.

Semeraro, Angelo. *Il sistema scolastico italiano*. Rome: Carocci, 1999.
Talanti, Anna Maria. *L'industrializzazione edilizia in Italia*, vol. I, *1945–1954*. Milan: Associazione Italiana Prefabbricazione per l'Edilizia Industrializzata, 1970.
'Walls and partitions: Curtain wall office block in Milan', *The Architects' Journal* 3328 (December 1958): 69.
Whiteley, Nigel. *Reyner Banham: Historian of the immediate future*. Cambridge, MA: MIT Press, 2002.
Zaffagnini, Mario (ed.). *Documentazione sul programma e sul sistema del CLASP*. Florence: CNR, 1967.

15
Post-war British church architecture and the Italian model

Lorenzo Grieco

The Festival of Britain, which opened in London in 1951, eloquently formalized the rebirth of post-war British architecture, but it lacked any reference to churches. As noted by Joseph Rykwert in a passionate article of 1956, the failure to acknowledge the role of religion in the making of the city demonstrated the backwardness of the British discussion on liturgical innovation. Rykwert drew an unfavourable comparison with the influence exerted by contemporary church design in France and he highlighted the importance of three exemplary modern Italian churches: San Vincenzo de Paoli in Matera; and Santa Maria Nascente and Madonna dei Poveri in Milan, which all manifested a precise 'pauperist' tendency.

Rykwert's article was one of the few British investigations into Italian churches. By contrast, the key British texts on liturgy and architecture published between 1950 and 1960 made no reference to Italian models. *The Modern Church* (Mills, 1956), and *Liturgy and Architecture* (Hammond, 1960), referred to Swiss, German, American and French examples of church design, but did not mention Italian ones. In the few cases in which they were cited, Italian churches were sharply accused of theatrical exaggeration and regarded as irrelevant to the development of a liturgically conscious architecture. Only in the late 1960s did the impetus of the Second Vatican Council (1962–5) for liturgical reform prompt a rediscovery of Italian church architecture, the great absence in the British post-war architectural debate.

No country for new churches: The Festival of Britain, 1951

Among the events more characteristic of the direction of British architecture and its role in reconstructing the country in the aftermath of the Second World War, the Festival of Britain emerged as the most symbolic public 'act of national reassessment'.[1] Opened in London in 1951, the festival was widely considered as one of the first occasions for the formalization of new architectural and urban objectives, in line with the post-war British policies on city planning and social welfare.[2] Pushed by the consistent insertion of new capital following the approval of the Marshall Plan, the reconstruction of British cities had been proceeding swiftly since the New Towns Act of 1946. If the 1943 exhibition on 'Rebuilding Britain', organized at the National Gallery by the RIBA and sponsored by the building industry, had been limited to a primitive and functional reflection on land planning, the Festival of Britain explored the connection between the city and human life. Indeed, the South Bank exhibition focused on the renewed social function of the city, embodying in its pavilions the British search for an architectural style to visually express the 'Welfare State' massively promoted by the Labour Government.[3] At the heart of the South Bank Exhibition, the Royal Festival Hall, a bright building designed in a modernist ardour by Leslie Martin (1908–2000), represented the new image of sociality in a pleasant section of London.[4] In direct dialogue with the river Thames, just along from County Hall and almost opposite Parliament, the building recovered a space of post-war dereliction and damage, particularly of industrial infrastructure. Sections of the exhibition dealt with daily aspects of living in the reborn country, from farm to housing and industry, to sports, television and tourism.

Nevertheless, as underlined by a young Joseph Rykwert (b. 1926) in 1956 in the English Catholic magazine *Blackfriars*, commenting on the words of John Summerson (1904–1992) in the catalogue of the festival, the exhibition was completely lacking any reflection on religion.[5] This absence, according to Rykwert, was the symptomatic result of a void in British architectural culture, attesting to its retardation in the discussion on church architecture and liturgical innovation.

In fact, even though the main exhibition barely mentioned religion, religious architecture was exhibited at a secondary location. Indeed, the South Bank exhibition was accompanied by parallel events in other venues, as the 'live architecture' exhibition, organized as a branch of the festival and visited in a tour through the brand new Lansbury Housing Estate, in Poplar, east London. One of the main architectural emergences of the estate was the Trinity Congregational Church, completed by 1951 on a design by Cecil Handisyde and Douglas Roger Stark: a modern structure of reinforced concrete frames filled with yellow bricks and copper, 'designed to be light and airy'.[6] Just a few miles away, during the festival, on 7 October 1951, Cardinal Bernard William Griffin (1899–1956) laid the foundation stone of the Catholic church of Saint Mary and St Joseph by Adrian Gilbert Scott (1882–1963).[7] The church, among the first to be funded by the War Damage Commission, would be completed in 1954, boasting a revivalist Byzantine-Romanesque style.[8] The aesthetic distance from the nearby Congregational church was clear. In fact, the two churches underlined the distinction between modernism and tradition, fuelling the aesthetic conservatism of the English Catholics, well expressed in the words of Cardinal William Godfrey (1889–1963), Archbishop of Westminster, who recalled the visual recognizability of the traditional old-fashioned church.[9] The presence of religion exclusively in the architectural exhibition proved how churches were regarded as one among the many typological possibilities of architecture, rather than a social tool influencing people's life and worthy of being included in the main sections of the festival. Their confinement on one hand expressed the distance of welfare politics from religion (probably meant to mitigate the religious contrast that would explode in the late 1960s with the Troubles in Northern Ireland); on the other hand it presented ecclesial architecture, in the two solutions of Handisyde/Stark and Gilbert Scott, as a mere question of style, independent from liturgical and communal arguments. Lacking a serious discussion on religious architecture even in the Poplar exhibition, the Festival denied the identification between religion and society that had been the core of the British historical religious movement, from Catholic distributism to the Anglican 'Parish and People Movement'; an identification that had inspired the evolution of twentieth-century Anglican liturgy, as attested by the title of one of its key texts, *Liturgy and Society*, published in 1935 by Arthur Gabriel Hebert (1886–1963).[10]

The context of Rykwert's article was therefore an architectural chapter in which Catholics and often even Anglicans remained linked to traditional iconography of the church, while modernist designers seemed to snub religious architecture completely or, at best, merely gave the appearence of modernity to buildings with traditional layouts. Religious architecture was indeed treated with different expressive means, as a subcategory of architecture that was not engaging with modernist style but rather expressing a new revivalism, in which symbolism was favoured over functionalism. Until the completion of Coventry Cathedral (1956–62), designed by Basil Spence (1907–1976), who had won the competition in 1951, not a single church in Britain could be compared to the modern temples that were being built abroad. Conscious of such a gap, clearly expressed in the programme of the Festival of Britain, Rykwert compared the status of religious architecture in Britain to the modernization of language in church design that occurred abroad, especially in France and in Italy.

Between theatrical exaggeration and transparent poverty: Seeing Italy from Britain

The decision to take Italy as a term of comparison was surely influenced by Rykwert's interest in modern Italian architecture and its peculiar expressive language.[11] To fund his comparison, he brought up three built projects that had just been published in the Italian magazine *Casabella*[12]: the church of Saint Vincent de Paul in La Martella (1951–3), Matera, by Ludovico Quaroni (1911–1987); the Nativity of Mary (1953–5) at the Quartiere Triennale 8 in Milan, by Vico Magistretti (1920–2006) and Mario Tedeschi (1920–2005); and the church of Our Lady of the Poor (1952–4) in Baggio, Milan, by Luigi Figini (1903–1984) and Gino Pollini (1903–1991). The three churches cited by Rykwert, all built in new estates, reinterpreted the traditional typologies of Italian churches with a modern language and a functionalist approach. For example, the Milanese church by Figini and Pollini offered a 'reinterpretation of the traditional basilica ... but a reinterpretation in the spare, harsh terminology of modern technique'.[13] The same church would even be included in the history of church building that Rykwert wrote (1966) for the series of *Faith and Fact Books*, promoted by the Catholic Lancelot C. Sheppard.[14] On the other hand, the church at QT8, dedicated to the Virgin, calls to mind the studies of Rudolf Wittkower (1901–1971) on centrally planned churches.[15] In effect, Wittkower had exerted a strong fascination on Rykwert since his lectures on 'the Classical Tradition', attended while still in secondary school, and his studies on Italian renaissance and baroque architecture had an undeniable influence on an entire generation of British architects.[16]

The churches cited by Rykwert clearly incarnated the perception of Italian church architecture in Britain, swinging between a sentiment of

Franciscan 'transparent poverty' and a mannerist exuberance.[17] This double interpretation would distinguish the British approach to the Italian model, described by the oxymoronic combination of theatrical eloquence and humble deprivation. Certainly, all three cases selected by Rykwert embodied a harsh pauperist tendency of the Italian architectural culture, which was in line with the severe neorealism of the national film industries. It is probably not incidental that in the same journal, the year before, Maryvonne Butcher had written an article on 'the Future of Italian Films', praising the Italian neorealist cinema.[18] Nevertheless, despite fostering a neorealist dryness through unadorned surfaces, Italian churches were habitually regarded as the product of a baroque rhetoric. This opinion was still alive in 1964, when the American photographer and architectural critic George Everard Kidder Smith (1913–1997) published in London *The New Churches of Europe*, with a consistent section on Italy.[19] The author's comments on Italian churches highlighted the theatrical character of the buildings, evoked in the comparison between the modern church of the Redeemer in Turin (1956–7), by Nicola (1899–1986) and Leonardo Mosso (1926–2020), and Guarini's Sindone chapel or in the use of the adjective *dramatic* to describe St Mary the Great in Francavilla al Mare, Abbruzzo (1948–9) by Ludovico Quaroni.[20] His reading, accentuated by his training as photographer, relied on the unrestrained use that Italian churches made of light, a distinctive element hardly findable in other European countries, and which he referred to as of baroque descent. Accordingly, Kidder Smith was very impressed by the dramatic integration of direct and indirect lighting in the Milanese church of Figini and Pollini, whose lantern worked as the lens of a camera catching the light. Captured in a series of vivid black and white pictures, the church opened the Italian section of the book: 'The interior, on the other hand, provides a powerful, near-brutal, statement of strength in church architecture: This power, it should be noted, emanates from the lighting, both natural and artificial, even more than from the structure'.[21] The church even attracted Reyner Banham (1922–1988), who praised it in *The New Brutalism: Ethic or Aesthetic?* of 1966 (originally published in *The Architectural Review* in 1955).[22] Banham, particularly critical of the effects of Wittkower's principle on modern design, despite recognizing the proportioned renaissance-like layout of the church, put stress on its bare walls. These unadorned surfaces affirmed, according to him, the existence of a 'Protestant connection', in the sense of a 'puritan aesthetic' which deliberately lacks 'obvious finishes'. Banham had caught the spirit of poverty incarnated by the church, even if Figini himself, quoting St Francis and praising the mystic marriage between sacred architecture

Figure 15.1 Luigi Figini and Gino Pollini, church of Our Lady of the Poor, Milan, 1952–4

Photo Lorenzo Grieco

and poverty, had denied any connection with Protestantism, which he rather associated with misery.[23] In contrast with Figini, Banham regarded the concept of proportional harmony as a certain sign of classicism, which he believed to be among the most dangerous trends of contemporary arhitecture, both in Italy and in England. Although in line with Banham on the frontier against the Wittkowerian classicists, Peter Smithson (1923–2003) had instead tried to recover the link between modern and baroque architecture by affirming the predominance of plastic language over the Wittkowerian principles of classicity: 'The great Baroque churches are not at all theatrical in the expressionist (or Gordon Craig) sense, but rather communicate their meaning primarily by space, and by absolute consistency of plastic language. And these tools are still available – in fact are the only tools of architecture'.[24]

Renaissance and baroque categories provided critics with a vocabulary through which they could describe contemporary Italian church architecture and, sometimes, also comment on those British churches that exhibited a more Italianate language. For instance, in 1967 Gillespie, Kidd and Coia's seminary building at Cardross (1966) would be targeted as 'more Baroque than of conventional modern design' for its monumentality and the disinhibited use of light sources.[25] Indeed, the production of Giacomo Antonio Coia (1898–1981, also known as Jack), among the founders of the firm, showed many affinities with contemporary Italian churches, to the point that recent studies have compared it to the trend inaugurated by the Milanese Our Lady of the Poor.[26] Particularly, the churches of the Holy Family (1959) and that of Charles Borromeo (1959–60) in Glasgow, the last to be designed directly by Coia himself, could be inserted in a very Italian trend of churches with traditional basilical plan. Their expressive deprivation of finishes, materialized in exposed brick walls and folded concrete roofs, was not far from contemporary Italian churches, such as St Charles in Cà Granda (1957–60) and the Miraculous Medal church (1960–1) that Luigi Grigioni and Guglielmo Giani were building in Milan, or St Basil (1952–63), designed by Augusto Baccin (1914–1998) in Rome.[27]

Figure 15.2 Augusto Baccin, church of St Basil, Rome, 1952–63
Photo Lorenzo Grieco

The stylistic similarities between the churches could be explained by Coia's personal connections and by his frequent travels to Italy, through which he encountered an architectural context otherwise rarely investigated by British publications. Suffice it to say that during the 1950s, despite British interest in Italian engineering, sanctioned by the Royal Gold Medal awarded to Italian engineer Pier Luigi Nervi (1891–1979) in 1960, Rykwert's article remained one of the few glimpses into contemporary Italian church building. The destiny of the Italian churches built before the war, tainted as the work of Fascist bombast, was even more ill-fated. Almost totally neglected by the critics, they were only quickly recalled by Edward Maufe (1882–1974), who frequently travelled to Italy as principal architect (1944–69) of the Imperial War Graves Commission.[28] In his publication on *Modern Church Architecture* (1948), funded by the Incorporated Church Building Society, Maufe presented some examples built in Italy before the Second World War: the church of Christ the King (1920–34) in Rome by Marcello Piacentini (1881–1960); the Santissima Annunziata church (1933–5) in Sabaudia by Gino Cancellotti (1896–1987), Eugenio Montuori (1907–1982), Luigi Piccinato (1899–1983) and Alfredo Scalpelli (1898–1966); St Fabian and St Venantius (1934–6) in Rome by Clemente Busiri Vici (1887–1965).[29] As Maufe wrote in the text, the apse of the latter had been decorated by the English artist, theologian and women's rights activist Joan Morris (1901–1988). Morris had directed in 1937–8 a review on *Modern Sacred Art*, where she had published the contribution of foreign artists and critics, including the Italian painter Gino Severini (1883–1966) and the Catholic historian Monsignor Guido Anichini (1875–1957). The review was the source of many of the illustrations used in Maufe's book, and it is likely that even the inclusion of St Fabian and St Venantius was due to the willingness of Morris.[30] For Maufe, the danger of publishing churches built under the Fascist period was that he might be easily accused of rhetoric. Therefore, in the preface, he was keen to point out that 'Frequently we may think that these foreign architects are "showing off"; if this really be so, it is a sin, but we must guard against condemning effects which have truly arisen from circumstances very different from our own.'[31]

If Maufe found a way to deal with the Italian church architecture built during the Fascist period, probably the link with politics prevented other British critics from investigating the field of post-war church architecture in Italy, which still saw the contribution of architects who had been very close to the regime. For instance, among the British key texts on church architecture, *The Modern Church* (1956) by Edward David

Mills (1915–1998), which constituted a practical handbook on designing and building a church, gave a list of exemplary projects of churches built in England, Switzerland, France, Finland, Sweden, Germany, North America (the United States and Canada) and South America (Venezuela and Brazil), but did not mention any church built in Italy.[32] Equally, *Liturgy and Architecture* (1960) by Peter Hammond (1921–1999), who, as it happens, had also participated in the invasion of Italy, took as examples many churches from Switzerland, Germany, the US and France.[33] However, modern Italian examples were almost absent, limited to a mention, within the theme of circular-planned churches, to the church of St Marcellinus (1932–5) in Genoa by Luigi Carlo Daneri (1900–1972), accompanied by the author's remark that 'the way in which the six secondary altars are set in shallow recesses all around the eucharistic room gives the church a decidedly baroque flavour'.[34] The term *baroque* again seems to imply a negative judgement, especially if the section on St Marcellinus is compared to a passage of *Toward a Church Architecture* (1962) in which Hammond reproaches Edward Maufe for having praised, in his book on churches, the presence of secondary altars in a church to 'greatly improve the value of the design'.[35] Besides this brief entry on Daneri, when it came to describing post-war church planning in Western Europe, Hammond only acknowledged that 'Italy has in the last few years produced a number of interesting new churches, including two or three based on a circular plan'.[36] No other words were spent to describe the contemporary design of church buildings in the peninsula, although he openly recognized the fertile impact on architecture of events like the international congress held in Assisi in 1956.[37]

The Bologna National Congress on Religious Architecture and the Second Vatican Council

Despite the almost deafening silence on Italian church architecture, the Mediterranean country was leading an enthusiastic reflection on the theme of architecture and liturgy, fostered by figures such as the bishops Giacomo Lercaro (1891–1976) and Giovanni Battista Montini (1897–1978), who would be Pope (1963) as Paul VI. Nevertheless, the British press did not cover it and the only information arrived in Britain mainly through the articles of Irish and American scholars. In May 1956, the Irish architect Wilfrid Cantwell (1921–2001) wrote in the Irish Catholic magazine *The Furrow* about 'the Italian Model' of church architecture. In the article, Cantwell did not specifically mention examples of built churches. Indeed, despite having travelled to northern Italy in 1946 with his colleagues from the office of Michael Scott (1905–1989), the only building he referred to as evidence of Italian talent was a secular one: the new Termini Railway Station in Rome, made famous by the contemporary international press (which presumably he did not see if he had travelled around the north only). Instead, his analysis focused on the factors determining the success of the Italian church building programme, including the liturgical propaganda, the institution of the Central Pontifical Commission of Sacred Art and the International Institute of Liturgical Art, finally, in spite of the split economical competences laid down by the Lateran Treaty (1929), the conspicuous state funding for new churches.[38]

The theological studies on liturgy and art, fervidly debated in Italy, and their subsequent institutionalization in congresses and committees far before the Second Vatican Council, emerged as a stirring sign of the modernity of the Italian Catholic world. Rykwert himself pointed out the relevance of such manifestations of consciousness, like the First National Congress on Religious Architecture, held in Bologna in 1955. Among others, the congress gained the support of many British institutes, like the Royal Institute of British Architects, the Architecture School at Cambridge, as well as the Pontifical Scottish College of Rome; of British magazines such as *Architectural Design* and publisher Faber and Faber; of architects like David Rodney Burles of Burles, Newton and Partners, and of architectural historians like Nikolaus Pevsner (1902–1983). Diplomats including the Minister to the Holy See Sir Douglas Frederick Howard (1897–1987), A.D.M. Ross and P.H.P. Thompson, lent their support too. The event occasioned a vibrant speech by Cardinal Giacomo Lercaro, Archbishop of Bologna (1952–68), who praised 'the spirit and liturgic functionalism of paleochristian basilicas', which had to be entrusted to a contemporary language.[39] The programme of the congress, the conference proceedings, the list of participants, and a selection of projects for churches designed in the last 20 years, were collected in a book published in 1956, which included translations of the principal speeches in French, English and German.[40] They were given by Cardinal Giacomo Lercaro, the Oratorian Giulio Bevilacqua (1881–1965), the Dominican Tarcisio Piccari, and the architects Giovanni Michelucci (1891–1990) and Ludovico Quaroni.[41]

The congress had a relevant echo in the Liturgical Movement and was the source of a consistent renewal of the aesthetics of Catholicism. This was clear to Father Cloud Meinberg (1914–1982) of Saint John's Abbey in Collegeville, Minnesota, who praised the meeting in his article on 'the New Churches of Europe', published in *Worship* and *The Furrow* in 1957.[42] Although presented in respectively American and Irish magazines, the text was known in English Catholic circles. Meinberg, an architect himself before joining the Benedictine order, was an ardent supporter of liturgical reform and used to discuss architecture. He would have, for example, a long dialogue with Marcel Breuer during the construction (1953–61) of his brutalist abbey with the annexed church, which, due to its innovativeness, would have required just few adjustments after the Second Vatican Council.[43] Meinberg, who had travelled throughout Europe and met personalities such as the Cardinals Celso Benigno Luigi Costantini (1876–1958) and Giacomo Lercaro, wrote in the said magazines a commentary on church architecture in Europe. By analysing the several national approaches to the theme, he delineated a difference between the architectural style of northern countries (Germany, Belgium, France and Switzerland) and that of southern ones (above all Spain and Italy). In particular, Italian churches showed, according to the Benedictine, a baroque footprint that transpired from modern trappings, in a revivalist approach often overlooking pastoral needs.[44] However, he claimed that Italy had the potential for a sacred architecture 'worthy of her past', able to embody the warm spirit of its inhabitants: 'The genius largely is in the south. Italy, where so many of the cultural movements of Western Europe have been born, where men know how to live fully and to be happy although poor, where Catholicism often makes a rather disappointing showing on the exterior but where perhaps the Catholic soul lies deeper – for something must explain the enormous unmatched vitality of this people – this Italy is stirring. So far the new churches of Europe tend to be clear and cold – like the frosty dawn of an early spring. The warm sun of Italy is still to come – I hope'.[45]

Meinberg even cited the significant exhibition of modern German church architecture held at the Lateran Museum in Rome in 1957, sponsored by the Cardinals Josef Frings (1887–1978) and Joseph Wendel (1901–1960), with a catalogue introduced by a text by Romano Guardini (1885–1968) on 'the Religious picture and the Invisible God'.[46] A few years later, in 1961, Guardini would be asked to enter the Liturgical Preparatory Commission of the Second Vatican Council, while Cardinal Frings would be among the animators of the Council called by John XXIII in 1959.

The Second Vatican Council opened in 1962 and concluded in 1965. Its original ecumenical energy was the occasion for English liturgists to meet other national realities and, especially, the Italian one. Indeed, Pope John XXIII himself wanted some external observer to represent other faiths and to report the work of the council to their own leaders. For the Anglican communion, the Archbishop of Canterbury decided to employ as representative Bernard Pawley. In the meantime, John XXIII organized several ecumenical meetings: on 2 December 1960 he received the Anglican Archbishop of Canterbury Geoffrey Francis Fisher (1887–1972), and on 10 May 1962 the bishop of Edmundsbury and Ipswich Arthur Harold Morris (1898–1977). Parallel to institutional meetings, a series of informal initiatives led British Anglicans to dialogue with the Roman Catholic Church.[47] Although the outcomes of the council on Catholic church architecture and furnishing were not immediate and the principles expressed in the *Constitution of the Sacred Liturgy* (1963) would be fully received only around the 1970s, the discussion of the council arrived long before in British Catholic and Anglican circles. The rapid reform of the Roman Catholic Missal pushed forward the Anglican Liturgical revision, whose first official expression, the *Vestments of Minister Measure* (1964), authorized ministers to wear eucharistic vestments, till then considered a 'popish' practice. The new stress on corporate action and on eucharistic service, shared with the Roman Catholic reform, would deeply influence the modelling of the *Alternative Service Book*, used from 1980, and the following *Common Worship*, in use from 2000, whose sections can be easily compared to the Vatican II Missal.[48]

A new dawn

Under the driving liturgical forces of the Second Vatican Council and the miracle of the Italian economic boom, a new dialogue finally began between Italian and British church architecture. The British attitude towards industrialization became the occasion to know new Italian prefabricated architectures and to rediscover the Baranzate glass church. The building by Mangiarotti and Morassutti was published in 1964 in Kidder Smith's already mentioned reportage, as well as in *Churchbuilding*.[49]

The magazine was the official organ of the New Churches Research Group, guided by Peter Hammond and the architectural duo Robert Maguire (1931–2019) and Keith Murray (1929–2005), who would include the same church even in their selection of *Modern Churches of the World* (1965).[50] In the pages of *Churchbuilding*, the Italian church was compared to another foreign masterpiece, the church of St Christophorus in Köln-Niehl (1954–9) by Rudolf Schwarz (1897–1961). Neglecting its innovative technologies, the comparison seemed to be particularly harsh on the former. Indeed, the article blamed the 'depressing',

Figure 15.3 Angelo Mangiarotti and Bruno Morassutti, church of Our Lady of Mercy, Baranzate, 1956–8
Photo Lorenzo Grieco

'pseudo-primitive yet highly sophisticated' exterior look of the Baranzate church, as well as the 'picturesque irrelevance' of the pool near its baptismal font.[51] The interior, despite being described as charming and full of light, 'gives the impression of a modern building re-ordered for a medieval liturgy' and was again condemned for its over-sophistication. The text closed with the reaffirmation that, although no comparable churches had been built in Britain, the Italian church only embodied a superficial understanding of the liturgical movement when compared to German examples.[52]

Four years later, in 1968, the book *New Directions in Italian Architecture* by Vittorio Gregotti was published in London. It presented some examples of contemporary church architecture, all expressing a new aesthetic of Italian building, departing from the bareness praised by Banham to reach a new expressionist afflatus, more in keeping with its baroque background. The *eloquentia* of the trend was embodied by the project (1949) of Ludovico Quaroni for a church in the Prenestino quarter, Rome, the entry submitted by Enrico Castiglioni (1914–2000) to the competition for the sanctuary of Siracusa (1957) and the church of St John the Baptist on the A11 highway (1960–4) by Giovanni Michelucci.[53]

From an opposing viewpoint, in 1970 a monographic number of *Manplan* dedicated to 'Religion' presented the church of the Holy Heart

Figure 15.4 Guido Maffezzoli, church of the Holy Heart, Milan, 1962–6
Photo Lorenzo Grieco

Figure 15.5 Giovanni Michelucci, church of St John the Baptist, Campi Bisenzio, 1960–4
Photo Lorenzo Grieco

(1962–6) in Milan by Guido Maffezzoli (b. 1921) again praised for its almost Protestant mood: 'shorn of its Baroque past, the form retains immense human appeal'.[54] The church was even selected by German architect Reinhard Gieselmann (1925–2013) in his book on *Contemporary*

Church Architecture, published in London in 1972, to represent Italy along with its baroque nemesis, Michelucci's highway church.[55]

In fact, cited by international critics and inserted among the examples of the new architecture by the *Encyclopædia Britannica*, Michelucci's church architecture started to register a growing interest, finally enshrined in the exhibition that the RIBA dedicated to the Italian architect in 1978.[56] The same year, the picture of Michelucci's church in Longarone (1975–82) appeared on the cover of the April issue of the *Architectural Review*, with the headline 'Viva Michelucci', while Rykwert wrote on the Italian architect in the *RIBA Journal*.[57] The success of Michelucci's churches in the UK attested to the increasing interest in Italian religious architecture and the progressive dismantling of that 'Baroque anathema' that had cursed the destiny of previous Italian churches. The warm sun of Italy had finally started, as it were, to shine in Britain!

Acknowledgements

The present study was produced within the frame of the PhD research *A 'Disturbing Influence': Directions and cross-fertilisation in English church architecture, 1945–1970*, conducted at the University of Rome Tor Vergata, under the supervision of professors Claudia Conforti and Maria Grazia D'Amelio, and at the University of Kent, under the supervision of professors Manolo Guerci and Gerald Adler. The author thanks the supervisors of the research, as well as Lorenzo Ciccarelli, Ambrose Gillick, Andrea Longhi, Alan Powers, and Robert Proctor, for their valuable suggestions. I refer the reader to my thesis for further details.

Notes

1. Cox 1951.
2. On the directions of British urban planning after the Second World War see Ciccarelli 2019.
3. Burstow 1996, 5.
4. Martin was appointed to lead the design of the Festival Hall by Hugh Casson (1910–1999), who had overall architectural direction of the festival.
5. Rykwert 1956.
6. Mills 1959, 94; McGregor Dunnett, 2017. The building would be converted in 1975–6 by Edward Mills into Methodist Trinity church. From 1995 it would operate as the Calvary Charismatic Baptist church.
7. Proctor 2016, 15.
8. Although already completed in 1954, the church was consecrated only in 1960. It is strange to note how the 'Lombardic tiles' used for the covering of the lower roofs, whose format is not common in English constructions, are used to gain a certain Romanesque atmosphere.

9 Proctor 2016, 16–7.
10 Hebert 1935.
11 In particular, Rykwert looked at Ignazio Gardella, BBPR, Giuseppe Pagano, Figini and Pollini, and to the masters of Italian Rationalism: Baird 2002, 18.
12 *Casabella-Continuità*, 208 (November–December 1955).
13 Rykwert 1956, 174.
14 Rykwert 1966, 121–2.
15 Wittkower 1949, 11–32.
16 On Rykwert and Wittkower see Baird 2002, 13. Many texts have investigated Wittkower's influence on modern architecture. See Millon 1972; Payne 1994.
17 The definition of transparent poverty is taken from Capellades 1962.
18 Butcher 1955.
19 Kidder Smith 1964, 190–219. The Italian section includes the already mentioned Our Lady of the Poors by Figini and Pollini, followed by: Santa Giustina in Mesola (1954) by Pierluigi Giordani (1924–2011); the church of the Blessed Immaculate Virgin (1956–61) in Bologna by Glauco Gresleri (1930–2016); the Baranzate church (1956–8) by Angelo Mangiarotti (1921–2012) and Bruno Morassutti (1920–2008); the SS Redentore in Turin (1956–7) by Nicola (1899–1986) and Leonardo Mosso (b. 1926); San Luca Evangelista in Rome (1955–8) by Studio Passarelli (and structures by Riccardo Morandi); finally Santa Maria Maggiore in Francavilla al Mare (1948–9) by Ludovico Quaroni.
20 Kidder Smith 1964, 210 and 216.
21 Kidder Smith 1964, 190.
22 Banham 1966, 125. The Protestant churches to which the Milanese building is compared are the Reformed church in Nagele (1960) by Johannes Hendrik van den Broek (1898–1978) and Jacob Bakema (1914–81), and the Markuskyrka in Stockholm (1956–63) by Sigurd Lewerentz (1885–1975).
23 In particular, he noticed the shadow of a Protestant misery in those church buildings that were prefabricated without any unavoidable reasons, representing an unnecessary privation of the spatial harmony and richness that stimulated in the faithful a mysterious invitation to the worship of God: 'Ormai nel costruire sacro una scelta si impone tra i tre termini scalari in gioco: ricchezza, povertà, miseria … Quanto alla miseria … di fronte allo squallore di certe "prefabbricate" (tali anche dove non ve ne sia vera e improrogabile necessità), non si può non pensare per analogia a una certa "forma mentis" di sapore nihilista, affine al "cupio dissolvi", e a un autolesionismo rinunciatario di colore protestantico … Quanto alla povertà, non sarà certo fuori luogo qui, nella terra di S Francesco, tesserne ancora una volta l'elogio, parlare di nozze mistiche dell'architettura sacra con Madonna Povertà', from Figini 1965.
24 Peter Smithson, *Spiritual exercise for churchmen and architects*, from a talk at the University of London, autumn 1959, from Hammond 1962, 10.
25 Nuttgens 1967, 248, cited in Walker 1985.
26 Robertson 2014; Robertson 2017, 245–96. For the suggestion on Figini and Pollini's church as inspiration: Stamp 1994, 51.
27 On the style of Baccin's St Basil see Contessa 2016.
28 Maufe had travelled to Italy several times to visit the office of the Southern Regional Commission in Rome, since 1964 in Via Cornelio Celso 4. During one of his last visits, he had the occasion to see new Italian architectures, including the new Hilton Hotel in Monte Mario by Ugo Luccichenti, Emilio Pifferi e Alberto Ressa, with structure by Pier Luigi Nervi; Nervi's Palazzo dello Sport and the newly complete building of the EUR quarter. For the rest, he remained in the city centre and did not visit modern church buildings, which were mainly being built in peripheral areas of the city. The diary of his 1964 travel is in the RIBA Library Collection, MaE 140.
29 Maufe 1948, 46–9.
30 Morris 1938.
31 Maufe 1948, 8.
32 Mills 1956.
33 Hammond 1963.
34 Hammond 1963, 65–6.
35 Hammond 1962, 27, n. 12; Maufe 1948, 9.
36 Hammond 1963, 81.
37 Hammond 1963, 79. The first International Congress of Pastoral Liturgy took place in Assisi and in Rome from 18 to 22 September 1956.

38 Cantwell 1956, 296–9.
39 On the use of primitivism in modernist architecture see Gombrich 2002.
40 Centro di Studio e Informazione per l'Architettura Sacra di Bologna 1956.
41 Centro di Studio e Informazione per l'Architettura Sacra di Bologna 1956, 48–53. On the conference see Zito 2013, 21–2. Father Bevilacqua wrote the introduction to the first Italian edition of *The Spirit of the Liturgy* by Romano Guardini, see: Guardini 1930.
42 Meinberg 1957.
43 Thimmesh 2011, ix; Young 2014.
44 'In Italy the issue between the old styles and modern is not clear. Consequently eclecticism is rife – sometimes of Renaissance origins, often of Baroque, and sometimes of modern' or again 'there is still, for example, the multiplicity of altars in parish churches ... are they the old Baroque shrine-altars mainly for special devotions ... ?', from Meinberg 1957, 366.
45 Meinberg 1957, 372.
46 Meinberg 1957, 368–9.
47 The Jesuit Charles Boyer is a key figure in this ecumenical dialogue. Professor at the Università Gregoriana in Rome, in 1945 Boyer founded in the heart of the city the Unitas Centre, a focus for ecumenical studies, whose ideas were diffused through the homonymous journal, *Unitas*, which was published in four languages. He was soon joined by the Ladies of Bethany, a congregation of nuns from the Low Countries with the mission of approaching people, even from different religions, who founded in 1950 the Foyer Unitas. From 1962 in Palazzo Pamphilj in Piazza Navona, it offered a place to sleep to non-Catholic pilgrims who had arrived in Rome, and above all to the observers called to the Council. Many Anglican priests frequented the place, from Bernard Clinton Pawley (1911–1981) to John Moorman (1905–1989).
48 Yates 2008, 147–55.
49 Catt *et al.* 1964.
50 Maguire and Murray 1965. The New Churches Research Groups, founded in 1957, included many liturgists and architects, such as Nigel Melhuish, Lance Wright and Peter Ansdell Evans of the firm Melhuish Wright and Evans; Robert Potter; Austin Winkley; Gerard Goalen; George Gaze Pace. On the group see Adler 2012, 75.
51 Catt *et al.* 1964, 9, 'Seen from a distance, the church stands out clean and bright ... Closer to, the outside of the church is rather depressing, because the building hasn't worn well ... The glass is crackling, the glass fiber is going yellow and the paint is peeling off the steelwork'.
52 Catt *et al.* 1964, 17: 'It is also probable that the greater depth of understanding evident in Schwarz's building when compared to the church designed by Mangiarotti and Morassuti [sic] is due as much to the development of liturgical understanding in Germany as to the greater maturity of Schwarz in this respect'.
53 Gregotti 1968: 43 (Quaroni), 78 (Castiglioni), 86 and 89 (Michelucci).
54 *Manplan* 5 Religion (1970), 224.
55 Gieselmann 1972, 40–2. A sentence of Claudia Conforti on the baroque look of Michelucci's church in San Marino (1961–7) could easily fit the highway church: 'I diaframmi diversamente traforati che sfumano le ombre perimetrali; la luce che penetra obliquamente da un taglio del tetto accarezzando gli arconi, lambendo le superfici curve e inclinate, e dileguandosi nell'intensa penombra dell'aula: sono tutti fattori che accostano la chiesa di Michelucci alla grandiosa inattualità di un teatro barocco, più che alla cruda drammaticità di una scenografia espressionista', from Conforti 2006, 308.
56 'Architecture' 1965; Naldi 1978; for the critical fortune of Michelucci see Dulio 2006.
57 'Viva Michelucci' 1978; Rykwert 1978.

References

Adler, Gerald. *Robert Maguire and Keith Murray*. London: RIBA, 2012.
'Architecture', *Encyclopædia Britannica*, vol. 2, 35–9. Chicago: Encyclopædia Britannica, 1965.
Baird, George. 'A promise as well as a memory: Notes toward an intellectual biography of Joseph Rykwert'. In *Body and Building: Essays on the changing relation of body and architecture*, edited by George Dodds and Robert Tavernor, 2–27. Cambridge, MA: MIT Press, 2002.
Banham, Reyner. *The New Brutalism: Ethic or aesthetic?* London: Architectural Press, 1966.

Burstow, Robert. *Symbols for '51, the Royal Festival Hall, Skylon and Sculptures for the Festival of Britain*. London: Royal Festival Hall, 1996.
Butcher, Maryvonne. 'The future of Italian films', *Blackfriars* 36 (April 1955): 121–7.
Cantwell, Wilfrid. 'The Italian model', *The Furrow* 7, no. 5 (May 1956): 296–9.
Capellades, Marie-Robert. 'Transparent poverty', translated by Keith Harrison, *Churchbuilding* 7 (October 1962): 4–8. Originally published in *L'Art sacré* (January–February 1958).
Catt, John and Murray Maguire. 'Milan and Cologne: Two churches', *Churchbuilding* 12 (April 1964): 8–17.
Centro di Studio e Informazione per l'Architettura Sacra di Bologna. *Dieci anni di architettura sacra in Italia 1945–1955*. Bologna: Ufficio tecnico organizzativo arcivescovile, 1956.
Ciccarelli, Lorenzo. *Il mito dell'equilibrio: Il dibattito anglo-italiano per il governo del territorio negli anni del dopoguerra*. Milan: Franco Angeli, 2019.
Conforti, Claudia. 'Santuario della Beata Vergine della Consolazione'. In *Giovanni Michelucci*, edited by Claudia Conforti, Roberto Dulio and Marzia Marandola, 304–11. Milan: Electa, 2006.
Contessa, Alessandra. *Augusto Baccin architetto 1914–1998*. Rome: Edizioni Preprogetti, 2016.
Cox, Ian. *The South Bank Exhibition: A guide to the story it tells*. London: H. M. Stationery Office, 1951.
Dulio, Roberto. '"Quel moderno che gli fo io": La fortuna critica'. In *Giovanni Michelucci*, edited by Claudia Conforti, Roberto Dulio and Marzia Marandola, 38–59. Milan: Electa, 2006.
Dunnett, Harding McGregor. *1951 Exhibition of Architecture: Guide to the exhibition of architecture, town planning and building research*. London: Routledge, 2017.
Figini, Luigi. 'La povertà delle chiese'. In *Architettura e Liturgia*, edited by Pina Ciampani, 119. Assisi: Edizioni Pro Civitate Christiana, 1965.
Gieselmann, Reinhard. *Contemporary Church Architecture*. London: Thames and Hudson, 1972.
Gombrich, Ernst Hans. *The Preference for the Primitive: Episodes in the history of Western taste and art*. London: Phaidon, 2002.
Gregotti, Vittorio. *New Directions in Italian Architecture*. New York: George Braziller, 1968.
Guardini, Romano. *Lo Spirito della Liturgia*. Brescia: Morcelliana, 1930.
Hammond, Peter. 'Foreword'. In *Towards a Church Architecture*, edited by Peter Hammond, ix–xi. London: Architectural Press, 1962.
Hebert, Arthur Gabriel. *Liturgy and Society: The function of the church in the modern world*. London: Faber and Faber, 1935.
Kidder Smith, George Everard. *The New Churches of Europe*. London: Architectural Publishing, 1964.
Maufe, Edward. Extracts from Maufe's diary-journey by ship and train to Italy and visit to Rome with his wife. RIBA Library Collection, MaE 140.
Maufe, Edward. *Modern Church Architecture*. London: Incorporated Church Building Society, 1948.
Meinberg, Cloud. 'The new churches of Europe', *The Furrow* 8, no. 6 (June 1957): 364–72.
Millon, Henry A. 'Rudolf Wittkower, architectural principles in the age of humanism: Its influence on the develoment and interpretation of modern architecture', *Journal of the Society of Architectural Historians* 31, no. 2 (May 1972): 83–91.
Mills, Edward D. *The Modern Church*. London: The Architectural Press, 1956.
Morris, Joan. *Modern Sacred Art: An international annual review*. London: Sands and Co., 1938.
Naldi, Fabio (ed.). *Giovanni Michelucci*. Florence: Modulo, 1978.
Nuttgens, Patrick. 'Review of New Seminary: St Peter's College, Cardross', *The Clergy Review*, March 1967, 248.
Payne, Alina. 'Rudolf Wittkower and Architectural Principles in the Age of Modernism', *Journal of the Society of Architectural Historians* 53, no. 3 (September 1994): 322–42.
Proctor, Robert. *Building the Modern Church: Roman Catholic church architecture in Britain, 1955 to 1975*. London: Routledge, 2016.
Robertson, James. 'Ecclesiastical icons: Defining Rome through architectural exchange'. In *Rome, Postmodern Narratives of a Cityscape*, edited by Dom Holdaway and Filippo Trentin, 137–54. London: Pickering and Chatto, 2014.
Robertson, James. 'Gillespie, Kidd and Coia: Ecclesiastical architecture, 1931–1979'. PhD thesis, Manchester Metropolitan University, 2017.
Rykwert, Joseph. 'The churches we deserve?', *Blackfriars* 37, no. 433 (April 1956): 171–5.
Rykwert, Joseph. *Church Building*. London: Burns and Oates, 1966.
Rykwert, Joseph. 'Giovanni Michelucci Master of Italian Architecture', *RIBA Journal* 3 (March 1978): 105–6.

Stamp, Gavin. 'Postscript', *Mac Journal* 1 (1994), 51–6. Monographic issue: Gillespie, Kidd and Coia.

Thimmesh, Hilary. *Marcel Breuer and a Committee of Twelve Plan a Church: A monastic memoir.* Collegeville, MN: Liturgical Press, 2011.

'Viva Michelucci', *The Architectural Review* 974 (April 1978): 197–8.

Walker, Paul. 'Developments in Catholic Churchbuilding in the British Isles, 1945–1980'. PhD thesis, University of Sheffield, 1985.

Wittkower, Rudolf. *Architectural Principles in the Age of Humanism*. London: Warburg Institute, University of London, 1949.

Young, Victoria. *Saint John's Abbey Church: Marcel Breuer and the creation of a modern sacred space*. Minneapolis: University of Minnesota Press, 2014.

Zito, Carla. *Casa tra le case: Architettura di chiese a Torino durante l'episcopato del cardinale Michele Pellegrino (1965–1977)*. Cantalupa: Effatà, 2013.

Index

The main text and figure captions are indexed, but not the endnotes or references. Figure references are in italic.

A-frame ix, 160–3, 170–1
Aalto, Alvar 22, 164, 213
Abbagnano, Nicola 133
Abercrombie, Patrick 22, 24–7, 150, 151, 165, 168
Acquapendente 30
Adam, Robert and James 163
Addis Ababa 147
Adelphi 163
Adorno, Theodor 90
Agrigento 36
Ahrends, Peter 70
Aix-en-Provence 117, 159, 166, 167
Alatri 30
Albini, Franco 1, 51, 65, 70–6, 78–81, 112, 113, 115, 120
Albini, Marco 73
Alexander, Cristopher 67
Algiers 118, 163
Alison, Filippo 101
Althusser, Louis, Althusserianism 89, 91, 92, 102
Alton Estate 165
anarchism 98
Anderson, Benedict 6, 9
Anderson, Perry 91
Andriello, Domenico 145–52
Anglo-Saxon 21, 53, 146, 149, 160
Anichini, Guido 243
anthropology 118, 159
Antonioni, Michelangelo 172
Archigram 49, 89, 90, 92, 94, 99, 101, 205
Architects' Co-operative 224
Architects Co-Partnership 180, 186, 190, *192*
Architects Journal 71, 110, 111, 219
Architectural Association 22, 23, 30, 87, 96, 100, 101, 107, 109, 111, 112, 120, 134, 158, 166, 173, 223, 224
Architectural Design 71, 89, 96, 180, 182, 245
architectural historian, role of 51–3, 184, 245
Architectural Review 31, 32, 34–6, 45, 46, 60, 61, 71, 74, 77, 78–80, 113, 158, 159, 173, 180, 185, 191, 199, 200, 208, 209, 218, 224, 250
Archizoom 48, 49, 86, 87, 89, 99
Arendt, Hannah 180, 181, 185, 194
Arenzano 62, 221
artifice 46
Arts and Crafts 77, 164, 165, 187
Assisi 31, 244
Associazione per l'Architettura Organica (APAO) 21, 72, 148
Astengo, Giovanni 26–8, 148
Athens *130*, 189
Athens Charter 108, 111, 113, 117–19, 127, 136, 138, 141, 142, 159, 160
Athougia, Ruy 80
Attlee, Clement 21, 34
Aulenti, Gae 60, 65
Avezzano 30

Baccin, Augusto 242
Bakema, Jacob 62, 64, 66, 117
Banham, Reyner 1, 45–*54*, 60–2, 64–6, 158, 160, 161, 163, 170, 203, 218, 219, 221, 224, 231, 240, 241, 248
Baracco, Giuliana 137
Baranzate 236, 247, *248*
Barbiano di Belgiojoso, Lodovico 81, 111, 117
Barthes, Roland 93
Bath 32, 166, 171
Bauhaus 164
BBPR 59, *63*, 64, 72, 115
behaviour 90–1, 95, 98, 100, 136, 141, 156, 232
Benevolo, Leonardo 60, 66
Benigno, Celso 246
Bergamo 101, 107, 108, 110–12, 159, 223
Berlanda, Franco 110, 115, 223
Berlin 14, 95, 101
Bernstein, Levitt *157*
Bevilacqua, Giulio 245
Bianco, Mario 26
Biella 226, 227
Bill, Max 213
Birmingham 152
Black, Misha 220
Bloomsbury *157*, 158, 163, 164
Bo, Carlo 139
Boccioni, Umberto 162
Bologna 236, 244, 245
Bolsena 29
Bombay 130
Bon, Christoph 70
Bottoni, Piero 107
Boyarsky, Alvin 87, 97, 98, 101
Branzi, Andrea 99
Brawne, Michel 80

Breckman, Warren 90
Brett, Lionel 180, 186, 209
Breuer, Marcel 78, 246
Bridgewater 111, 113, 136
Brighton 14, 180
British architecture 1, 12, 13, 36, 76, 185, 236–7
Britishness 11
Brockhouse Steel Structures 216
Brooke, Thomas 29
Browne, Kenneth 32, 159
Brunswick Centre 156–74
brutalism 48, 179, 203, 240
Buccinasco 228
Buchanan, Colin 81, 151, 168, 169
Buenos Aires 51
Bullock, Nicholas 71
Bunshaft, Gordon 50
Burles, David 245
Burton, Richard 70
Busiri Vici, Clemente 243
Butcher, Maryvonne 240

Cadbury-Brown, Henry Thomas 109
Calini, Leo 46
Calza Bini, Alberto 148
Cambridge (MA) 142
Cambridge (UK) 71, 73, 78–81, 169, 186, 187, 202, 245
Campbell, Louise 186
Campi Bisenzio *249*
Cancellotti, Gino 243
Candilis, Georges 81, 117, 118, 159
Cantwell, Wilfrid 244
Capon, Kenneth 109, 179, 180, 184, 186, 190, 191–5
Carbonara, Pasquale 10
Caruso, Martina 2
Casabella, Casabella Continuità 52, 57, 59–61, 71, 73, 89, 95, 118, 119, 121, 201, 202, 205, 206, 219, 239
Case a gradinate 161
Caserta 232
Cassi Ramelli, Antonio 223
Castiglioni, Enrico 248
Cederna, Antonio 146, 147
Celant, Germano 91, 94, 97, 101
Cerdà, Ildefondo 141
Cervinia 74, *75*
Chamberlin, Peter 70
Chermayeff, Serge 77
Chicago 11
Chiodi, Cesare 147
Chiusi 29
CIAM 42, 64, 72, 77, 78, 107–14, 116–22, 131, 136, 138, 141, 159, 167, 221, 223, 224
CIAM summer schools v 107, 109, 121–2
Ciccarelli, Lorenzo 1, 2, 145
Cid, Pedro 80
CLASP 47–8, 214–19, 212–13, 225–7, 229–32
Coalbrookdale 13
Coates, Wells 77, 112
Cocchia, Carlo 148
Coderch, Josep Antoni 213
Coia, Giacomo 242
Colchester 190
Coleman, Alec 169
Collegeville 245
Colletta di Castelbianco 139, 140
Cologne 8, 247
Colombini, Luigi *75*
community 25, 26, 71, 78, 114, 131, 133, 136, 151, 169, 180–2, 185, 190, 191, 194, 195, 206, 209
Concise Townscape 159
concrete 65, 78, 156, 162, 163, 169–70, 173, 238, 242
Conran, Terence 222
construction industry 213–15
continuity 31–2, 59–60, 62, 71–3, 128, 157, 160, 163–4
conurbation 152–3
Conway 14
Cook, Peter 89
Coppola Pignatelli, Paola 203
Cortona 19
Cosenza, Luigi 148
Costa, Lucio 115
Costantini, Luigi 246
Coventry 33, 186, 187, 225, 239
Covre, Gino 74
creativity 72, 100
Cretella, Michele 148
Croft-Murray, Edward 29
Crooke, Patrick 107, 115
Crosby, Theo 158
Cuccia, Francesco 148
Cullen, Gordon 32, 33, 159
cultural exchange 1, 4–5, 9, 17, 121, 213
Culture of Cities 132, 137, 164
Cumbernauld 35
Curtis, Penelope 80

d'Avoine, Pierre 166
Daneri, Luigi Carlo 244
Darby III, Abraham *13*
David, Elizabeth 166
De Andrade, Alfredo 9
De Carlo, Giancarlo 36, 62, 80, 115, 119, 121, 127, 131, 136–41, 159, 160, 203–6
De Luca, Giulio 148
De Mendonça, Maria José 80
De Wolfe, Ivor 159, 191
De Wolfe, Ivy 159
Deakin, Ralph 31
democracy 146, 149, 158, 179, 186, 188, 194, 195
derivative 49
détournement 95
Detti, Edoardo *200*, 201, 208
Dewey, John 133
didacticism 87
Dikanski, Michel 146
Doglio, Carlo 137, 138, 140, 152, 207
Domus 61, 71, 97, 217, 224
Dorfles, Gillo 61, 94
Doxiadis, Kostantinos 134, 135
Drew, Jane 108
Dubrovnik 118–20

Eccles, David 220, 222
Eco, Umberto 94, 95
Edallo, Amos 148
Eddy, David Hamilton 170, 173
Edinburgh 127, 129–31, 187, 202
Ellis, Roger 29
Ellis, Tom 22
Elmhirst, Dorothy 134
Elmhirst, Leonard 134
English Gothic 8, 164–5
English Heritage 71, 161, 187
Englishness 12, 14
Eno, Brian 101
Enthoven, Roderick 29–31, 35
Erten, Erdem 194
existentialism 133, 165

Fanfani, Amintore 122, 214, 215
Fano 30
Fellows, Philip 220
Fera, Cesare 221
Ferentino 30
Ferraris, Tommaso 220
Festival of Britain 156, 164, 165, 224, 236–9
FIAT 49
Figini, Luigi 236, *239–41*
Finland 164, 243
Fisher, Geoffrey 247
flats 156–7, 170, 194
Florence 2, 30, 89, 94, 101, 199–202
Foligno 30
Ford, Henry 49
Forlì 101
formalism 46, 59–61, 73, 112, 159
Forshaw, John Henry 22, 24–7, 165, 168
Fort l'Empereur 160, 163
Forum (journal) 118, 159
Fossombrone 30
Foundling Estate *161*, 165
Fourier, Charles 207
Franco, Fausto 115
Frings, Josef 246
Fry, Maxwell 92, 107, 109, 111
Fuller, Buckminster 98, 101
Fulton, John 187
Furneaux Jordan, Robert 1, 107, 111, 112, 159
Fuselli, Eugenio 148
futurism 45–7, 160, 162, 165, 173, 174
futurist city 160
Fyfe, Hamilton 12

Gabetti, Roberto 57, *58*, 60, 74
Gabo, Naum 77
Gardella, Ignazio 62, 65, 72, 113, 115, 120
garden city 151, 152, 206–8
Gardner, James 222
Gardner-Medwin, Robert 47, 49
Garroni, Emilio 93, 94
Gaudí, Antoni 60
Geddes, Patrick 109, 127–37, 139–42, 152
Geneva *8*, 9
Genoa 74, 80, 224
Gentili, Eugenio 59, 60
Georgian architecture 164–5, 166, 169
Giani, Luigi 242
Gibberd, Frederick 22
Gibson, Donald 216
Giedion, Sigfried 111, 113, 134–7, 184, 185
Gieselmann, Reinhard 249
Gilbert Scott, Adrian 238
Gillespie, John 242
Giovannoni, Gustavo 146, 147
Glasgow 101, 226, 242
Global Tools 87, 99, *100*, 101
Gnecchi Ruscone, Francesco 107, 110, 111, 222–32
Godfrey, William 238
Gorio, Federico 148
Gowan, James *200*, 201, 208
Gradara 30
Gray, Patience 218
Grcic, Konstantin 222
Gregotti, Vittorio 51, 57, 60, 115, *200*, 201, 208, 209, 248
grid, gridiron 87, 89–90, 95, 108, 118, 137, 216
Griffin, Bernard 237
Grigioni, Luigi 242
Gropius, Walter 108, 109, 114, 165
Gruppo 9999 86, 87, 89, 99
Gruppo Sturm 97, 99
Guardini, Romano 246
Guarini, Guarino 240
Gubbio 29
Gubler, Jacques 8
Guccione, Margherita *140*
Guidi, Ignazio 147
Gutman, Robert 117

Habitat Charter 166, 117, 136, 159
habitat 117, 136, 137, 159, 166, 167, 172
Hall, Gordon 117
Hall, Peter 140, 158
Halsey, Albert 184
Hamilton Eddy, David 170, 173
Hammond, Peter 244, 247
Handisyde, Cecil 238
Hansen, Oskar 111
Harlow 16, 34
Harvey Court 79, 169, 170
Harvey, David 184
Hastings, Hubert de Cronin 32, 34, 159, 191
Heathcote, F.W. 216
Hebert, Arthur 238
Helg, Franca 51, *76*, 80, 81
Hénard, Eugène 146
Henderson, Graham 112
Herron, Ron 90
Heynen, Hilde 184, 185
high-density 34, 156, 158, 167
historic centre 29, 31, 32, 34, 36, 62, 64, 139, 147, 159
Hitchcock, Henri-Russell 203
Hitler, Adolf 72
Hobsbawm, Eric 5, 6
Hoddesdon 113–15, 122, 136, 159, 167, 169
Hodgkinson, Patrick 70, 79, 156–73
Hoffmann, Josef 221
Holden, Charles 15, 172
Holford, William 15
Hope Reed, Henry 32, 33

Horkheimer, Max 90
housing 2, 21, 23, 34, 36, 61, 70, 74, 78, 86, 110, 136, 140, 152, 156, 158, 160, 162–8, 172, 173, 194, 237
Howard, Douglas 245
Howard, Ebenezer 151, 152, 206, 207, 210
Howard, Maurice 182
Howell, William 117
Hunstanton 166

identity 5, 9–12, 14, 17, 71–2, 75, 99, 120, 140, 146, 151, 173–4, 187
ideology 91–2, 159–60, 172, 186, 208–9
Independent Group 46, 64, 78
Indore 130
International Laboratory of Architecture and Urban Design (ILAUD) 121
International Style 65, 72, 74, 77, 112, 159
Isola, Aimaro 57, *58*, 60
Isozaki, Arata 11
Israel, Lawrence 22
Istituto Nazionale di Urbanistica (INU) 21
Italian Contemporary Architecture (exhibition) 1, 107, 112, 159, 224
Italian heritage 20, 29–31, 34
Italian modernity 49–50, 53–4
Italian urban planning 21, 26, 145
Italianness 11
Italy 1–3, 4, 8, 9–12, 20–6, 28–32, 35, 36, 45–53, 61, 62, 67, 70–2, 90, 93, 108, 110, 112, 114, 117, 119, 122, 127, 131, 132, 137, 145, 146, 159, 167, 180, 194, 195, 199, 202, 206, 208, 213, 214, 217, 219, 222–229, 231, 232, 236, 240, 242–6, 249, 250
  architectural heritage 20, 29
  national identity 10, 11
  relationship to modernism 46, 239
  post-war reconstruction 16–17
  urban planning 26
Ivrea 62

Jencks, Charles 65, 66, 96
Jerusalem 130
Johnson, Philip 137
Jowsey, Diana 100

Kahn, Louis 67, 170, 194, 201
Kallemann, Gerhard 150
Kant, Immanuel 50
Keil do Amaral, Francisco 80
Kern, Stephen 146
Kidd, William 242
Kidder Smith, George Everard 240, 247
King George VI 24
Knight, Richard Payne 14
Koolhaas, Rem 95–100
Kopp, Anatole 141
Koralek, Paul 70
Korn, Arthur 109
Korsch, Karl 90
Kosik, Karel 90
Kropotkin, Peter 129, 133, 140, 141
Kuwait City 81
Kyoto 11

La Sarraz 119, 120, 138
Lacey, Dan 221, 225
Lancaster 180
Las Vegas 67
Lasdun, Denys 35, 193
Lastra a Signa 139
Le Corbusier 24, 65, 72, 77, 108, 113, 115, 116, 134, 137, 138, 159, 160, 163–5, 182
Le Play, Frédéric 128
Leeds 181, 209
Lefebvre, Henri 141, 187
Leipzig 223
Leonidov, Ivan 95
Lercaro, Giacomo 244–6
Lethaby, William 164
Lingeri, Pietro 107
Lisbon 9, 80
listing 158, 161, 173
Liverpool 46, 181
London *15*, 21–30, 34, 45, 46, 66, 72, 77, 78, 81, 87, 91, 97, 98, 107–12, 115, 116, 122, 134, 158, 159, 162–165, 167, 173, 220, 222, 223, 224, 236–8, 240, 248, 249
  County of London Plan 24, 26, 28, 165
  greenbelt 27
  local communities 24–6, 27, 151, 163, 165
  pollution 12
  post-war rebuilding 33, 71, 168, 172, 237
London County Council 34, 78, 110, 165, 172
Longarone 250
Loreto 29
Los, Sergio 92
Loughborough Estate 168
low-rise 158, 167, 172
Lubbock, Jules 182, 186
Lucca 31
Lukács, Georg 90
Lutyens, Edwin 76
Lynch, Kevin 142
Lyons, Edward 22
Lyons, Eric 22

Macciocchi, Maria Antonietta 91, 92
Mackintosh, Charles Rennie 101, 221
Maffezzoli, Guido 248, *249*
Magistretti, Vico 62, 221, 236, 239
Maguire, Robert 247
Manchester 181
Mangiarotti, Angelo 236, 247, *248*
Mango, Roberto 148
Mannheim, Karl 146
Marcenaro, Caterina 117
Marghera 117, 120
Maritain, Jacques 133
MARS 31, 77, 78, 107–12, 122, 136, 223, 225
Marseille 111, 130, 163, 165
Marsoni, Lina 206
Martin, Leslie 1, 70, 71, 73, 74, 76–81, 165, 168
Matera 62, 138, 239
Matte-Trucco, Giacomo 50
Maufe, Edward 243, 244
Mazza, Luigi 152
McGrath, Raymond 77

McKean, John 182
McLuhan, Marshall 135
megastructure 48–9, 158, 160–1, 163, 165,167, 172–3
Meinberg, Cloud 245, 246
Melhuish, Clare 2
Melnikov, Kostantin 77
Melograni, Carlo 61
memory 81, 194
Menai 14
Mendelsohn, Erich 165
Menna, Filiberto 90, 91
Merrell, D.H. 225
Mestre 120
Metron 16, 21, 23, 71
Michelucci, Giovanni 149, 245, 248, 249, 250
Milan 45, 47, 49, 51, 52, 59, 61, 62, 64, 71–4, 80, 87, 101, 138, 139, 161, 213, *214*, 220, 221–4, 226–9, 239, *241*, 242, 248, *249*
Milan railway station, Sant'Elia project for 161
Mills, Edward 236, 243
Mingardi, Lorenzo 159
modern movement, modernism 47, 53, 57, 59–66, 72, 73, 77, 78, 112, 127, 218, 221
modernity 32, 46, 49–50, 53–4, 73, 113, 146, 160–1, 181, 184–5, 194, 218, 219, 224, 231, 245
modernization 146, 182–4, 187, 215, 239
modesty 80
montage 87, 89, 95, 98, 100
Montaner, Josep Maria 62
Montgomery, Bernard Law 28
Montini, Giovanni Battista 222, 244
Montpellier 130, 131, 139
Montuori, Eugenio 46, 243
Monza 228
Morassutti, Bruno 236, 247, *248*
Moretti, Luigi 46, 47, 49, 50, 61, 65
morphology 159
Morris, Arthur 247
Morris, Joan 243
Morris, William 207
Morrison, Jasper 222
Moschini, Francesco 87
Mounier, Emmanuel 133
Moya, Hidalgo 70
Mumford, Lewis 132, 133, 135, 137, 142, 152, 164, 165, 169
Murray, Keith 247
museology 80
Mussgnug, Florian 2
Mussolini, Benito 32
Muthesius, Stefan 182, 186, 194
Muzio, Giovanni 213
mythologies 159

Nairn, Ian 32, 34
Naples 29, 101, 146, 148, 150, 229, 232
Nash, John 14
Natalini, Adolfo 1, 87, 88, 97–101
nation building 6–7
national identity 10, 12, 14, 17
national narratives 4–5, 6–8, 10, 11, 17
nationalism 5–6, 8
Navone, Paola 99, 100
negative space 164
neighbourhood 24, 25, 26, 27, 33–6, 65, 150, 156, 163, 167, 169, 172, 173, 206
neoliberty 45–7, 50, 53, 59–62, 65, 218
NER 89
Neutra, Richard 22
new towns 14–16, 26, 32, 34, 35, 182, 203–8, 237
New York *88*, 95, *96*, 101, 151, 164
Nicholson, Ben 77
Niskanen, Aino 81
nomadism 89–90
Norwood, L.W. 222
Nottingham 77, 187

Olivetti, Adriano 119, 131–3, 148, 203
Olmo, Carlo 92, 150
Olmstedt, Frederick Law 142
OMA 95
Orefice, Roberto 59
organic 21–7, 34, 72, 74, 136–7, 148–9, 150, 191
organic city 149–50
orientalism 10
Orlandoni, Bruno 99, 100
Otterlo 62, 119–21
Oxford 71, 169, 182, 202

Paci, Enzo 231
Padovan, Richard 166
Pagano, Giuseppe 73
Palanti, Giancarlo 73
Palladio, Andrea 4
Pane, Roberto 148
Pannunzio, Mario 147
Paris 77, 91, 99, 109, 114, 118
Patrick, Michael 112, 113
Pavia 204
Pawley, Bernard 246
Pedroni Zanuso, Billa 138
Pelliccia, Carlo 205
People's Detailing 164
Peressutti, Enrico 81, 107, 111, 112
Pericoli, Giovanni 223
Perry, Clarence 151
Persico, Edoardo 73
Perugia 31, 160
Pessoa, Alberto 80
Pevsner, Nikolaus 12–16, 32, 45, 76, 113, 159, 180, 184, 186, 220, 236, 245
Philadelphia 201
Philipe, Gérard 115
Piacentini, Marcello 243
piazzas 31, 33, 34, 114, 159, 179, 182, 188, 192
Piccari, Tarcisio 245
Piccinato, Luigi 120, 146–9, 151, 243
picturesque 14, 190, 193, 247
Pidgeon, Monica 78
Pienza 30
Pietilä, Raili 81
Pietilä, Reima 81
Pistoia 29

place 14, 15, 32–4, 58–9, 72, 81, 90, 114, 128–9, 135, 138–9, 157, 162, 166–8, 171–3, 204, 208
Pollini, Gino 236, 239–*41*
Ponti, Gio 46, 48, 51, 217, 220, 223, 224
Ponti, Lisa 220
Pope, Alexander 14
Popescu, Carmen 9
Pordenone 48
Portaluppi, Piero 223
Portoghesi, Paolo 50, 60–2, 65
postmodernism 48, 57, 65
Powell, Geoffry 70
Powell, Philip 70
Powers, Alan 194
Prato 31
precinct 15, 150, 151, 156, 157, 169, 172
prefabrication 214–16, 221, 229–32
Pretoria 134
Price, Cedric 98, 204, 205
Price, Uvedal 14
Pritchard, Thomas *13*
Prosser, Trevor 221
Proudhon, Pierre-Joseph 140
public space 34, 129, 156, 157, 159, 160, 167–71, 174
Puddu, Sabrina 2
Pugin, Augustus Charles *7*, 8
Pugin, Augustus Welby Northmore *7*, 8
Purini, Franco 201

Quaroni, Ludovico 47, 52, 61, 138, 236, 239, 240, 245, 248
Queen Elizabeth 24

Raboni, Bianca 203, 204
Ragghianti, Carlo Ludovico 115
Ramos, Carlos 80
Ranger, Terence 6
rational, rationalism, rationalization, rationalizing 27, 52, 59, 60, 62, 64, 72–4, 87–9, 95, 141, 159, 163
Reclus, Elisée 137, 140
Reclus, Paul 131
reconstruction, post-war 16, 17, 20, 22–5, 33, 70, 71, 107, 134, 138, 150, 152, 157, 158, 170, 172, 173, 186, 215, 237
regional planning 26, 72, 112, 129–31, 135, 148, 152, 203, 204
regionalism 112, 129, 135
Reilly, Paul 220
Renacco, Nello 26, *27*
RIBA 1, 22, 23, 29–31, 70, 71, 107, 112, 159, 185, 224, 237, 250
Richards, Alan 120
Richards, James Maude 31–4, 72, 111, 115, 159, 220
Ridolfi, Mario 59, 67, 80
Rigotti, Giorgio 28
Rivière, John Henri 80
Rivolta Biffa, Matilde 202
Rizzotti, Aldo 26, *27*
Roehampton 16
Rogers, Ernesto Nathan 1, 51, 52, 57, 59–62, 64, 66, 72, 73, 89, 107, 108, 110–15, 118–20, 137, 138, 159, 167, 169, 218, 219, 221, 223, 231
Rome 2, 22, 29, 32–4, 49, 51, 72, 74, *76*, 92, 147, 148, 159, 170, 179, 189, 203, 229, 232, 242–6, 248
Ross, A.D.M. 245
Rossari, Augusto 72
Rossi, Aldo 59, 64, 67
Roth, Alfred 108
Rothblatt, Sheldon 183
Rowe, Colin 170
Rowse, Eric 134
Royaumont 121
Russell, Gordon 220
Rykwert, Joseph 92, 114, 159, 166, 170, 171, 173, 186, 203, 236–40, 243, 245, 250

Saint-Dié 24
Samonà, Giuseppe 35, 72, 112, 113, 115, 120, 207
Samuely, Felix 163
San Francisco 101
San Gimignano 31, 179, 193, 194, 231
San Marco, Piazza 31, 114, 159
San Marino 122
San Quirico d'Orcia 30
Sant'Elia, Antonio 45, 47, 160–2, 165, 170
Sartogo, Piero 205
Sartre, Jean-Paul 90, 133
Scalpelli, Alfredo 243
Scarpa, Carlo 36, 65, 117
Schevenels, Conrad *192*
Schinkel, Karl Friedrich 13, 14
school buildings 2, 25, 47, 48, 50, 71, 129, 151, 168, 181, 213–19, 221–9, 231, 232
Schwarz, Rudolf 247
Schwarzer, Mitchell 7
Scimemi, Gabriele *121*
Scolari, Massimo 87
Scott Brown, Denise 120
Scott Brown, Robert 120
Scott, Felicity 87
Scott, Michael 244
Scrivano, Paolo 1
Segre, Roberto 92
semiotics 93–4
Sennett, Richard 156, 170
Sert, José Luis 111, 134, 136, 137
Settis, Salvatore 146
Severini, Gino 243
Sharp, Dennis 99
Sharp, Thomas 150
Shepheard, Peter 109
Sheppard, Lancelot 239
Sheppard, Richard 22
Siena 122, 194
Sierks, Hans Ludwig 146
simulation 49
Singer, Oscar 108
Siracusa 248
Sitte, Camillo 141, 146
Sjöstrom, Cyril 22
Sloman, Albert 183, 190, 194
Smithson, Alison 64, 66, 67, 81, 117, 119, 120, 137, 138, 159, 166, 173, 193
Smithson, Peter 62–4, 66, 67, 81, 117, 119, 120, 137, 138, 159, 166, 173, 193, 241
sociology 128, 130, 145–6, 159

Sorkin, Michael 99
South Bank 164, 237, 238
Southampton 188
spectacle 86, 99
Spence, Basil 22, 179, 180, 184, 186–90, 193, 194, 195, 202, 239
Spina, Davide 160
Stark, Douglas 238
Steinberg, Saul 114
stepped section 158, 163, 170
Stevenage 16, 34
Stirling, James 35, 36, 164
Sullivan, Louis 142
Summerson, John 66, 237
Superstudio 48, 86–90, 92, 94–6, 99–102
Sutri 30
Swedish empiricism 159

Tafuri, Manfredo 49, 53, 65, 86, 87, 89, 99
Tange, Kenzo 201
Taut, Bruno 11, 136
Taylor, Gordon 22
Team X 62, 66, 78, 117, 119, 121, 131, 141, 159, 166, 167, 172
technomorphous architecture 89, 94
Tecton 77
Tedeschi, Mario 236, 239
Telford, Thomas 14
Tentori, Francesco *108*
Terni 29
terrace 131, 164, 165, 167–8, 172
Terrassenhauser 160
Testa, Virgilio 148
The Italian Townscape 34, 159, 191, 192, 194
Thompson, P.H.P. 245
Tokyo 201
Toronto 101, 135
town and country planning 1, 22, 122
town room 156–7, 167–72
townscape 31–4, 159, 160, 173, 182, 190–2, 194, 195, 231
tradition, traditional, traditionalism 6–7, 9–11, 14, 22, 31, 46, 50, 57, 59, 61–2, 67, 71–3, 76, 77–9, 98–9, 112, 146, 152, 160–1, 163–8, 170, 173, 179–81, 183–91, 193–5, 202, 205–7, 210, 215–16, 219, 230–2, 238–9, 242
transdisciplinary 141
transnationalism 129, 134
Triennale 47, 64, 74, 80, 87, 138, 213–15, 217, 219, 220–6, 239
Trincanato, Egle 115, 117, 120
Tripp, Alker 151
Tschumi, Bernard 98, 101, 102
Turin 9, 26–8, 48, 57, *58*, 60, 240
Tyrwhitt, Jacqueline 109, 111, 127, 133–8

Unité d'Habitation 163
United Kingdom 1–4, 9, 11, 14–17, 60, 67, 74, 107, 108, 158, 160, 170, 172, 173, 199, 202, 203, 206, 207, 213, 217, 221, 222, *225*, 232, 250
United States of America 22, 25, 53, 89, 114, 142, 145, 146, 166, 243
university buildings and campuses 70, 78, 129, 139, 160, 167, 169, 172, 179–95, 199–209
Ur 29
urban life 152
urban planner 20–4, 26, 31, 35–6, 138, 141, 142, 146–51, 153, 166
urban planning 14, 20, 21–4, 26, 33, 36, 67, 93, 108, 111, 121, 122, 132, 134, 136, 137, 138, 141, 142, 145–52, 159, 167, 170
Urbino 36, 66, 122, 139, 160
use- versus sign-value 50
utopia, *eutopia* 71, 86, 90, 102, 151–2, 180, 182, 207
Utzon, Jørn 81

Vagnetti, Luigi 46
Valle, Cesare 147, 148
Valle, Gino 48
Valle, Nani 117
Van den Broek, Johannes Hendrik 115
Van der Rohe, Mies 165
Van Esteren, Cornelius 111
Van Eyck, Aldo 117, 118, 159, 213
Venice 31, 36, 72, 92, 107, 108, 112–22, 148, 159, 203
Venturi, Robert 67
Veroli 30
Vienna 101
Viganò, Vittoriano 51
Vincent, Leonard 16
Vitale, Daniele 88
Vittorini, Alessandra 140
Vittorini, Elio 138
Volker, Welter *130*, *135*
Volterra 29
Von Moos, Stanislaus 98
Voysey, Charles 72, 164

Ward, Colin 140
Ward, Stephen 145
Warwick 180
Watkin, David 14
Weber, Max 127
Weil, Simone 133
Welfare State 2, 20, 21, 36, 158, 179, 182, 183, 237, 238
Wendel, Joseph 246
Williams, Owen 77
Willson, Edward James *7*
Wilson, Colin St John 78, 79
winter gardens 161, 170
Wittkower, Rudolf 194, 239, 240
Wood, John 117
Woods, Shadrach 117, 118, 159
Woolley, Leonard 29, 30, 35
Wright, Frank Lloyd 22, 24, 60, 72, 116, 142, 148, 149, 219

York 180

Zanuso, Marco 51, 220
Zenghelis, Elia 100
Zevi, Bruno 16, 17, 21–5, 28, 34, 35, 51, 53, 61, 62, 65, 66, 72, 148
Zuddas, Francesco 2

www.ingramcontent.com/pod-product-compliance
Lightning Source LLC
LaVergne TN
LVHW052017300826
846742LV00020B/80
* 9 7 8 1 8 0 0 0 8 0 8 4 3 *